W9-BKL-419

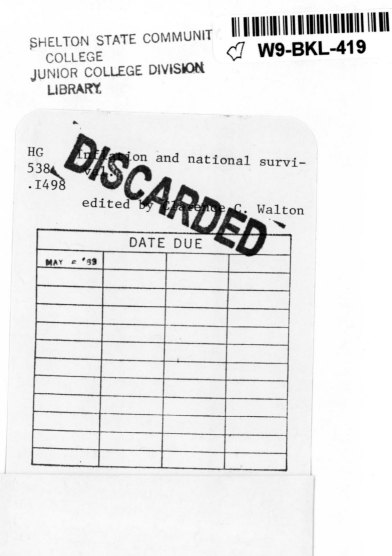

HG
538
.I498

Inflation and national survival

edited by Clarence C. Walton

DISCARDED

Inflation and National Survival

Inflation and
National Survival

Proceedings of
The Academy of
Political Science

Volume 33
Number 3

Edited by Clarence C. Walton

The Academy of Political Science
In conjunction with
The American Council of Life Insurance
New York, 1979

Contents

Preface

Rarely in peacetime has the United States been faced with a situation that poses as grave a threat to national survival as that created by inflation. Every segment of society is affected, although some more seriously than others. Understanding the reasons for inflation and determining how it can be controlled will continue to challenge the best minds in the nation for the next decade. Whatever decisions will be reached, it is evident that there is no easy solution.

The Academy of Political Science is indebted to the American Council of Life Insurance for permission to edit and publish in modified form the essays that the Council commissioned as working papers for a conference at Williamsburg, Virginia, in February 1979. The authors are distinguished scholars from universities, research institutions, and the government service who have been concerned with the study of various aspects of inflation. The views they express, however, are their own and do not necessarily reflect the position of the institutions with which they are associated. Neither are they an expression of the position of the Academy nor of the Council regarding what should be done about inflation. Rather, it is the purpose of this collection of essays to shed light on the scope of the problems created by inflation, examine its causes, and assess possible solutions.

The Academy particularly wishes to express its appreciation to Blake Newton, president of the American Council of Life Insurance, to J. Edwin Matz, chariman of the John Hancock Mutual Life Insurance Company, who chaired the Council's project, to Professor Clarence C. Walton, of the Graduate School of Business, Columbia University, who directed the project, and to William Farr, Frederick Wegener, and Arthur Adler for their editorial assistance.

ROBERT H. CONNERY
President of the Academy

Contributors

ROBERT H. CONNERY is Professor Emeritus of Public Law and Government, Columbia University, and President, The Academy of Political Science.

CLARENCE C. WALTON, formerly President, Catholic University of America, is Professor of Business, Graduate School of Business, Columbia University.

BARRY P. BOSWORTH is Director, Council on Wage and Price Stability, and formerly Senior Fellow, The Brookings Institution.

DANIEL YANKELOVICH, a social research executive, is President, Yankelovich, Skelly, and White, Inc., New York City.

PHILLIP CAGAN is Professor of Economics, Columbia University, and Research Associate, National Bureau of Economic Research. He is the author of the forthcoming *Persistent Inflation*.

ROBERT W. CRANDALL is Senior Fellow, The Brookings Institution. He has served as Deputy Director, Council on Wage and Price Stability.

MARTIN J. BAILEY is Professor of Economics, University of Maryland.

PHILIP SAUNDERS, JR., is Vice President, JUDITH MARKLAND is Director, Economic Research Department, and BENJAMIN W. WURZBURGER is Associate Economist, The John Hancock Mutual Life Insurance Company.

MORTON D. MILLER is Vice Chairman, The Equitable Life Assurance Society of the United States.

KENNETH E. BOULDING is Distinguished Professor of Economics, University of Colorado at Boulder; President, American Association for the Advancement of Science; and a past-president of the American Economic Association. He is the author of *Stable Peace*.

JAMES W. KUHN is Professor of Industrial Relations, Graduate School of Business, Columbia University.

EDGAR R. FIEDLER, who served as Assistant Secretary of the Treasury for Economic Policy, is Vice President, Economic Research, The Conference Board. He is the author of *Measures of Credit Risk and Experience*.

EDWARD M. GRAMLICH is Professor of Economics and Public Policy, The University of Michigan.

ROGER E. BRINNER is Director of Research, Data Resources, Inc., Lexington, Massachusetts.

HENRY C. WALLICH, formerly Professor of Economics, Yale University, is Member, Board of Governors, Federal Reserve System.

JOEL POPKIN, who served as Senior Staff Economist, Council of Economic Advisers, is Director and President, Joel Popkin and Company, Washington, D.C.

MICHAEL L. WACHTER is Professor of Economics, University of Pennsylvania.

JOHN W. KENDRICK, formerly Chief Economist, U.S. Department of Commerce, is Professor of Economics, The George Washington University. He is the author of *Understanding Productivity*.

CARL H. MADDEN was Professor of Business, The American University. He also served as Chief Economist, U.S. Chamber of Commerce.

Divergent Views of Inflation

CLARENCE C. WALTON

After fourteen years of inflation, Americans need no tutelage on the grim consequences of an inflationary economy that has cut their purchasing power in half during the past decade—and threatens to cut it by an even greater percentage in the coming decade. The nation's gospel of progress, buttressed by a hundredfold rise in the gross national product (GNP) since 1900 and by a reasonably low unemployment rate averaging 4.7 percent up to 1966, is fast disintegrating before the high inflation and high unemployment that have simultaneously afflicted the nation during the past decade. Traditional optimism has been badly shaken, and each month brings added evidence that confidence will not be restored soon.

When inflation is considered along with other disturbances to the economy that have occurred since the late 1950s, reasons for pessimism mount. In the late 1950s per capita income in the United States was twice that of either West Germany, the United Kingdom, or France; today it is equal to that in each of these three countries. In short, the country is no longer the unassailable economic giant on the world economic stage. Further, during the past decade the world economy has been in a condition of persistent disequilibrium; additional shocks have resulted from the 1971 breakdown in the fixed exchange rates international monetary system, the sharp reversal from a $5 to $6 billion surplus in the American trade balance to massive deficits, and the explosion of raw materials prices triggered in part by the OPEC increases in oil prices.

The issue, however, is not simply one of economics. Behind the so-called problem of the dollar are other disturbing realities, especially a new philosophy that has led to the formation of what has been called the welfare state. By this term is meant the widely shared conviction that government must not only cushion individuals against unforeseen or unavoidable disasters but also must go beyond that to provide the "good life," however defined, for all citizens. The welfare state rests on an appealing concept—namely, happiness for all. Unfortunately, citizens of a democracy sometimes demand more than existing resources can supply. Consequently, some would argue that in a democracy a key factor in controlling inflation rests on the willingness of citizens to accept the sacrifices that control will entail. The sad experience of democracies in Western Europe faced with a similar problem points to the importance of the public's clearly understanding the problem and necessity of united action.

That inflation exists in the United States none will dispute. How it came about, its causes, whom it affects most, and how it can be controlled produce divergent answers. Some Americans believe that big business, the government, or labor unions are to blame and only one bold action by legislative bodies can put the nation's economy on a sound basis again. The following essays do not support such a simplistic solution. Indeed, the authors emphasize the complex nature of the problem. Moreover, as one essay by Daniel Yankelovich points out, the political and social aspects are as important as the economic factors in finding an answer. What the American public believes to be the causes and cure of inflation are almost as important as solutions put forward by experts.

Views of the Citizens

To sample American public opinion about inflation, the American Council of Life Insurance (ACLI) placed advertisements in major newspapers and news magazines urging Americans to express their views on the subject in letters addressed to the author. The most important question the letter writers were asked was how inflation was affecting their lives. The thousand letters received in response to the advertisement suggest that Americans are angry over inflation and expect leaders in the public and private sectors to take action. Most of the letters were handwritten, long, thoughtful, and constructive. The writers rejected a viewpoint expressed in one of the house organs of the Price Waterhouse accounting firm that "inflation is invisible, noiseless, odorless, and usually painless—at least in its earlier stages." To these Americans inflation is visible in escalating prices, stirs noisy rumblings against its harmful effects, generates malodorous divisiveness among classes, and causes pain that is deep and pervasive.

To give some notion of what the letter writers were like, it is useful to develop a composite or profile before reporting their most frequent recommendations. While the respondents did not always indicate their age, work, or education, some rather clear notions can be derived. Respondents were generally male, white, between fifty-five and sixty-five (over half who stated their age were over fifty), and generally well educated. The writers came from the District of Columbia, Puerto Rico, and every state except Idaho; men outnumbered women by ten to one, but the "housewives" were numerous and were generally most indignant over recent price rises and pricing practices.

The signals indicate that Americans who had been longest in the work force and had acquired a home and some savings were most distraught by the ravages of inflation. Data on formal schooling suggest that, by a ratio of two to one, the respondents had completed college and possibly graduate work as compared to those who had only completed high school. Of the professional groups, educators and lawyers were by far the most vociferous, while representatives from small business outnumbered those from large corporations by a three to one ratio.

In sum, to the degree that data from the sampling are accurately read, the segment of society most troubled by inflation is the middle class, which has contributed significantly to the nation's prosperity, reaped a modest harvest from its efforts, and wants to keep that harvest safe. Given the age and educational levels, it is not surprising that the response indicated that opinions were shifting toward the right. A second feature of the responses is the growing skepticism Americans have toward economists and government. What Secretary of the Treasury W. Michael Blumenthal (himself a Ph.D. in economics and former chief executive officer of the Bendix Corporation) said is widely believed: "I really think the economics profession is close to bankruptcy in understanding the present situation." Clearly the public shares the economists' perception of themselves; the halcyon days of the 1960s, when economists were felt to have all the right answers, are over. In light of the expressed skepticism, it is worth recalling that of the sixteen cabinet-rank officers in the Carter administration, five have doctorates in economics and only four are lawyers—a rather startling reversal of the historic pattern of professional representation in the highest levels of government.

Typical is this excerpt from a letter by a Carbondale, Illinois, resident: "A particularly disturbing fact is that the current inflation has been, in a large part, actively brought about by professional economists. . . . It is also useful, if depressing, to look at the array of professional economists holding high positions in the present administration who have worked actively to promote the cost-push interpretation in inflation and to heap unremitting pressure on the Federal Reserve not to slow down the monetary growth." The viewpoints often echoed what a *Fortune* writer said: "I don't trust any economist today."

Another interesting fact regarding possible solutions should be noted. Most respondents, either directly or by implication, do not agree with those who share Senator William Proxmire's view that "gives employment a clear priority. It has priority over inflation; it has a priority over any economic policy in this country." The senator was referring, of course, to the Humphrey-Hawkins bill, which, by its passage in Congress, presumably established national policy. This law requires the president to specify, at the beginning of each year, an employment-rate target for the year and policies for achieving it. This act involves spending federal money and, in addition, requires the Federal Reserve Board to report to Congress twice a year on the manner in which its monetary objectives are bringing the nation closer to the president's target. So if inflation is the most important problem in the minds of some Americans, unemployment is most important in the views of those committed to Humphrey-Hawkins. In this conflict lies a very important lesson: in periods of high employment, Americans clearly favor all measures to bring inflation under control, but it is less clear that, in periods of recession and high unemployment, such a resolve would hold. This creates the political dilemma in all of its classic forms.

To complete the profile, one final point should be made. Some of the writers, especially among the women, critically note the pervasiveness of hedonism in contemporary life: Americans seek instant satisfaction and gratification; they behave petulantly even when satisfied, and they react angrily when frustrated. One writer urged "an exercise in economic genealogy" to demonstrate that "compared to other nations and compared to our forefathers, we are indeed rich beyond measure." She goes on to ask: "Does every couple need a $10,000 wedding? Would a smaller house suffice? Would we buy used appliances and paint old furniture?" Her answer is straightforward: "We have been guilty and are still guilty of promoting materialism." A woman from Elizabethtown, Pennsylvania, talked of the need to reform the American psyche: "Instead of developing things and using people, we must develop people and use things. . . ." She wryly noted that in the ACLI's advertisement "most of the men . . . look as if they never have lived or enjoyed themselves." A Los Angeles woman added that Americans "should buy only what they can afford in order to reduce the huge credit card debt. . . . Our people should be convinced that they must use self-discipline and common sense in handling their financial affairs."

While it is difficult to conclude that the foregoing assessments represent a consensus, it is appropriate to indicate that the themes touched on these issues: economists are no longer to be trusted in their proposals to control inflation, the nation's first priority—though stated in Humphrey-Hawkins as unemployment over inflation control—is not fully accepted by the public, and a pervasive hedonism (perhaps more significant than concern for social justice) encourages a psychology of entitlement, which in turn propels the welfare state toward further spending.

To turn now to specifics, the following major recommendations are listed according to the frequency with which they appeared in the letters. First, "balance the budget" is the battle cry. The people are saying that, with one-sixth of the labor force working for government and with government expenditures approaching 40 percent of the GNP, the time has come to call a halt. A retired Alabama resident wrote that, while his thoughts on controlling inflation are probably so "old fashioned" they will make no headlines, he still felt he was right: "Essentially, they are first associated with balancing the Federal Budget and even paying off some of the vast debt." There is, of course, the irony that much of the government's growth and consequent cost is due to public demands for more and more material goods. Insufficiently stressed in the letters was that, whether measured by employment share or by tax share, the government has grown from 75 to 100 percent faster than the private sector during much of American history. The fact is that government has always been expanding. But has it reached its limits? If its present growth rate continues, by the year 2000 the government will take about 45 percent of the GNP in taxes and employ about 25 percent of the labor force. If the trend is not stopped, within another century the government will take everything—all of the GNP—in taxes. And though the government will employ about 50 percent of the labor force, all the others will in effect "work with the government." Though rarely mentioned by name, the mood was favorable to the proposal made last year by Representative Jack Kemp (Republican, New York) and Senator William Roth (Republican, Delaware) to cut more than $100 billion from federal reserves during the next three years—a proposal, incidentally, that lost by only twenty-three votes in the House in April 1978.

While the purpose here is to report rather than appraise, a few critical notes are appropriate. First, this popular outcry for a balanced budget is not new; as a matter of fact, the cry has been heard for nearly half a century. The call for balanced budgets stems from the popular belief that deficits automatically cause inflation. Yet there have been deficits practically all the time since 1929, and there has not been inflation all the time. Moreover, the assumption may be mistaken that, since deficits permit undisciplined spending, removal of deficit-spending privileges will restore a much needed discipline on Congress. But the public clearly feels that it has not seen anyone offer better rules for fiscal policy than a balanced budget philosophy.

There were occasional hints of dissatisfaction with both unions and corporations in the sense that the large corporations and large unions were viewed as seeing big government as more of an ally than an adversary. One writer recalled Friedrich von Hayek, who won the 1974 Nobel Prize in economics, as a prophet because he advanced the notion that freedom is not simply precious, it is also efficient; therefore, the free market system is infinitely to be preferred to government planning. While one could not say that a "Proposition 13" mentality was apparent in the responses, there was the clear and vehemently expressed view that government spending was out of hand. Tax collections have increased at a compound annual rate of 6.4 percent since 1972, and, in real terms, taxes seem to be doubling every thirteen years. There is a fear that government spending has reached a danger point; if one takes into account the debt for local, state, and federal governments, the United States is at the $900 billion level—or around $4,000 for every individual in the country.

What these Americans seem to want is a fiscal policy that brings spending issues to the public's attention and forces the White House and the Congress to select priorities from competing spending proposals. Limits on government size and spending are sought. There is the vaguely expressed sense, however, that business is not doing all that it should to support those in government who seek to exercise fiscal responsibility. This support is essential because of a decisive difference between the market system and the political system. The market produces a distribution of income that is disproportionate to the distribution of votes; therefore, those with the lowest incomes use the political process to increase their share. It takes political courage to fight the trends, and such freedom fighters need support from every influential quarter.

"Stop the money flow" is the second battle cry. One writer from Seattle, Washington, said that "inflation is one hundred percent government created and only Washington can solve it." The uninterrupted money printing since

1913 has "led us to the brink of financial collapse." A man from Coraopolis, Pennsylvania, wrote that "we now have a dishonest currency. The unit of currency is, or should be, a measure of value. . . . The American dollar has none, it represents nothing, it is an orphan. Such a currency will always diminish in value because it is like the salt block left out in the rain. The natural elements gradually erode it away and nothing ever builds it up again." A builder from Vincentown, New Jersey, suggested that the Federal Reserve Board be required to reduce the currency by 2.5 percent immediately and then cut an additional 0.5 percent each month for the next ten months. The total reduction would be 7.5 percent, which would, in his judgment, curb the rush to dump dollars.

Reducing government regulation is the third most frequently stated demand. In view of the widespread public discussions on the excesses of regulation, it is not surprising that the public should be concerned. A Government Accounting Office study in 1978 showed that Americans spend at least $4.75 billion a year—and probably more—to comply with the federal government's paperwork demands. Most people think that the Department of Health, Education, and Welfare is the biggest culprit, but actually it is the Federal Communication Commission. It is estimated that preparing reports required of broadcasters takes 30 million hours of work each year. One letter enclosed a newspaper clipping that described the experience of Fletcher Byrom, chairman of the Koppers Company headquartered in Pittsburgh. Mr. Byrom came across a price increase for one of his products that he thought was excessive and noted that it was the third increase within a fifteen-month period. It was a product, furthermore, that enjoyed a favorable share of the market, so Koppers could risk a price increase. Concerned, Byrom called a meeting of his division personnel and asked if they really thought the last increase was reasonable. The response was that safety and environmental regulations had driven costs up. He concluded: "After listening to them, I was convinced I would have made the same decision to raise prices." Another writer enclosed a Mobil Oil advertisement on the "regulatory octopus" that called for the appointment of a commission authorized to recommend elimination of regulations no longer needed and provide for the demise of all new regulations and regulatory agencies unless their charters were periodically reviewed by Congress. There were also multiple proposals for economic impact statements for all proposed regulations and for greater professional competence among those who serve regulatory bodies.

Holding the line on wages and prices was the fourth recommendation. A typical view was that although mandatory controls "lead us to a regulated society, it is a better alternative than our present anarchistic fiscal policy." One had a sense that there was not much confidence in voluntary wage and price controls and that the administration's proposals are viewed as simply postponing the day of reckoning. They seemed to endorse the view expressed by Professor Laurence Klein of the University of Pennsylvania, who said in a *New York Times* article dated June 16, 1978, that voluntary control "is like watering a lawn with a hose that has ten holes in it."

Some correspondents focused on the income side, and three letters were worthy of note. One concerned housewife from Demarest, New Jersey, said flatly that "no man is worth more than $200,000 per annum. . . . Sad but true, most corporate executives are replaceable." This comment may represent a fragile straw before a strong wind, but there are some signs of restlessness over executive salary ranges. Concern was also expressed that large unions had insulated their workers from any normal shocks in the economic system and that the experience of the past three decades, when wage increases consistently outran productivity increases as measured by output per manhour, has to stop. As a former business school dean put it, the country has "too much sail and too little anchor." Proposals to effect change went from a call for "the dissolution of the present union and closed shop system" and "reestablishment of a right-to-work principle" to a suggestion that because "the major virus creating and nourishing the disease of inflation is the failure of collective bargaining to relate wage adjustments to changes in productivity (thus denying the possibility of achieving reasonable stability and real unit cost of delivering prices and production)," there must be "a modification of the anti-trust exempt status of labor."

One writer from Nathrop, Colorado, presented this ingenious idea: since "the fundamental cause of inflation is the payment of more money for labor that produces the same (or less) output," one must distinguish between the kinds of salary or wage rises to be allowed. He suggested three classes of pay raises. The first class would include promotional raises given, for example, to someone who succeeds a retiring individual. Since the promoted man would be simply filling a vacated slot, there would be no difference in the total cost of labor. The second class of raises would be for those who perform at a rate of productivity equal to, or greater than, the cost of the raise. This is the best type. The third class would refer to raises in wages given to those who "do the same job at the same productivity level." This, by definition, is inflationary and harmful. The first and second classes of wage increases would be allowed, but the third class, in the writer's view, must be stopped if the inflationary spiral is to be halted. He suggests, therefore, that a law be enacted that would make it "unlawful for any business, industry, or private institution to raise the price of their goods or services as a result of granting a raise of the third class to any of their employees; and it shall be unlawful for any government . . . or governmental agency to raise taxes or increase budgets to pay for such a raise granted to any of their employees."

Some hostility was expressed toward salaries earned by public officials, and one writer urged that limits be placed on the salary earned by the president, and then scale-down efforts could be systematically carried out at all levels of government. Another insisted that overtime for federal and state employees be reduced to an "absolute minimum." Still a third would achieve an appropriate wage stability goal by imposing a "ten percent cut in the budgets of all federal bureaus."

Examples were also given of pricing practices that irritate consumers. A fairly typical view was expressed by a writer from Frederic, Wisconsin, who said that he was tired of "profiteering" by supermarkets and quoted his own experience in seeing a certain brand of motor oil that cost 84 cents on one shelf and 89 cents on another. In another store he compared brand-name cat food and reported differences of 4 cents to 5 cents per container. The Census Bureau, in its January 1979 report, indicated that price rises between 1976 and 1977 practically offset the 7 percent income gain, and this phenomenon has obviously worried and angered consumers.

If one can judge public opinion by this relatively small sampling, one may conclude that Americans are getting the message (articulated by President Carter, Secretary of Energy James Schlesinger, and others) that the boom years of economic growth have ended. The bad news was authoritatively delivered in the annual report of the Council of Economic Advisers. From 1950 through 1965, productivity grew at an annual rate of over 2.5 percent, from 1965 through 1972 at roughly 2 percent, and from 1973 to the present it has averaged 1 percent. This dramatic decline is ominous, and Americans sense the damage and the need for corrective measures. That the worry expressed by the writers was not matched by imaginative proposals to improve productivity should occasion no surprise. Even the experts are unsure. But the average citizen seems to feel that the government's traditional focus on aggregate demand management must be reversed. Public policy (as expressed in tax law and job-training programs) should emphasize investment instead of consumption, work instead of leisure, and rewards for performance instead of mere compliance.

Beyond the five recommendations that have been reported were other comments relating to the need to cut the abuses of credit card systems, the growing pressures arising from transfer payments coupled with a worry about where the money to support such payments is to come from, a feeling that foreign aid programs should be overhauled and substantially reduced, and that "Buy American" may be a good philosophy under existing circumstances. Concerning the military aid programs, one retired soldier wrote: "I have been a first-hand witness as to how this aid has been administered, and it has been a waste of time and money. Laos, Thailand, Turkey, Iran and the Republic of China, are excellent examples of this waste." Following these suggestions would save the country hundreds of millions of dollars.

One lingering impression was the feeling that Americans wanted and, at the same time, resented the various developments that have led the United States away from a market economy. One writer concluded that the basic problem is that "we have made large numbers of Americans—union members with strong unions, social security recipients whose receipts are indexed—so powerful that each dose of inflation creates another one since much of the economy can demand and get protection against inflation. Obviously, I also include farmers who get price supports from our government, doctors whose customarily unreasonable fees are adjusted upward each year, and industries which plead poverty as they raise prices. . . . The primary inflation source is, therefore, government and government-backed quasi-monopoly groups like labor unions and aggregates of farmers."

Disturbed, frustrated, and *angry* were adjectives that appeared with great frequency in the letters. But also expressed was a belief that the nation had the will and the resources that, properly harnessed, could halt an inflation that threatens the stability of a free society as well as the other societies of the free world that depend on America.

Whatever else the public response indicated, it showed that many Americans had lost faith in the experts—in this case primarily the economists. Part of the reason may be that experts tend to speak a language that only their peers can comprehend. If a solution is to be found for the nation's inflation, it must be with the advice of experts. But no matter how sound a program may appear to the experts, an opportunity must be provided for a public debate, free discussion, and the development of a consensus. The present attitude of the public provides a frame of reference within which such efforts should take place. A skeptical American public must be convinced that whatever program the experts offer is the best solution.

Views of the Experts

All the contributors to this volume stress a common theme: inflation is far more than simply an economic problem. In most cases, they invite readers to weigh the trade-offs between control of inflation and the development of a recession. Invariably they recommend cautious action. The inflation, they note, has been under way for a long time and it cannot be brought to a sudden halt without prohibitive social and political costs. But they agree that inflation cannot be allowed to continue since its overall effects are devastating to the social and political stability of the nation.

One strategy to diminish inflation is the tax-based incomes policies (TIP) suggested by Henry C. Wallich, a member of the Federal Reserve Board, and others. Developed in cooperation with Sidney Weintraub of the University of Pennsylvania, the basic idea is to permit firms to raise wages and prices but to make it unprofitable for them to do so. In óne proposal, business firms that exceed the "acceptable" level of prices and wages would be subject to an added tax; in another plan, workers who took small salary increases would receive a tax credit. No censensus on the feasibility of a TIP policy has been achieved. Some writers suggest it would lead to an administrative nightmare; others say TIP only touches the top of an economic iceberg and is doomed to fail; still others feel that it is politically unacceptable because large unions will oppose it. Nonetheless, there is strong sentiment that the tax-based incentive program should be studied further to determine how to correct its alleged deficiencies.

The relative decline in productivity, even as measured in the conventional output per labor hour unit used by the Department of Labor, is of great concern to the experts. Price rises can be more easily resisted when output increases.

Between 1948 and 1966, productivity rose by over 3 percent a year; in 1966 the deceleration began and has continued to the present. To increase productivity, recommendations were made by the experts to allow tax credits to those industries characterized by high rates of research and development (R&D) because such industries have shown a consistently higher rate of productivity than those marked by low R&D efforts. Better uses of manpower are suggested, but management lacks a sophisticated understanding of what motivates employees to work efficiently.

Government policies and practices receive the sharpest criticism. Public officials have become masters at disguising costs of government: inflation itself is one device; financing public policies (toward farmers, for instance) through the price support level is another. Since billions of taxpayer dollars are involved, the argument is made that these sums should be disclosed so that voters know how much they are asked to give in support of specific sectors of the economy. Perhaps most vexatious are the increasing costs of government regulations and the absence of cost-benefit analyses on the newer regulatory commissions—such as the Environmental Protection Agency (EPA). A recent study by the Arthur Andersen accounting firm showed that the incremental costs of forty-eight companies to comply with the regulations of six federal agencies were over $2.6 billion. If extended to all major American enterprises, the costs would be staggering.

So far as wages and prices are concerned, the essays indicate that in a depression, under a free market economy, prices are likely to decline more quickly than wages. Indeed, among the major industrial nations of the world, year-to-year wage flexibility is lowest for the United States while the nation's price flexibility seems to be average. The basic reason is structural—business firms and unions have sought, rather successfully, to exempt themselves from the law of supply and demand. Changing the structures is a major political challenge to Congress and the White House and indeed to the American public.

There are other questions that the essays discuss. What, for example, is the impact of transfer payments on the economy? Of the defense industry? Of rapidly escalating health costs? Of the declining value of the dollar on the international money markets? Of labor power? And, finally, since fear of a rise in unemployment has been widely viewed as the price for controlling inflation, is there a more realistic figure for an "acceptable" unemployment rate than the present 4 percent?

Economists need to expand their analytical apparatus so that the nation will have adequate means to combat inflation. For example, they are just starting to understand the total impact of the financial system on inflation and particularly the problem of the structure of interest rates at different maturities, as well as the relative role of short-term bonds, long-term mortgages, and the like. In short, a fair amount is known about the nation's income but not enough about the nation's assets. Yet the assets structure may well be a major clue to the dilemma of inflation.

America has experienced other historic debates—over ratification of the Constitution, over states' rights, over slavery, over gold and silver, and over war and peace. The test of a democracy is not speed or efficiency—but logic and fairness. Given time for testing, the American response will be salutary if proposed anti-inflation policies are logical and carefully explained, if the burdens associated with achieving stability are equitably shared, and if leadership is consistent and courageous.

The Carter Administration's Anti-inflation Program

BARRY P. BOSWORTH

One of the great difficulties with inflation is that people do not agree on what ought to be done about it. There is also a wide divergency of opinions about what causes inflation. As a result, the United States has really done nothing about the problem. To be sure, the government has periodically addressed the problem but then found that many of the recommended cures would increase the rate of unemployment. That led to a reversal of its course before any of those economic policies could have any impact. But it is possible to analyze the nature of inflation by considering the problems of the private sector and then of the government.

One problem in the private sector has resulted from a decade of continuing inflation and expectations that inflation is going to continue. Most people are caught in a vicious circle. Wages and prices are rising rapidly—not so much because of any evidence of excess demand or the classical explanation of too much money chasing too few goods but chiefly because of a purely self-defensive type of mechanism. People believe that prices will continue to go up, so they are demanding wage increases to catch up with price increases. The same thing is happening in business. Only occasionally, in fact, is business able to get increases in excess of cost increases. Business concerns are simply trying to catch up and protect themselves against what they think is the inevitable inflation of other sectors. Nobody is willing to moderate their demands, even though they realize that their own efforts are futile, because they have no confidence that anyone else will do the same thing.

There have been broad institutional changes in the structure of the American economy that make it possible today for wages and prices to be determined not by competitive pressures in the marketplace or the interaction of supply and demand. Instead, individual groups have varying degrees of ability to dictate what their own wage increase is going to be or to dictate what their own price increase is going to be.

The fundamental reason for this is that, contrary to popular belief, America does not have a competitive economic system today. In fact, neither do the American people want a competitive economic system. The nation spent over fifty years trying to modify a competitive economic system to make it more equitable. The organization of labor unions, the technological changes in production, and the growing role of government in the economy were responses to specific problems. But as a result of these actions, people have more and more discretion to dictate to some extent what their own wage or price increases will be.

The momentum of that process has increased wages followed by price increases and price increases followed wage increases in a fashion that is difficult to explain by any economic rationale, such as excess demand in the marketplace and shortages either in product markets or in labor markets. Fundamentally, shortages are not increasing automobile prices. Neither will shortages determine the outcome of the teamsters' union negotiations, nor have they anything to do with the oil worker negotiations.

There has been a steady underlying rate of about 6 percent inflation ever since the middle of 1975, and it continued through 1976 and much of 1977. In 1978, because of food shortages and pressures in some individual markets, the rate has accelerated dramatically. Today it is probably closer to 7.5 percent and perhaps even as high as 8 percent. The international shocks that the United States has been subjected to in recent years have tended to increase the rate of inflation and to become embedded in the wage and price decisions within the industrial sector. Thus they are perpetuated long after they have run their course.

Even more dramatic have been the changes in the way that government impacts on the economy. This impact goes far beyond balancing the budget or regulating the rate of growth of the money supply. While these factors are important, they present an incomplete picture of the impact of government on the economy. The rapid growth of two other aspects of government has also had significant implications on the course of inflation. The first aspect is the rapid growth of noneconomic business regulations, such as pollution abatement, health and safety regulations, fuel economy standards, and various occupational safety measures that have had an inflationary effect. One might almost speak of government regulations as a new industry. It began in the mid-1960s, with the passage of the environmental protection acts. The nation has had less than a decade of experience with regulatory agencies, and economists would probably conclude that—like most new industries and particularly most new industries run by government—they have failed to function adequately.

The cost of government regulation shows up mainly in the fact that there has been a sharp decline in the rate of growth of productivity in the United States. Regulations do not raise the profit margin, and they do not raise wage rates. But they do slow the rate of growth of measured economic productivity, and this is one of the fundamental problems with the current inflation that has to be dealt with. The rate of productivity growth in this country in the 1950s and through much of the 1960s averaged 3 percent a year. In the last decade it was down to less than 2 percent a year.

In the last two years, and in the midst of a strong economic recovery, the rate dropped to less than 1 percent growth and productivity annually. That is an impressive decline. The Council of Economic Advisers is now estimating that the trend rate of productivity growth may be little more than 1 percent in the years immediately ahead. This means that the improvement in the average American's living standards has been reduced to one-third of what it used to be, requiring an adjustment that most people find difficult to make. Consequently, it is difficult to convince Americans to moderate their wage demands or their price increases.

It would be a gross exaggeration to say that regulation by government has been responsible for all of the decline in productivity, but economic studies have indicated that it is a very real and important component of it. Probably the impact of government regulations on the rate of productivity growth is running about half a percentage point. Thus the government's regulatory activities have a rather substantial influence on productivity.

The needs of society are often offered as a justification for government regulations. Too much attention, one may argue, has been given to the goals of regulation. Some people maintain that the environmental goals are too rigid and too high. People question what exactly are the goals, and it is a difficult question to answer. How does one value the environment? How does one value a human life?

But not enough attention has been given to the question of the means of achieving the goals. This is the problem receiving most attention in the Carter administration at the present time. Is the government, through regulation, trying to achieve an improvement in the environment by the cheapest possible means? Are there cheaper alternatives to achieve an equally substantial improvement in the environment, in health areas, or in occupational safety?

The second major aspect of government that is new and rapidly growing and having a substantial impact on inflation can be called special interest legislation. The growing tendency for people suffering from economic disadvantages on cyclical downturns in their own industry now seems to be to seek from the federal government some form of restriction on competition—restrictions on foreign or domestic competition, a guaranteed minimum wage, a guaranteed minimum price, or similar actions.

The difficulty of dealing with these situations is illustrated by one currently before the Congress—the sugar bill. The world price of sugar is about .075 cents a pound. It has been proposed by the administration and in Congress that the American support price be set at about 16 cents. In other words, it would be more than double the current world price of sugar.

Why do congressmen support such issues? There are 13,000 sugar producers in the United States and 220 million consumers, and one would think the sugar producers would lose in that sort of situation. But when an issue like sugar comes up, the sugar producers will vote for or against a congressional candidate solely on the basis of his vote on sugar. They do not care what his stance is on any other issues. In the next election they will contribute to his campaign, and they will vote for him on the basis of whether he supported sugar legislation.

The rest of the people in the country will never know what happened. They will observe that sugar prices went up a bit. They will probably blame big business for the price increase, but people have little understanding of what really happened. If one argues that the legislation is inflationary, the answer is that it will not raise the consumer price index more than .001, and that will have a small impact on the inflation rate.

There is probably no action by government that can raise consumer prices in an economy as big as the United States by more than a tenth of a percentage point, but in the next session of Congress there will probably be thirty to fifty such actions taken, and the cumulative effect on inflation will be substantial. For example, during 1978, various types of special interest legislation and regulatory actions passed by Congress including the regulatory actions had an impact of well over a percentage point on the rate of growth of the price level.

Congress is now deciding how to allocate a fixed, overall total amount of budget funds, but the budgetary process is never extended to costs of special legislation. Regulation is treated as something outside the budget, and, as a consequence, its costs have grown very rapidly. There has been little attempt to ensure that the costs provide the maximum amount of benefits.

The nation has to face major problems, such as stopping the momentum of inflation and dealing with government actions at home and overseas that increase the inflation rate. In each area there are unpleasant alternatives. Two major policies can be guaranteed to stop the momentum of inflation in the industrial sector. The first would be fiscal or monetary restraint. Those who argue that fiscal or monetary restraint will not be successful in stopping this inflation miss the point. Fiscal or monetary restraints must be extensive and applied over a long period of time. Unfortunately, sole reliance on fiscal or monetary restraint is simply too costly in terms of unemployment. There is really little disagreement among economists that if the rate of inflation is reduced by 1 percentage point, 1 percent more people in the work force will be unemployed for at least a two-year period. That means about 1 million people will be put out of work for every 1 percent decline in the rate of inflation. Thus if measures are taken to bring the current inflation down to half of what it is now within the next two years, the levels of unemployment will be of double-digit magnitudes, an extremely high price to pay.

People will differ on whether they think that fiscal or monetary restraint is paying the penalty of high unemployment, depending on whether they believe they will be employed. If one is a tenured professor of economics at the University of Chicago, for example, he will think such policies are worthwhile because very few tenured college professors have ever lost their jobs in a recession. If one grew up in an urban ghetto and tends to vote for the Democratic party, he would think such things are a disaster. The nation has debated these questions for many months but has not been able to reach a conclusion.

One of the problems is that people like to speak in euphemisms about fiscal or monetary restraint. It is trite to say that balancing the budget would bring inflation to an end, or if the government did not print money, it would not have inflation. The second argument is true, of course, by definition. But the public should be told that balancing the budget by itself is not going to have any impact on wages or prices anywhere in the economy. A lack of growth in the money supply itself would not have an impact on any wage decision, and particularly not on the teamsters' negotiations or any other price dispute. Instead, if the restraints are really to have an impact on the rate of inflation, government expenditures must be reduced, and aggregate demand, production, and employment must also be reduced. The result will be to throw a few million people out of work. To be sure, if enough of them are out of work, they will cease asking for wage increases. No one likes to say that, but that is what lies at the heart of the proposal for fiscal or monetary restraint.

If the rate of growth of the money supply is held down and interest rates increased, housing will collapse, and investment, production, and employment will decline. The fundamental problem with those policies is not that they have not been tried in the past. Indeed, they have been tried again and again but not for long, because the social costs were always too high. During economic expansions, everyone gets upset about inflation and calls for fiscal restraint. The government provides it, the nation goes into a recession, unemployment rises, and everyone panics and demands that something be done about unemployment.

As a result, the economy over the last decade has looked like a roller coaster. The planning of business investment in various industries has been disrupted, and all that has happened is high levels of unemployment and of inflation. Consequently, as long as the issue is unemployment versus inflation, it seems the nation will do nothing about inflation.

On the other hand, some people argue that mandatory wage and price controls are the answer to inflation. Certainly, if legislation is passed making it illegal to raise prices and wages, they probably will not rise. But at the same time, the nation should be told that this policy will bring with it all the inequities and distortions that made people so concerned about inflation in the first place. The American people probably would support wage and price controls for about six months. Then, as individuals, they would discover that *their* wages were being controlled and at that point public support would disappear.

The Carter administration admits that the government simply does not know how to administer wage and price controls. On the price side, the issues are too technical. The personnel of the Council on Wage and Price Stability has been tripled in size in the last few months. But one may doubt that it has the expertise to determine the correct level of three prices in the economy, much less what 3 million ought to be.

Most Americans would agree that it would be most unfortunate if wage rates were determined in Washington, D.C., over a long period, because it would divide the nation between those who were wage earners and those who were not. In the past the United States has successfully avoided this situation. Instead, the inflation program of the Carter administration offers a middle course to deal with this problem of momentum. The experience of the 1960s proved that wage and price guidelines cannot be substituted for responsible fiscal and monetary policy, and the early 1970s proved that price controls cannot replace responsible fiscal and monetary policy.

One might ask whether the Carter program of voluntary standards can be successful if guidelines and controls fail. The answer probably would be that there is a fundamental difference in the way they are applied. This time the program includes a restrictive fiscal and monetary policy combined with wage and price standards.

It is evident that fiscal and monetary restraint is needed in order to moderate the rate of inflation. But to rely on that alone would mean that the cost in terms of unemployment would be too high. The present effort is, first of all, to create an environment with fiscal and monetary policy that will be conducive to a moderation of inflation and then to try to use some voluntary measures to see if the rate of wage increases and price increases can be reduced at less cost in terms of unemployment than would otherwise be the case. It is therefore crucial in evaluating the use of standards to realize that they are being combined with the fiscal and monetary policy that is also restrictive. But this policy attempts to avoid the mistakes of the past, particularly a return to high levels of unemployment.

A very long period of time will be required to find a way to deal in an intelligent fashion with the issue of social regulations and to determine a means of evaluating properly their cost and benefits. Ultimately the nation will try to establish a budget for federal regulations, a budget with the costs measured in terms of the cost to the economy and with the benefits balanced against the costs. To establish such a budgeting concept, more progress will have to be made in finding a means of determining the benefits and the costs of regulation. The first step in this undertaking is to require all the regulatory agencies to make an economic analysis of the benefits and the costs of a proposed program as well as a statement of the costs of alternatives. Some time within this decade, it may be possible to establish a new budgetary framework. Currently a system exists in which the Environmental Protection Agency (EPA) proposes a regulation and the Council on Wage and Price Stability opposes it. In order to be effective, for every EPA there should be another agency of equal size to argue the other side of the case, and that is not a very intelligent way to determine government policy. But at the present time EPA has no incentives whatsoever to regulate in an efficient fashion. It regulates business activities in the simplest and most direct fashion because the cost in economic terms is irrelevant to the EPA.

The only way this can be changed is to require regulatory agencies to operate within a budget that states the economic cost imposed on the economy. This would ensure the maximum environment benefits for the money spent. But any progress in this area will take a long time to achieve. The Carter administration has been surprised by the extent of cooperation that it has received from labor as well as from business groups. On the whole, the program has gone very well. Some labor leaders have expressed their concern for the equity of the program, but in general labor has been cooperative.

Business has produced rhetoric in favor of the program, but the January wholesale price index indicated that some real concern exists, particularly among the small and intermediate size companies. Some people are convinced that mandatory controls are inevitable, and consequently there has been a lot of anticipatory pricing in the business community. The national income accounts will show extremely large increases in corporate profits the first quarter of 1979 that will raise some of the same concerns about whether the administration's program can be made effective as far as prices are concerned. The administration, therefore, has more of an obligation to make sure that the price side of this program does not fall by the wayside.

Other problems make it particularly difficult to do anything about inflation in 1979. Productivity probably will continue to grow at slow rates. Thus real incomes from productivity alone will probably be up at most 1 percent over the next year. Half of that will be taken away by increased federal taxes to finance social security. The remainder might in theory accrue to workers, but food prices will be increasing 4 or 5 percent more rapidly than other prices. Housing prices are rising at about 12 percent a year, and there is little the government can do about it in the short run. Energy prices are going to rise substantially as a result of OPEC price actions. The American worker may be willing to agree to a voluntary program and hold down his wage increase. But when his real income declines, what will happen?

Labor options are more limited than those of business, and labor is taking more risks than any business firm is. A business firm can say it will go along with the government's program, but if it does not work, two months later it can raise its prices. When labor signs an agreement, it does not have that option. Even nonunion workers usually find their wages are determined only once a year. Thus with the uncertainty about prices, real wage insurance becomes even more crucial than ever. The Carter administration wage insurance program is essentially an attempt to provide some assurance that people who support the program and try to moderate their wage demands will get some protection. To be sure, the only way that full assurance can be given is with wage and price controls. But if the nation does not want controls, then the alternative is to give workers some sort of an insurance contract, recognizing that they are taking more of a risk.

Most of the administrative difficulties that were forecast by economists for the wage insurance program earlier were greatly exaggerated. It has not been nearly as complicated as some people thought. If everyone in the nation went along with the wage standards and was therefore eligible for real wage insurance, the chances that the rate of inflation could exceed 7 percent would be about zero. If only a few people go along with wage standards, the government would have to make insurance payments. But if there were very high rates of inflation, with labor income making up 70 percent of the total national income, by definition there could not be many workers who would be eligible for the 7 percent rebate. So with high rates of inflation the government would have to pay high insurance but not to very many people. At low rates of inflation, there would be a lot of people qualified, but none of them would receive much.

The second aspect of the wage insurance program became apparent from the data developed to determine its cost. Inflation, by placing people in higher tax brackets, generates more revenue to the federal government. In past years taxes have been reduced about every two years, and everyone gets a tax rebate. This program has cost almost the same amount as the impact of inflation on the progressive income tax structure. There are rebates, but not to everyone. Instead, those who tried to hold down their wage increases get the rebates as part of an incentive plan. So this budget cost of wage insurance is extremely limited. Furthermore, any payout that has a maximum dollar amount to any one individual drastically narrows potential cost. When workers are asked to moderate their wage increases in a two- or three-year contract, there should be some assurances that they are not going to lose simply because nobody else approves of the program.

To be sure, the proposal for real wage insurance has upset a lot of people. They say it is gimmicky and radical. But when one looks at the alternatives, unless something like this works, wages can be held down only by creating fear that workers are going to lose their jobs. The costs in unemployment are very high in this alternative.

The Carter program has a reasonable chance to succeed. It will require not only fiscal or monetary restraint and not only standards, but it will also require the government to deal with the problems of the low rate of productivity growth. It will take a long period to achieve this. In the next twelve months, however, there will be substantial reductions in the rate of price and wage increases, and the rate of inflation will moderate.

The Noneconomic Side of Inflation

DANIEL YANKELOVICH

For the public today, inflation has the kind of dominance that no other issue has had since World War II. The closest contenders are the cold war fears of the early 1950s and perhaps the last years of the Vietnam war. But inflation exceed those issues in the breadth of concern it has aroused among Americans. It would be necessary to go back to the 1930s and the Great Depression to find a peacetime issue that has had the country so concerned and so distraught. From the public's point of view, such an intractable problem demands close cooperation between business and government in the search for solutions and in the call to responsible public action.

Inflation is a problem with economic effects, but its causes are only partially economic, and its solutions may also be only partially economic. It would be a great mistake to address the problem of inflation exclusively in economic terms, thereby failing to come to grips with it as a social-political issue. Due weight must be given to the noneconomic features of the problem—the social, political, and psychological factors. If these are not confronted as directly and cogently and seriously as the purely economic factors, a proposed solution may be academically or technically correct but it will not be implemented or, if implemented, will not work.

One of the essays in this volume states that during periods in the recent past when the Federal Reserve Board increased the money supply at rates that helped fuel inflation, men like Arthur Burns were at the helm—and Arthur Burns can hardly be dismissed as an easy money radical. The failure of the Federal Reserve Board to implement the sacred tenets of the "old time economic religion" did not result from a lack of economic "right thinking" or from a lack of understanding of the role of economics in the larger social and political realities. On the contrary, it reflected an appraisal of political realities. Economists are well aware of the nature and importance of political and psychological realities, but they do not systematically take them into account when proposing solutions. Such a position is entirely correct and proper for economists as professionals. They are exercising proper restraint in not making pronouncements in fields other than their own. But the purpose of these essays is to develop a clear understanding of the root causes of inflation. This cannot be done without giving as much attention to the noneconomic aspects of inflation as to the economic ones.

The interplay between the economic and noneconomic factors is complex and confusing. It is not a question of either economic medicine or political willpower but of both simultaneously. This problem of mixed causal factors arises often in psychology. For example, a person who has acrophobia, a pathological fear of heights, and lives on the side of a mountain has a problem that can be approached in two ways. He can be given psychotherapy to help him overcome his fear of heights, or he can be persuaded to move off the mountain. Either method may work, and they are clearly not mutually exclusive. Obviously, one should try both.

For more than a year, the government has been trying to administer some weak and occasional economic medicine, but the patient has been climbing farther and farther up the side of the mountain. The steeper the height, the less effective the medicine; and the more severe his pathology, the worse his fall will be when it finally comes.

To combat inflation both economic and psychosocial approaches must be applied, and they must be coordinated. The nation's expectations must be changed—its habits, behavior, and calculations—and it must also exercise control over fiscal and monetary policy. Harsh doses of economic medicine unaccompanied by correct political and psychological strategies may not work or may ultimately kill the patient. A few examples will show how political and psychological factors interact with economic variables and why both noneconomic and economic approaches are necessary.

The problem of productivity will be considered first. Since the mid-1970s, the postwar average of more than 3 percent annual increase in the rate of productivity has been cut in half, and in 1978 there was no increase at all. Among the Western industrial nations, the United States finds itself with England at the bottom of the ladder. Moreover, the formal productivity measures badly understate the severity of the problem. The narrow economic measure of productivity—output per person hour of labor—does not take into account such factors as poor product quality, pilferage, bad service, low morale, not caring, and the costs of layers on layers of managerial and supervisory controls that add to the costs without contributing to the product.

In the post-World War II period, one important reason for the low inflation rate in the United States was the fact that increases in productivity kept pace with wage increases, resulting in real gains in the American standard of living. Now wage increases are geared to inflation and regularly outstrip productivity gains.

A purely economic analysis of the causes of the declining rate of productivity increases would stress the slowing of investment, the aging of plant and equipment, the cost of environmental controls, the increase of other government regulations, the change in composition of the work force, and so on. Although these factors are important, another category of factors should be considered. In the late 1960s, almost half of all employed Americans viewed their work as a prime source of personal fulfillment; now that number has plunged to fewer than one out of four. An overwhelming 84 percent of all Americans have come to believe that it does not pay to work hard and live by the rules. The University of Michigan recently repeated a survey it conducted in the late 1950s. It showed that, twenty years later, twice as many people have difficulties on the job, while fewer consider their work a source of satisfaction and happiness. Only 13 percent of working Americans now find their work more meaningful and important to them than their leisure time.

There can be no doubt that there is a growing gap between people's motivations—what they require to stimulate them to work harder—and the existing incentive system. It would certainly overstate the case to attribute all the current ills of the American economy to a less involved, less committed work force. But it is a fact that Americans are making less of a commitment to their jobs than in the past.

In recent years, people's work motives have changed enormously, but the incentive systems have not. Corporate management has not faced up to the changes in worker attitudes and motivations or to the need for revised incentive systems as a method for improving productivity. In management circles, aside from lip service there is great resistance to the idea that human resources are a key to improving productivity and competitive efficiency. The conventional wisdom rather holds that capital investment, technology, and management systems are more important than people's motivations. Some executives regard the motivation to work hard as being of negligible importance, while others think it is important but not very important. The reason is that in the past, technology and capital investment were the key factors, and, in addition, they were easier to deal with than people.

Today the United States has an outmoded incentive system that is a major cause of productivity decline and, consequently, of inflation as well. In the past, management had ready tools for motivating people to ensure ever-increasing productivity, but this is no longer true. In the past, management could always count on four key tools: the fear of loss of a job and the ensuing economic insecurity; the use of money as an incentive to get people to work harder; the use of production techniques such as the assembly line that did not make productivity as dependent on individual motivation; and the work ethic, that is, the desire to do a good job. Today all four have lost strength. There is less fear of economic devastation from loss of jobs, and that is a good thing. Making more money is important to people, but only a fraction of today's workers are motivated to do a better job by money increases. In fact, many people work less hard when they make more money because they then have the means to enjoy their leisure—and the implications of this point are rarely understood. Also, the national economy has changed so greatly that 70 percent of all jobs today are of the service type, and techniques to increase productivity depend less on workers' motivations. Finally, when people feel that they are not getting as much out of their jobs as they are putting in, they are likely to be less involved and less committed to their work, and the work ethic suffers accordingly. These are not mysterious changes that have to be accepted passively. All too frequently policymakers assume that something can be done about the economic variables but that nothing can be done about the social-psychological variables. But once these are analyzed and taken seriously as drains on productivity, remedial action can be taken. For example, the United States has an extremely pluralistic work force—the most diverse and best educated work force in history. But the incentive system assumes that it is homogeneous and that money and status rewards will universally motivate people to give everything they have to the job.

This is a serious mistake. In selling products and services to the American public, the diversity of the marketplace is recognized, and consequently products and services are customized to suit every taste. But when these very same consumers are encountered as employees, no allowance for individual differences is made. Some employees value time flexibility, while others are motivated by educational opportunities, longer vacations, variety and diversity, the challenge of the job, attention and feedback, the inherent interest of the work, more participation and involvement, or the social world afforded by the job.

In this age of the computer, it is quite possible to put together a whole range of cafeteria-style incentive systems to fit each individual's preferences. This is not done, because the new motivations of the American workers are not understood, and management does not think these motivations affect productivity. The psychological factors have been pushed aside and only the economic variables considered, even though there is no real evidence that they, by themselves, account for the diminution of productivity.

The methods of paying and reimbursing the costs of medical care illustrate even more dramatically how noneconomic factors interact with economic variables. The people who devise the methods for reimbursing physicians and hospitals—lawyers, accountants, legislators, and bureaucrats—hardly consider anything as academic-sounding as the sociology of the doctor-patient relationship. But the "mind set" of the medical profession must be considered. One has to take into account the profession's aura of medical absolutism with respect to costs and the belief that cost should not be a consideration when dealing with people's health. Allied to this proposition is the value judgment that nothing is more important in America than quality medical service regardless of its cost. Another factor that influences costs is medical uncertainty. If a physician is not sure of a diagnosis, he inevitably orders more tests, which incur added expenses. Ironically, in today's state of advanced knowledge, diagnosis grows ever more uncertain as the number of tests that can be done increases with new technology.

Another consideration is the practice of defensive medicine—the feeling that a physician must protect himself against malpractice suits, even when he does not feel more tests and other expenses are needed. Medicalization of social problems is yet another factor. Today all manner of social problems, such as care for the elderly and the disabled, have been put under medical supervision and costs have escalated. Finally, the economy suffers from a reversal of all known market principles. In every other field it is assumed that increasing supply will stimulate competition and lower prices. In medicine, Joseph Califano, secretary of health, education, and welfare, has publicly stated that the nation does not need more physicians, because every physician adds $300,000 of new costs. Under the prevailing cartel conditions of the profession, he may very well be right. If these factors are taken in combination, they add up to a total absence of cost consciousness and an unprecedented opportunity to spend and to waste resources.

If the devil himself had an understanding of these conditions and if he had been asked to invent a system of financing medical care that would guarantee waste and escalate costs to multiples of what they had been, he would have developed the present system of third-party payments and cost-plus contracts. Those who conceived the present cost system planned it within a single, largely economic frame of reference, and it seemed to make sense within that frame of reference. However, if the system is examined in relation to other social factors, it does not make sense. In fact, it virtually guarantees that health service costs will continue to escalate.

The third and most important example has to do with the need for public cooperation in carrying out a successful anti-inflation program. The best possible paper plan for controlling inflation will not work if the public does not understand it or does not believe it or does not accept it. Most policies can be planned and implemented by experts without much public understanding or even attention. Full public comprehension and acceptance of every policy that America implements is not necessary. But in the areas of inflation, energy, jobs, and taxes, public acceptance is indispensable.

What happened to the energy program is an instructive and disastrous example that should not be repeated in the domain of inflation. When the president gave his famous "moral equivalent of war" speech, experts had been agonizing over the need for a national energy policy for at least a decade. In that speech, the president asked Americans to reverse direction and to change attitudes and behavior that had been encouraged for more than three decades—a life-style centered on big automobiles, big homes, and other energy intensive products.

The president's twenty-minute speech illustrates the dramatic difference between an engineer's conception of communication, based on facts and information, and that of a psychologist. The engineer president checked off the items on his list as he gave the country the facts about the seriousness of the problem. He was dramatic. He used all three television networks to reach a massive public audience. His speech conveyed a tone of urgency, but once he made his speech about energy he turned his attention to the next crisis. There was no follow-up. There was no public debate, no presentation or discussion of alternative policies and their advantages and disadvantages for the citizens of the country. As a result, people were left more confused, cynical, worried, and inert after the speech than before it.

Psychologists have learned that effective communication with the public is far more complex. Communicating factual information in a single speech bears little resemblance to the process of convincing people that they must reverse deep-seated attitudes and behavior. Psychologists use the term "working through" to describe a complex process that has three or four distinct phases. If people are to make changes in basic attitudes and behavior, they need time to live with new ideas that conflict with their established views. They need time to fight against a new idea, resist it, ask questions, challenge, probe, and argue. Only after this complicated process, which may take days, weeks, months, or years, can they begin to accept a new idea and change their attitudes accordingly.

On energy, it must be admitted that the Carter administration faltered twice. It failed to understand the public's need for time to digest and "work through" choices when fundamental values and changes of life-style are involved. It also failed to present to Congress and to the people real alternative approaches to the energy problem. The result of this dual failure is a cynical public, a bedeviled administration, and a frustrated Congress. The country still does not have an energy policy, and the president did not even mention energy in his State of the Union address in 1979.

In America's present mistrustful, skeptical state of mind, leadership is not just a matter of giving the public the facts; it is a matter of helping to launch and direct a real public dialogue so the citizens can wrestle with hard choices they must make as a mature, responsible electorate. A successful approach to the problem of inflation must consider the economic, political, social, psychological, and ethical aspects of the problem. Particularly important is the ethical aspect. The country is hungry—almost desperate—for the return of public policy to traditional values based on honesty, integrity, leadership, and fairness in the sense of rewarding people who work hard and live by the rules and not rewarding those who flout the rules.

Americans will have to make some painful choices before the problem of inflation is solved. First, however, they must understand what these choices are. Only then will they accept the discomfort that accompanies responsible choice and decision.

Inflationary Effects of
Government Interference in Markets

PHILLIP CAGAN

Government interference in markets has two effects on prices that are not always clearly distinguished but are quite different in their significance for inflation. One is to raise a particular price relative to the general price level. The removal of this interference would lead to a one-time decrease in the price relative to the general price level. The second effect reduces the responsiveness of the price to changes in market conditions and thus reduces price flexibility. This is important for the problem of inflation, because the necessary condition for subduing inflation—slowing the growth in aggregate demand—tends to produce accompanying short-run reductions in output and employment, the magnitude of which depends on general price flexibility. Hence greater price flexibility is thought to improve the short-run trade-off between output and prices in pursuing an anti-inflationary monetary and fiscal policy.

This essay surveys the main government measures that have these two effects on prices. The removal of government interferences that raise prices could be expected to produce a decline in the affected prices; but, unless such interferences were removed on a broad scale in unison, the effect on the general price level, however desirable, would be small and could not perceptibly reduce the rate of inflation over a year's period. Not much should be expected from such reforms, but new and expanded interferences during periods of serious inflation that exert upward pressures on prices should be postponed or stretched out.

Increasing the responsiveness of prices to demand conditions, particularly so that they would rise less rapidly as demand slackened, could greatly improve the effectiveness of anti-inflationary restraints on aggregate demand. The evidence does not support the argument that government is mainly responsible for the general decline in the responsiveness that has occurred in recent decades. But the government does reduce the flexibility of many prices, and some improvement could be made.

The Problem of Reducing Inflation

The upward trend in the United States rate of inflation since 1965 has been arrested three times—by a minirecession in 1966–67, a mild recession in 1969–70, and the most severe recession since World War II in 1973–75. Each time the rate of inflation was cut approximately in half during the recession and the ensuing recovery period. But each time it subsequently turned up and continued to rise as business recovered and expanded. The trend of inflation has been unmistakably upward; each business expansion has started from a higher rate of inflation than did the previous expansion. During the present business expansion the inflation rate fell from the high rates of 1973–74 to 5 percent in early 1976 but has since stubbornly edged higher despite quite high unemployment and excess productive capacity. When unemployment finally fell below the full-employment level of 6 percent in early 1978, the inflation rate had reached the 6 to 7 percent range and was clearly rising further and more rapidly. Thus the severe recession of 1973–75 briefly reduced the inflation rate to 5 percent, which was well above the average rate of 1972 before the outburst of 1973–74; and during 1977 the inflation rate did not fall but began rising even before the economy reached full employment.

In the light of this experience it is widely believed that inflation is largely self-propelled and cannot be easily arrested, not even by ordinary business recessions, and that many years of excessively high unemployment are required to stop it. Given this pessimism, it is not surprising that the business community remains in constant fear of the reimposition of mandatory price controls, despite official denials, and that unusual schemes of using taxes and subsidies to affect the setting of prices and wages directly have been proposed and discussed.

Why do prices continue to rise even when there is slack in the economy? This phenomenon is the source of much public confusion about the inflationary process. The answer is that economic units come to expect that recent inflation trends will continue, and wages and prices are regularly adjusted upward on the presumption that the ongoing average rate of inflation will prevail in the future. Expectations will seldom be exactly correct and will normally require adjustments in the light of experience, but imprecise expectations of some positive rate of inflation have proved to be far superior to the assumption that the general level of prices will remain constant. As each wage and price is raised either to catch up with past inflation not yet adjusted for or to anticipate future increases until the next adjustment is made, the increases raise costs in each stage of production, which in turn require increases in other prices, and the resulting price increases in final goods and services raise the cost of living, which feeds back on wage adjustments. The process is continuous; there is no moment at which it can be stopped by fiat without leaving some wages and prices too low because they had not yet fully adjusted to past cost increases. Inflation cannot suddenly stop; at most, it can only unwind.

Recognition that inflation proceeds as a series of interrelated step-by-step adjustments is important. At any moment most prices and wages are not in equilibrium in relation to each other or to aggregate demand. This is the main reason why price and wage freezes cannot be maintained over long periods and why effective price and wage controls are impossible to impose equitably and without distortions of economic efficiency. It is also the reason why policy restraints on growth in aggregate demand do not appear to have any immediate effect on the inflation rate, which continues under its own momentum. But this does not signify that aggregate demand is unimportant to inflation. Over the long run the rate of inflation is governed by the growth rate of aggregate demand. Aggregate demand in turn is determined by government policies, particularly over the long run by monetary policy. Hence monetary policy determines the long-run rate of inflation. It is important to keep this basic fact in mind in order to avoid misinterpreting the significance of short-run influences on inflation.

Empirical studies confirm that a slowing of demand growth reduces inflation. Since the process works slowly, however, the initial effect of monetary restraint in slowing demand growth is to reduce employment and output. The inflation rate continues for a while along its previous path, which reflects the previous effects of aggregate demand and expectations of the future inflation rate. Continued restraint on aggregate demand pulls actual price increases below the expected path and eventually reduces the expected inflation rate, which feeds back to diminish price and wage increases pushed along by expectations, thereby further reducing the actual inflation rate.

But why does the rate of inflation not only fail to decline but actually rise during business expansions, long before all idle labor and productive facilities have been put back to work? The answer is that, as aggregate demand fluctuates over the business cycle, the rate of inflation fluctuates correspondingly. Nevertheless, apart from the fluctuations, the average rate of inflation can decline from one business cycle to the next if the expected rate of inflation declines. The expected rate declines when aggregate demand fluctuates around a declining growth trend. This is associated with a higher average rate of unemployed resources over the business cycle. The excess unemployment associated with a reduction in the annual inflation rate by 1 percentage point from one business cycle to the next is estimated to average about two-thirds of a percentage point. Thus, reducing the inflation rate by 3 percentage points, say, would result in excess unemployment of 2 percent for a business cycle of four years.

All such estimates, however, are derived from the experience of the past twenty-five years during which doubts have multiplied whether an effective anti-inflationary policy would be carried through. If policy were now to demonstrate, over the course of a business cycle, that continuing measures to reduce inflation were in force and would undoubtedly persist, expectations would more quickly adjust and contribute to a declining rate of inflation, and the associated unemployment would be lower. But credibility in government pronouncements of opposing inflation has become quite low. Credibility can probably no longer be raised in short order except by an act of Congress directing the Federal Reserve to reduce annual monetary growth by, say, 1.0 to 1.5 percentage points each year. Barring that resolute action, at least a full business cycle will be needed to determine whether an anti-inflationary policy can survive a business cycle in which pressures to do something about unemployment intensify. Policymakers are thus hemmed in by skeptical expectations, which are difficult to dissipate because of the slow response of prices and wages to policy restraints. The initial effect of restraint imposed on aggregate demand mainly reduces output and may precipitate a recession. Given the belief that reductions in output and the associated increases in unemployment are unacceptable to the public, policymakers believe that they have no choice but to accommodate increases in prices and wages at prevailing rates, and expectations that they will do so contribute, of course, to the maintenance of the ongoing rate of inflation.

The dynamic behavior of the economy has not always been so prone to continuing inflation. During the 1920s and earlier periods, prices displayed considerable variation over business cycles. Although wages were generally unresponsive to mild business cycles, in the severe business contractions of 1920-21 and 1929-23 they declined sharply. In the first post-World War II recession of 1948–49, considerable price flexibility remained. But thereafter a progressive decline of the response began. The declines in the level and rate of change of prices in the post-World War II recessions progressively diminished, and the overall variability of prices was appreciably less in these recessions than in those of the 1920s.

This development did not go unnoticed at the time; it was widely discussed as a new phenomenon of "creeping inflation." In his famous Fordham lectures of 1957, *Prosperity Without Inflation*, Arthur Burns warned of the dangers of the new situation and discussed possible policy solutions. He noted the decreased flexibility of prices. At that time the problem was viewed as "downward rigidity" of wages and prices, whereas today it is not the absence of declines in level but the inflexibility of rates of increase that creates an inflationary ·momentum. What is clear today, and was not then, is that prices and wages tend to follow a trend path that changes only slowly, and inflexibility is characterized by resistance of prices to rising less rapidly than the trend path.

Burns attributed "creeping inflation" to the newly developed tendency of prices and wages in a mild business recession to stay rigid and fail to offset, through a decline, the increases that invariably accompany a business expansion. Hence, barring the unlikely avoidance of business expansions producing price increases, the absences of recessionary price declines made the trend of prices inexorably upward. Monetary policy had to accommodate the upward trend. Failure to do so would result in a protracted period of higher unemployment because rigid nominal wages would make real wages too high, and rigid prices would not allow markets to clear. In the 1950s, a persistent inflation of

3 percent a year was considered bad enough. But some commentators also worried that the dynamics of the situation could eventually turn "creeping inflation" into "galloping" or even "double-digit" inflation.

Burns attributed the decreased flexibility of prices to two developments. The first was the lessening severity of the business cycle due to improved government stabilization of aggregate demand. Burns also noted that prices and wages had developed decreased flexibility even in business cycles of the same severity as those of the 1920s and earlier. He identified a second development leading to decreased price and wage flexibility in increased government regulation of the private sector. The belief that government regulation is responsible for the weak effect of slack demand on prices is now widely held. But the diminished responsiveness of prices to business contraction is so pervasive across the economy that it is hard to believe that the growth in government interferences in private markets, vast as it is, has yet reached such a grand scale as to account for the decline in price flexibility. On the other hand, neither does the evidence support the other long-standing explanation that attributes it to a growing concentration of industry and a decline in competition in the United States economy. Economists simply do not have a satisfactory and complete explanation of the decline in price flexibility. It may be partly illusory because of inadequacies of the data and because of the changing composition of the economy (more manufacturers and services compared with agriculture), but probably most of it is an actual development related to lessened fears of cyclical catastrophes and to an uncertain and unanchored monetary standard. When the dollar was tied rigidly to gold before World War I and as it largely remained before the 1930s, only mild inflation was possible. Anything is possible today. This is bound to have affected expectations and the dynamics of the price system, but all the ramifications are not yet fully understood.

The diminished responsiveness of most prices does not reflect direct government influences. Nevertheless, a moderation of government controls over prices would help moderate inflation. The remainder of this essay will survey the main government effects on prices and then discuss how government controls might be lessened and what the results might be.

The Range of Government Effects on Prices

Only a few of the most important government effects on prices will be discussed here. It should be stated at the outset that critical remarks about any of these programs do not mean they necessarily could or should be eliminated. The purpose is to draw attention to the broad role of government and to suggest that modifications may be desirable and possible without complete removal of each item on the list.

Agricultural Price Supports. Many of these programs set minimum prices on a variety of products. Apart from preventing prices from falling below the minimums, whether these programs tend to raise prices depends on whether they restrict supplies. Commodity loans for grains, without acreage restrictions, do not restrict supplies permanently. Thus storable grains under the commodity loan program can put a damper on price increase because supplies are not forever removed from the market. But supplies are restricted, of course, by many of these programs and by limitations on domestic production, import quotas, and export subsidies. With restricted supplies, any increase in demand has a greater effect in raising prices. Acreage allotments and market orders for daily products do effectively restrict supplies. In an inflationary environment, however, it does not appear that these programs raise the average rate of inflation higher than it would be otherwise, even though they prevent declines in these prices.

Agricultural programs illustrate a conflict between the goals of raising and of stabilizing prices. A possible argument for agricultural price supports is that they should stabilize prices but not raise them on the average. Farmers complain of feast and famine in economic conditions. But in setting out to stabilize farm prices, these programs ultimately raise them, because decreases are prevented and increases allowed—that is, a floor but no ceiling is set. To even out fluctuations without raising the average level of these prices, a government storage program would buy when prices were "low" and sell when "high" and would stabilize without raising the prices if the definition of "high" and "low" were related to a "normal" price that always matched the level that would prevail on the average in a free market. But this reform would retain the stabilization goal and hence leave the prices less flexible—not a desirable result for fighting inflation. Yet such a reform, which entails selling stored farm products when prices are rising, would have anti-inflationary benefits on the upside, because it would contain an upsurge like the one in 1973 that tends to be passed on to other prices in the economy. Farm interests, however, would resist such a reform. "Stabilizing prices" has become instead a program to keep prices higher than free market levels, leaving both higher and less flexible prices.

Transportation Regulation. Railroads, trucking, and airlines have long had their fares regulated by the government. While the original purpose was to prevent high monopoly prices, open competition has been largely stifled in these sectors by limiting entry, and rigid cartel prices have come to be the standard arrangement. The prices in almost all cases are undoubtedly higher than they would be with free entry and no regulation, and their flexibility in response to short-run fluctuations in demand has been reduced almost to zero. Maritime shipping is a special case where government regulations and market forces have priced the United States out of the world market, producing massive federal subsidies and quotas on use of foreign vessels. These raise shipping costs and prevent price declines.

Import Restrictions. Foreign competition is limited by tariffs and direct quotas on a broad range of products far beyond agricultural items. Tariffs are equivalent to a sales tax, of course, and do not interfere with price flexibility unless the tariff is high enough, as it is in some cases, effectively to exclude certain foreign products from the domestic market. Quotas are another matter;

they cut off an important source of competitive supply for domestic markets. This makes the domestic price higher and also more volatile in the face of shifts in domestic demand, if no other restriction is put on domestic price changes. Quotas are not, however, an appealing way to introduce price flexibility. As economists have long pointed out, import restrictions protect certain domestic jobs, but only at the expense of jobs in export industries and of the purchasing power of the consumer.

Petroleum and Gas Controls. The government has long held down the price of interstate gas. Petroleum, on the other hand, presents a more complex picture; prices were raised by the pre-OPEC quotas on imports and are held down by present price ceilings. In this important sector, removal of all controls would lead to an increase in prices, but they would thereafter become responsive to market forces much more directly than they are now. The sorry record of government regulation in this sector has been widely discussed and has long defied the best advice of economists for improvement and did so again with the recent energy bill.

Environmental and Safety Regulations. These regulations operate to increase costs of production and hence to raise prices. They are the prime example of the government's contribution to inflation and the favorite complaint of those critics of government regulation who believe these measures were undesirable in the first place. They have a one-time effect in raising prices to a higher relative level, which can continue, however, for an extended period to keep prices rising. Investments to reduce factory noise and safety are just beginning and will continue for years to come. Much of this regulation is criticized for being too costly for the benefits produced, such as the publicized case of requiring expensive redesign of production facilities to reduce noise rather than simply providing earplugs. Automobile prices have been periodically raised for some years now and will continue to be for more years to come because of environmental standards. This is also true for industries, especially electric utilities, that must meet tightening environmental emission standards. Edward F. Denison has estimated that from 1967 to 1975 costs in the nonresidential business sector rose by 1.0 percent for pollution requirements and by 0.4 percent for employee safety and health programs.

Although dollar prices are raised in a theoretical sense, these increases are not necessarily inflationary. If the value of the environmental or safety benefits added to the total product is included, the price for the total value received may or may not be higher, even though the payment for the original product is higher. To be sure, these additions are socially mandated and are not demanded by individual purchasers; hence they could be paid for in a variety of ways. They are in fact covered by increases in the price of the product to which they are attached as a package. Thus automobile purchases pay for the environmental requirements that are attached. The price increases are inflationary, therefore, in the sense that alternative methods of financing (government subsidy, say, financed from the income tax) would not be. Covering the cost of automobile pollution devices by subsidy, and thereby reducing automobile prices, is considered undesirable, however, on the grounds that users of automobiles and not the general taxpayer should bear this cost.

One of the uncounted but not insignificant costs of environmental regulation is the uncontrollable time delays in conforming to conflicting regulations. The main example here is the conflict between environmental standards and energy requirements. Electric utilities are directed to make the nation less dependent on foreign petroleum but at the same time find that shifts to coal and nuclear facilities are blocked by environmental concerns. The time required to sort out the conflicting legal claims through the courts adds substantially to the development costs of the new facilities and eventually must be reflected in the price of electricity. The problem is an exacerbated version of the old political dodge in which Congress proclaims itself in favor of a "clean and safe environment," "cheap energy," and "independence from foreign sources." Vaguely written statutes to express these sentiments that ignore the inevitable conflicts are then passed on to administrative agencies for enforcement. When the conflicts arise, Congress keeps its distance. Administrative agencies, designed to determine technical details and to enforce clearly defined statutes, simply do not command the authority to untangle the thicket of conflicting political values, particularly when two or more agencies with differing mandates are involved.

The basic problem is that Congress is unable or unwilling to settle political conflicts that in a representative democracy only it can settle. The conflicts may eventually be resolved one way or another, but the method that has been adopted by default is very costly. The battles through the courts among administrative agencies, public interest groups, and affected economic organizations, guided only by vague and conflicting statutes, are inefficient and costly. When the construction of a needed electric utility threatens to harm the environment, there is no legal precedent for resolving that conflict in a court of law. It is a conflict of political values, though one with economic costs and benefits, that can only be resolved by a political entity representing the entire population—not just those interests that happen to have access to the regulatory process. Some economists think that a market in the purchase and sale of "pollution certificates," issued by the government, could be effective in allowing electric utilities to buy their authorization to build facilities, and environmental interests could bid against them, thus settling these disputes in the marketplace. But the belief that any such swift method of resolving conflicting interests will ever be instituted to shift these problems from the political sphere to the marketplace is unrealistic.

If these conflicts continue, as it appears they will, the proper solution is to establish a political body, elected to represent geographic units and patterned after the House of Representatives, which would be empowered to veto specific regulations and resolve conflicts among regulatory statutes and government programs. The vote of this body would be final, subject only to overrule by Congress itself. It would be a fourth branch of the government. The addition would reflect the growth to crisis proportions of economic externalities in the modern economy.

Sales and Payroll Taxes. Taxation cannot be eliminated, but it can be designed to have less effect on the price level. The 1978 increase in social security taxes, combined with the rise in the minimum wage, is projected to raise labor costs by 1 percent in 1979. It is generally thought that sales taxes raise prices and payroll taxes raise labor costs and thence prices, in contrast to income taxes, which do not affect prices from the cost side. The effects are more complicated than this simple dichotomy implies, because both income and payroll taxes to some extent discourage labor supply. It is probably true that a reduction in the social security tax on employers would be equivalent to a decline in wages and therefore anti-inflationary. But, while a reduction in the employee's tax would not affect the employer's costs, it would affect labor supply and might in the long run have the same anti-inflationary effect. It is generally assumed that it would not have such an effect on the grounds that the supply effects would not occur. It is likely that, whatever the supply effects in the long run, they would be small in the short run, and the assumption is therefore valid that a reduction in the employee's tax is not useful for anti-inflationary purposes. It is also sometimes argued that the employee social security tax is inflationary, because workers would press for higher wages to compensate for it, whereas the income tax would not have such an effect. This does not seem a valid distinction between payroll and income taxes; but, insofar as union demands gain success only to the extent that they are socially accepted and politically supported, it is possible that employee social security tax increases could thus raise wages and prices. Whether this is true of reductions is problematical.

Sales taxes have a more direct effect. They drive a wedge between the price of products and costs. It is possible to adjust to this wedge by lowering dollar payments to factors of production, which would leave the sales price the same. No one believes such an adjustment likely, however, and in the short run at least it is expected that the sales price will have the tax added on. Hence, reduction of the sales tax would, in the first instance, reduce the total sales price paid.

The difference between the sales tax and an equivalent income tax on workers is that wage payments remain the same for the income tax and the tax is taken from workers before they make purchases; hence they purchase less but presumably at the same price. Yet the real income of workers is the same whether the tax is added to the sales price or taken from income after it is received but before it is spent. The sales tax encourages a decrease in consumption in favor of saving, but aside from that difference it is hard to see that the long-run effect on the use and price of goods and services should differ from the effect of the income tax. But, again, that is long-run consideration. In the short run, income taxes are not expected to affect prices from the cost side.

Thus, if state sales taxes could be replaced by income taxes, it is alleged that the price level would benefit by an equivalent amount. However, real income would be the same overall if a reduction in the sales tax is offset by an increase in the income tax. The difference in their effects on prices rests on the convention of measuring sales taxes as part of price indexes rather than as deductions from pretax income. The attraction of the scheme for reducing sales taxes, however, is that "multiplier effects" are supposed to follow. The slower rise in prices is supposed to lead to reduced cost-of-living increases in wage negotiations, which in turn add less to costs and prices further down the line, and so on. It is possible to imagine such a series of consequences, but they depend critically on good timing and some questionable influences. Such an outcome must be viewed as highly problematical. The likely effects, if any, of slowing inflation by reducing sales or payroll taxes seem too slim to warrant interfering with a tax system that should be designed primarily for equity and economic efficiency.

Labor Restrictions. Government measures affecting the labor supply can have effects of considerable consequence for the simple reason that labor costs are a large part of the costs of production of most goods and services. Government policy supports and encourages labor unions, which have organized about one-fifth of the labor force. By intent and design they may make wages higher in dollar terms than they would otherwise be. But, in addition, they considerably reduce the flexibility of wages, a consequence that has been widely discussed. Labor unions have also become a political force, most recently used to pressure the government to reduce imports that compete with domestically produced goods in unionized industries.

In addition to unions, the federal government mandates minimum wages for many employments, forces up wages of construction workers on federally sponsored projects under the Davis-Bacon Act, and is instrumental in raising some wages and labor costs of production through affirmative action and minority hiring programs. Liberal unemployment benefits have tended to reduce labor supplies and to maintain wages, especially in periods of recession, though manpower programs that use general funds to train and place workers help to increase labor supplies. High marginal tax rates also reduce the labor supply; they make unemployment compensation and social security benefits more attractive than gainful employment and reduce the incentive for many workers to earn more. The reduction in labor supply raises pretax wages.

Much state regulation of occupations, while mainly a limitation on supply and a support of higher prices, also ultimately reduces flexibility. Many of the regulated professions and vocations are allowed to set up professional standards boards that may introduce fee schedules and limit advertising. Fixed real estate fees are an example of the former, and the widely discussed ban on advertising by doctors and lawyers is an example of the latter.

The only optimistic trend in the labor area is that these developments may not make inflation any worse in the future than they do now. Unions, despite their best efforts, do not appear to be gaining in size and importance. There is much that government reform could do to ameliorate restrictions on wage flexibility, but given the political opposition, whether much can be accomplished is questionable. A less unpopular reform would be to index wages more closely to the cost of living. Although this would accelerate their increase when inflation escalated, indexed wages would decelerate faster when inflation subsided.

Antitrust and Trade Laws. No general consensus exists on the overall result of government effects on competitive pricing. Antitrust laws can work to maintain competition and break up cartels—the electrical turbine conspiracy of the early 1960s is a dramatic example. But the Robinson-Patman Act of 1936 is often used to prevent aggressive competition and protect inefficient producers. Such limitations on competition should be eliminated.

While antitrust enforcement is a potential support of market competition and price flexibility, in reality it is doubtful that the government has the wisdom or competence to restructure concentrated and oligopolistic industries for purposes of achieving greater price competitiveness. Such endeavors are more likely to introduce inefficiencies than to affect price flexibility much. Government efforts in this area should be neither increased nor reduced soley for purposes of fighting inflation.

There is a group of developments that reflect the government's influence but are not directly or solely due to government programs or measures. These developments concern medical costs, product liability, and productivity.

The government has poured vast sums into subsidizing medical costs of the poor and the elderly, and this increase in demand concentrated in one sector accounts for a large part of the rise in prices of medical services. The manner in which the funds are supplied has also helped to inflate costs. Through the expansion of medical insurance, the public has little incentive to limit the demand for services or to be concerned about charges, particularly since much of the insurance provides coverage without deductibles or coinsurance. Such third-party payments for a heavily demanded service are custom-made to inflate costs. Combined with malpractice suits and the prevalence of hospitals that are not operated for profit, doctors are encouraged to provide and prescribe more extensive and more expensive medical services, and no individual patient covered by insurance has much monetary incentive to limit his use of these services. The marginal dollar cost to the individual is zero, while the total cost is paid collectively by all.

The theory behind free medical services is that the demand is completely inelastic because no one chooses to be ill or to need medical attention, but, as has been shown again and again, the demand is not completely inelastic. Although the government covers medical costs of the poor and the elderly largely without coinsurance, the low coinsurance in most private plans is not directly due to government measures, though the tax deductibility of medical insurance premiums contributes to it. The government could, in its own programs and through the removal of tax deductibility, induce coinsurance provisions in most medical insurance plans, but given the emotional attachment of the public to "free" medical services, the tide is moving strongly in the opposite direction. Putting a cap on hospital cost increases, as has been proposed, would not solve this problem.

It remains to be seen whether the projected oversupply of doctors in coming years will restrain the rise in medical costs. Here the government's subsidization of medical education is working to mitigate the problem. But a subsidized oversupply to satisfy an artificially stimulated demand is hardly the most efficient use of national resources. Medical programs can be supported as acceptable social policy only on the assumption that the allocating price of medical services should be set close to zero for most of the population. A price artificially set at zero is not a social policy that most economists would recommend.

Medical malpractice suits are only one aspect of the rising use of legal remedies to extract reimbursement for injuries connected with products and services. In recent years the degree of supplier liability for customer damages has expanded enormously. Changes in the law and legal precedents and new laws have made suits against suppliers easier and more likely to be successful. The old legal precedent that a product had to be defective and the primary cause of an injury before the manufacturer was liable has given way to the principle that the supplier of a product or service that is merely an instrument in an accident is liable. As a result, product and service liability insurance has skyrocketed, and the costs of production are thereby inflated.

No one contends that serious damages should not be litigable. But consumers are thus forced to pay for higher product insurance in the price of the product whether they want it or not. The law does not allow a doctor or a manufacturer to offer his services or product both at a low fee without the right to sue and at a high fee to cover insurance provisions for those who want it. Costs are thus inflated for everyone, and the consumer has little incentive to avoid the costs of injury. Can some way be devised to unpackage products and liability insurance?

A more general effect on the behavior of prices in the economy has reflected the growth of nonprofit sectors outside or inside the government, where the threat of profit or loss is not present to maintain efficiency and keep down costs. When nonprofit organizations are financed by the government in such a way that the services they provide are not directly paid for by those who consume them, there is reduced control over costs and efficiency. This is the basis of the argument that the growth of government is inflationary. These sectors are the government itself, such as municipal services and public education, and semigovernmental institutions, such as nonprofit hospitals and public housing. The effect is a kind of socialism in which no one is directly and individually concerned with and responsible for costs. In some of the specific cases cited above, particularly medical services, it can be an important contribution to inflationary pressures.

Another side to this growth of the nonprofit sector is often stressed. The governmental and nonprofit sectors of the economy are characterized by low incentives and opportunities to improve productivity, and these sectors are growing apace. Although productivity improvements in these sectors are largely unmeasurable, their productivity growth is undoubtedly low, and overall productivity growth in the economy as a whole has been decelerating. Consequently, the contribution of productivity growth to holding down price increases is diminishing. Nevertheless, the simple remedy to avoid the consequences of slower growth of output on the inflation rate is to reduce the rate of growth of nominal aggregate demand commensurately through the effective use of monetary policy.

Lessening Government Price Effects

As argued above, it is important to distinguish one-time effects from continuing effects of government measures on prices. A one-time effect leaves a price higher relative to the general price level but does not continue to raise it higher through time. A continuing effect, however, can be of two kinds. One is simply a one-time effect that is repeated, perhaps frequently, over a period of time or indefinitely. Prices rise each time the effect occurs, and the cumulative effect is a series of increases—a higher rate of increase of prices so long as the effect recurs. The continuing cost increases of meeting pollution requirements are an example.

The second kind of continuing effect is a single development that makes the economy prone to higher inflation rates—typically a change in the dynamic behavior of the price system. Less flexibility of prices makes the short-run trade-off between output and inflation less favorable and leads the authorities to pursue easier monetary policies. Because of the various possible meanings of price flexibility, it may be defined, for present purposes, as the change in a price per period of time that occurs when the intersection of the governing demand and supply curves has been displaced upwards or downwards by a given amount. Downward rigidity of wages is a special case of inflexibility, in which increases in wages and prices due to sporadic periods of strong demand cannot be reversed by periods of slack demand. Downward flexibility is less important to the present situation of persistent inflation, unless "downward" pertains to the rate of inflation rather than the level of prices.

In the present inflationary environment, prices need not decline to moderate inflation; they need only to rise less rapidly. Inflexible prices respond slowly to demand conditions, and that is generally true on the upside as well as the downside. Hence such prices do not spearhead a resurgence of inflationary pressures. But the inflexibility of regulated prices is still a problem, because it tends to make these prices inflexible in real terms. That is, although they may be slow to rise when other prices rise faster in an outburst of increased inflation, eventually they do respond, generally by rising sufficiently to make up for all lost ground and to maintain their historical relationship to the general price level. Slack demand in these markets has no effect in holding these prices down for any longer than the usual regulatory lag. When demand is slack in these sectors, competitive market pressures would, if given a chance to operate, prevent these prices from rising as much as they otherwise would—that is, they would decline relative to other prices for which demand was stronger. Regulated prices, by generally preserving the historical relationship to the general level, make this segment of the economy inflexible to demand pressures.

Removal of the one-time effects would produce a single decline in the affected prices relative to the general price level. If a large number of such declines could be made to occur in unison, a decline would occur in the general rate of inflation during the period in which these prices fell. Thereafter they would rise along with the general rate of inflation and have no further effect. Such a one-time decline in the rate of inflation, if matched by a corresponding slowing of aggregate demand, could reduce the expected rate of inflation and its contribution to the inflation momentum. There might therefore be a "multiplier effect" on the rate of inflation through reduced expectations, and conceivably the slowing process, thus initiated, could continue until inflation was eliminated. The corresponding decline in aggregate demand, of course, is crucial for the success of such a program.

Yet any selective removal of such effects would produce a negligible fall in the general price level within any short period of time and hence in the average inflation rate over an extended period, and the multiplier effects on expectations would not occur if the effects were almost imperceptible. Indeed, efforts spent in discussing and proposing a fight against inflation by removing these government effects may be counterproductive so far as inflation itself is concerned, if it diverts attention away from the aggregate-demand policies that are necessary for success. Removal of government effects should be pursued for their own sake, if found desirable, but a major reduction of inflation from them should not be expected or promised.

Nevertheless, as part of an anti-inflationary program of restraint on aggregate demand, the introduction of new cost increases, or the continuation of those with effects that occur regularly (such as the pollution controls) might be wisely postponed, especially when new inflationary pressures threaten or until policies of restraint imposed to reduce inflation have had a chance to operate effectively. Such cost increases can be magnified in inflationary periods, when every increase affects expectations of new outbursts and is built into the momentum of price trends often more rapidly than restraint on aggregate demand can hold it back.

Several major government effects may be amenable to amelioration. Pollution and safety controls with high marginal costs could be introduced on a slower time schedule, thus reducing the effect on prices per period of time. Something should be done about medical costs before the introduction of fully prepaid national medical insurance escalates them out of sight. In view of the pressures at work on medical costs, simple cost controls are unlikely to be effective. Market controls in this sector need to be strengthened, and that means the choice of services must somehow be reconnected with their payment. The delay due to regulatory battles over building new electrical facilities should be faced and reduced by resolving the conflicts. Runaway product liability needs to be brought under control. Since the law has evolved to enhance the growth of liability suits, it should be possible to reverse this growth trend. Contributory negligence needs to be restored as a major consideration in proving damages. As with the other items, it is a question of redressing an imbalance. Finally, the "economic impact" statement, introduced by President Ford and continued by President Carter, which seems to have had little influence so far, might be given more authority to moderate regulatory decisions throughout the government. It is true that this additional intrusion of paperwork and intragovernmental conflict will slow the regulatory process and in that respect add to costs, but during the present period of high concern over inflation it may readdress the nation's priorities and reduce regulatory costs in general.

Government effects on the flexibility of prices are pertinent to the rate of inflation if their removal would increase flexibility and lessen the adverse short-run trade-off between output and the inflation rate when aggregate demand is restrained. As noted earlier, the response of prices to changes in demand conditions has diminished, and any increase in response would enhance the ability of aggregate demand restraints to subdue inflation.

Some general guidelines might be applied in many areas. Government measures to protect either producers or consumers against changes in market conditions inevitably lead to controls over prices that reduce flexibility. Such controls should be loosened. Government services themselves also have notoriously inflexible prices, as is the case for government fees, pay scales, public transportation fares, postal rates, and so on. It would be desirable to introduce some allowable range of variation into governmentally fixed prices, so that they might respond in the short run to demand conditions. How this might be done would obviously depend on the circumstances of each case. An example is provided by the flexibility in airline fares, recently introduced step by step in a limited and experimental manner. So far it has proved successful and quite popular. One hopes that it will prove successful on a permanent basis and thus encourage similar action in other areas.

Other areas ripe for similar changes are the other sectors of transportation, particularly trucking, and petroleum. It might also work in such areas of government price fixing as postal rates, though here the absence of competitive suppliers undercuts the benefits to be expected. The lack of competition may inhibit such flexibility for municipal utilities, for which stability of price is important to locked-in customers. A remedy for lack of competition, of course, would be to allow it, starting for example with the monopoly of the U.S. Postal Service.

The labor market is the major area that would benefit most from more flexibility. Some eminent economists, such as Gottfried Haberler and Frederick Hayek, believe that the ability to avoid perpetual inflation depends critically on more flexibility in wages. This conclusion is not obvious, since only a fifth of the labor force is now unionized and subject to union wage contracts, and non-union wages display a similar historical rigidity of their own. But government impediments to flexibility are generally undesirable here, and some improvement would be beneficial. Many improvements could be made without conducting a frontal assault on unionism. If the proposition that labor markets should not have barriers to entry were generally accepted, reductions could be made in supply restrictions, such as occupational licensing, minimum wages for youths, apprenticeship rules, secondary boycotts, and jurisdictional disputes.

Some of the above proposals concerning one-time government effects on prices apply to flexibility as well, particularly medical costs, whose flexibility would be improved by moving away from the third-party payment system as well as by introducing more cost consciousness in the form of profit-making medical service organizations, especially hospitals. To shift the emphasis in this industry to cost control, more experimentation with small-scale and decentralized hospital services might also help.

Despite much talk about the inflationary effects of government interference in markets, it is doubtful that the total effect of removing interferences, given the obstacles, could amount to much in a year's period of time. It took many years from initial consideration to the first steps of deregulating air fares, and most other government interferences are equally or more complicated and the opposing interests more entrenched. The effort is worth making for its own sake but not as a panacea for curbing inflation. The reduction of inflation requires some hard-headed decisions about slowing the growth of aggregate demand, and the distasteful consequences for economic activity should not be hidden by sugar-coated pronouncements that there is a short cut. Nevertheless, a determined program of reducing market interferences by government can be indirectly helpful in reducing inflation through its effects on inflationary expectations. As argued above, inflation is resistant to slack demand in part because of expectations that policies to curb it will not be pursued long enough to be successful. If policies to slow aggregate demand are pursued, they will be successful in a shorter period of time and with fewer adverse consequences if government policies as a whole give evidence that a firm commitment to subdue inflation has been adopted.

Paying for Government Policy Through the Price Level

ROBERT W. CRANDALL

It is hardly new for the government to conceal the true costs of its policies by financing them through some mechanism other than taxes. Disguising the cost of government by simply increasing the supply of money is an ancient practice with many modern variants. As recently as the late 1960s, the United States government used inflation to finance a foreign war, ignoring the advice of its economists to pass a tax increase to finance it.

Today there is a disturbing tendency for government to finance its various policies through the price level, forcing the monetary authorities either to ratify these increases or to accept a reduction in social output. In part, this tendency may reflect a considered judgment that increases in certain relative prices are the best mechanism for financing the policy or for achieving the policy objectives themselves. Increases in highway user taxes, for example, could be justified in such a manner. In many others, however, burying the costs in the price level is the best way to conceal the true costs of the program. This is especially true for health and safety regulation, environmental policy, trade protection, and agricultural policy. If budget outlays of billions of dollars were utilized to subsidize producers of milk or steel, for example, or to pay for reductions in pollution, the electorate might rebel and instruct its representatives to reduce their zeal for protecting the citizens from the dangers of environmental pollution or market competition. But if these subsidies are underwritten by various price-enhancing mechanisms, the electorate might never know how much it is actually paying for the programs.

While it would be difficult to calculate the cost of all government policies that are financed through the price level, it is possible to identify the major contributors and to suggest alternatives that could at least contribute to offsetting recent rises in prices caused by government. The most important of these are agricultural policies, foreign trade protection, regulation, minimum wage legislation, and social security taxation.

This essay will attempt to measure the effect of some of the more important contributors to the price level in each category and to suggest some antidotes for this tradition of concealment. Providing a total estimate of the government's effect on prices would, however, be quite beyond its scope.

At the outset, it is important to stress the difference between inflation and high price level. A decision to underwrite the cost of government policy through a relative price increase is not necessarily inflationary. For example, raising the cost of cotton broadcloth by limiting imports raises only the price of cotton goods. In the absence of a change in monetary policy, this increase would require a reduction in social output, a reduction in other prices, or both. It would most likely cause some reductions in other prices, reduce output, and raise the general price level, but there is little empirical evidence on which to base such a prediction.

All of the possible government regulation—such as foreign trade protection, minimum wage legislation, agricultural output restrictions, and indirect taxation—would not affect the rate of increase in prices in future years. Real incomes of the average citizen would be lower because real output would be reduced by all of this excessive government regulation. Such policies, however, could not be called inflationary, only antisocial. Therefore, this essay will refer to the price-enhancing effects of government policies rather than their "inflationary" effects, even though they may be truly inflationary if their impacts are rising through time because of more and more government intervention.

Agriculture and Foreign Trade

Perhaps the best example of the political necessity for concealing the costs of a government program is to be found in the agricultural sector. While other forms of government intervention—such as economic and "social" regulation—may now outstrip agriculture as examples of the government's needlessly adding to the price level, agriculture has had the longest, uninterrupted run. Basically, agricultural policy is designed to ease the plight of the family farmer, who is no longer a major force in the economy, to reduce the volatility in agricultural prices and incomes, and to redistribute income from the average consumer to large holders of agricultural land. The first two goals can be promoted openly and even publicly financed, while the last requires more congressional discretion.

The dynamics of agricultural policy are well known. During periods of declining farm prices, Congress or the administration can attempt to stabilize farm incomes by utilizing support payments—equal to the difference between a "target" price and the market price. This tends to exacerbate the problem by increasing supply. Moreover, it exposes the Department of Agriculture to large increases in budget outlays, thereby creating pressures for crop restrictions. Acreage restrictions on plantings follow, driving up consumer prices. Throughout the process, a tension develops between the administration, seeking to stabilize general income and prices, and the agricultural interests in the Department of Agriculture and in Congress, seeking rises in the price level. Although direct payment programs to needy farmers would be the obvious solution to this problem, Congress cannot have checks written in sufficiently large amounts to stabilize the land values of large farmers, and it must limit the amounts paid to any farmer. Therefore, if Congress must aid the large farmer, price enhancement must be its policy instrument.

To see the large farmer bias in any price-enhancement policy, one need only examine the distribution of cash receipts and income from a cross-section of farms. As grain prices fell drastically from 1973 to 1976, the largest farmers—those with receipts of $40,000 a year or more—maintained and even increased their share of marketings to approximately 80 percent. Their share of total income fell slightly from 66 to 63 percent of national farm income, but these 17 percent of all farmers retained their roughly two-thirds share of income. While it is true that incomes fell substantially for large farmers from 1973 to 1976, their net income plus capital gains on their land gave them a return of between 23 and 29 percent on their investment in the latter year. Primary metals producers rarely do this well even in boom years.

Under one of the various income-support strategies for agriculture, the government uses land-retirement or purchase policies to raise prices. A $4.4 billion expenditure, which Senator Herman Talmadge advocated in 1977, leads to average increases of more than $16,000 in income for the largest farmers and only $57 to $353 a year for the small farmers with less than $10,000 in farms sales. (See table 1.) A target price system in which the government pays the dif-

TABLE 1

Returns per Farm from Alternative Hypothetical Policies for Distributing
$4.4 Billion to Farmers, by Size of Farm (1976 dollars)

| | Alternative Policies | | |
Farm Sales	Pure Price Enhancement	Target-price Income Supports with 1970 Government Payments Distribution	Income Supports with Equal Payments distribution
$100,000 or more	$16,842	$8,567	$1,577
40,000–100,000	2,896	3,716	1,577
20,000–40,000	1,382	2,346	1,577
10,000–20,000	711	1,585	1,577
5,000–10,000	353	918	1,577
2,500–5,000	182	553	1,577
Less than 2,500	57	217	1,577

Source: U.S. Department of Agriculture, Farm Income Statistics (July 1977).

ference between target and market prices generates a more equal distribution than the pure price enhancement strategy because of payment limitations that Congress feels compelled to place in the legislation and because of less than 100 percent participation in the program. A third income-support strategy, equal distribution of support funds, benefits the smaller farmers at the expense of the larger farmers when compared to current policy.

Clearly, if the objective of farm policy is to assist the struggling family farmer during periods of low prices, the direct payments policy is best designed to achieve this objective. Moreover, unlike the price-enhancement strategy, it does not add directly to the price level. Unfortunately, the direct-payments approach is too visible to the electorate and therefore tends to be avoided when substantial support is desired. As a result, during 1977-78 the administration and Congress used price enhancement to raise incomes for producers of milk, wheat, feed grains, and soybeans by $3.6 billion, or 0.2 percent on average prices. The "inflationary" cost of these initiatives could have been reduced by substituting an increase in target prices while allowing markets to clear at lower prices.

Another important example of income redistribution through government mandated price increases is foreign trade policy. In earlier years, most protection took the form of the imposition of tariffs or outright quotas. Recently, however, trade policy has taken a much more complex turn, leading to subtle effects on the prices of imported goods—effects that are difficult to measure.

While the United States still maintains a combination of tariffs and quotas on various products to protect American producers—textiles being perhaps the most expensive example of this combination—its trade policy tools are much more varied today. First the antidumping law was amended in 1974 to prevent exporters from selling below cost, however defined, if these sales injure United States industry. Second, trade remedies are available through the International Trade Commission (ITC) under the so-called escape clause covering situations in which the ITC determines that United States industry or employment is being injured by an increase in imports. Finally, countervailing duties are available for United States victims of unfair trade practices, such as government subsidy of exports.

Of these provisions, escape clause relief and antidumping duties are the most potent forms of government interference with free foreign trade and consequent upward pressure on domestic prices. The initial ITC decisions on escape clause relief for shoes and television sets would have added $1.7 billion to consumer costs, or 0.1 percent to the price level. These decisions were reached solely on the basis that increased imports—reflecting declining comparative advantage for United States producers—were damaging United States firms and their employees. Subsequently, orderly marketing agreements were substituted for the proposed ITC decisions, but it is difficult to measure the effects of these quantitative restrictions. These two cases provide ample warning that government can and will turn protectionist, adding billions of dollars in hidden costs to consumer prices, if and when the competitive tide changes in certain industries.

Among the most dangerous provisions of United States trade laws is the cost-of-production standard in the antidumping code. In times of declining demand, foreign producers are now required to raise their export prices to United States markets as their unit costs rise. For exporters to sell to the United States at prices below average costs is now unfair. This provision is not only antithetical to the operation of the price mechanism but is also highly inflationary. Prices are to be restrained only from decreasing when there is an excess supply in world markets. The United States is thus deprived of an important stabilizing force in the economy—a particularly unfortunate loss, given the tendency of the economy to emerge from successive recessions at higher and higher rates of inflation.

The obvious alternative to the price-enhancing effects of the escape clause and the antidumping provisions of the United States trade laws is a mechanism for easing the plight of those who are unexpectedly buffeted by foreign-trade competition. The United States now has a generous form of trade-adjustment assistance for labor. Workers certified by the Department of Labor as being unemployed because of the impact of imports may apply for supplemental unemployment benefits of up to 70 percent of their wages (not to exceed the average manufacturing wage) for fifty-two weeks. Any increase in this adjustment assistance might produce severe disincentive effects, worsening the unemployment-inflation trade-off or increasing the natural unemployment rate.

What is missing from trade-adjustment is an inducement to the firms adversely affected by trade developments. Large firms are essentially excluded from the program by loan limitations and a requirement that loans be extended only when unavailable from private capital markets. It can certainly be argued that it is not necessary to insulate firms from the business risk inherent in world markets, but inducing them to file antidumping suits instead is far from the best alternative. At present, industries threatened by imports can enlist their employees as allies and petition for price-enhancing relief from the Treasury Department. Some form of transitional trade adjustment, financed from the budget, would be better in this situation, but it is difficult to design such a program with sufficient safeguards to prevent abuses. How, for example, should the steel industry be eased through its current plight? Should the manufacturing of television sets, shoes, and steel be considered as declining industries in the United States or simply industries undergoing temporary disruptions from import competition caused by a number of nonrecurrent forces? There is probably no satisfactory mechanism for dealing with the loss of asset values brought about by declining comparative advantage, but the government should be less protective in responding to short-term shifts in trade.

Social Regulation

Perhaps the most inflationary form of government activity is the newest form of government regulation, the "social" regulation involving health, safety, and the environment. The costs of this type of regulation are increasing rapidly, although its form conceals its costs so well that reliable estimates of them are unavailable. The traditional form of regulation, involving entry limitations and maximum-minimum rate control, is a dying institution, enjoying a renaissance only because of the energy crisis.

Without any doubt, government intervention to protect the environment and the health and safety of workers and consumers has increased substantially since the mid-1960s. The establishment of the Occupational Safety and Health Administration (OSHA) and the Environmental Protection Agency (EPA) marked turning points in the government's willingness to specify the technique of production in United States industrial enterprise. In addition, the Federal Coal Mine Health and Safety Act of 1969, the Highway Safety Act of 1970, the Toxic Substances Control Act of 1976, and various statutes administered by the Consumer Product Safety Commission represent policies that in nearly every case require that costs be concealed in the cost of goods and services produced in the private sector.

Why should virtually every form of health, safety, or environmental regulation employ mandated technical standards as its mechanism for correcting a market imperfection? The answer is probably that it is the simplest approach for Congress to take. If a firm produces an unsafe product, utilizes a technology that is unsafe for workers, or generates pollution in its production processes, the easiest way to correct these abuses is to legislate a mechanism for setting standards that will eliminate them. Frequently, during the drafting of the legislation, little thought is given to minimizing the costs of regulation. There is often outright hostility to a comparison of benefits to costs. In fact, there may be no mention of costs or economics in the provisions for setting standards. For example, primary ambient air standards are to be set by EPA without regard to costs, but water standards are to be based partly on economic feasibility, while toxic substance control may or may not require consideration of economic effects depending on the statute being implemented.

A Congress more intent on making sure that regulation is efficient might have looked for more innovative approaches than technocratic standard-setting. For instance, market incentives could have been utilized much more extensively with firms actually paying taxes or charges for the externalities in question. But such standards would have had to be designed carefully and would have encountered substantial opposition from advocates of sharply reduced pollution, exposure to risk from occupational hazard, and so on. Moreover, they would have made the cost of the government's policies much more apparent to the electorate.

Environmental policy is difficult to summarize. EPA utilizes quite different policies in controlling air pollution, water pollution, solid wastes, noise, and toxic substances. For the most part, these policies involve a rather complex process of setting standards according to source for dozens of different pollutants. Many standards are set in cooperation with state authorities, and enforcement requires both EPA and state-local resources. A few generalizations are possible, however, each of which suggests a number of possible changes or improvements.

There is little attempt at benefit analysis within EPA, partly because the agency need not compare benefits with costs under current legislation. It is also a reflection of the absence of a comprehensive approach to the problem in the economics literature. EPA has at best imprecise estimates of control costs for each substance from each industrial source. The evidence it has, however, often demonstrates that control costs vary widely across industries for the same substance. Environmental monitoring and therefore standards enforcement are not well developed at EPA. Consequently, the agency frequently has no measure of individual point discharges and only imprecise information on air or water quality in various locations. Because it cannot accurately monitor each polluter, the agency is much more comfortable with what are in effect engineering standards rather than performance standards. Finally, standards for new plants are generally more stringent than those for existing plants. This reduces the incentive to retire existing facilities in favor of new ones.

Given the imprecision in the costs estimates for various regulations, it is obviously difficult to estimate the full social cost of EPA and state-local environmental policies. The Council on Environmental Quality estimates the costs of environmental controls for private industry (excluding mobile emissions from consumer-owned vehicles and municipal outlays for water and solid-waste facilities) at $24.4 billion in 1977. The author's estimate is $25.3 billion, rising to $44.7 billion by the mid-1980s. The crude estimates now available suggest that all environmental policies absorb roughly 1.5 to 2.0 percent of the social product. Edward Denison has found that business outlays for environmental control were growing rapidly enough by 1975 to absorb approximately one-tenth of the potential growth in output from labor and capital.

There is little doubt that environmental policy could be improved by a number of devices. If, for instance, EPA were to improve its ability to estimate industrial costs, it could set standards more efficiently. If it could monitor effectively, it could rely much more on performance standards, allowing firms to choose their own control techniques. More information on the benefits of environmental control would help policy formulation immensely, but it is not clear whether this would increase or decrease the stringency of regulation.

A movement toward pollution taxes would improve and simplify environmental policy. This change is not likely to occur very rapidly, however, given congressional and environmentalist antipathy toward it. For the present, the best that can be hoped for is the introduction of some form of transferable pollution rights in allocating air rights in the less developed regions of the country through the "prevention of significant deterioration" policy recently enacted by Congress. In addition, there should be a serious reconsideration of the policy of setting tight engineering standards on new facilities to determine just how much of an investment disincentive it provides. More retrofitting of existing sources may prove to be much less costly. Finally, a mechanism for rewarding those who achieve discharge or emission levels that are even lower than the standard should be devised. EPA has a penalties policy under development that could be altered to address this need, but the prospect of the government paying firms not to pollute may be too much for the congressional committees to tolerate.

At the beginning of the Carter administration, the Occupational Safety and Health Administration (OSHA) announced its intention to phase out most of its detailed safety regulations, concentrating instead on the bigger issues involving exposure to carcinogens and other dangerous substances. In fact, there has been only modest movement in this direction. Nevertheless, the occupational health regulations—covering exposure to benzene, lead, vinyl chloride, noise, cotton dust, and coke-oven emissions—are the most costly and should be given the highest priority.

At OSHA, two important biases underlie all regulations. The first is a bias against any form of quantitative benefit assessment. Since the value of reducing the risk of exposure to disease or accident is never calculated, there is no scientific method for setting standards. Each case is *sui generis*, allowing for enormous misallocation of resources.

Second, as with environmental policy, OSHA policy is biased toward the establishment of engineering standards. This bias is not only a reaction to the uncertainty of the monitoring-enforcement. process under a regime of performance standards, but it also reflects a strong preference for disallowing personal protective devices. If employers were required to reduce the exposure of their employees to dangerous substances, they might force them to wear protective devices—respirators, eyeglasses, or earplugs—rather than reduce the discharge of the substances into the workplace. Since engineering standards are much more expensive than using personal protective devices, this bias is costly indeed.

OSHA has not promulgated many health standards, perhaps because of the controversial nature of many of them. A review of OSHA's own inflationary impact statements for those standards proposed or promulgated provides an estimate of $4 billion for just eight major regulations. The average cost per worker protected varies from $2,285 a year (for the original cotton-dust standard) to nearly $70,000 a year (for the lead standard). Obviously, these costs are very large in proportion to value-added per employee. In many cases, the cost is probably above the bonus the worker would ask for to utilize the less convenient personal protective devices.

Whether the OSHA health and safety standards generate benefits equal to their costs is impossible to assess on the basis of existing data. Most standards are too new for their effects to be measured. However, the problem for the workplace is different from that of the general environment. A labor market exists in which workers respond to differences in perceived risk. If this market operates poorly, presumably because of insufficient information, OSHA could provide additional information to correct the "market failure." On the other hand, if transferring information to workers on the extent of the hazards involved is complicated and expensive, standards may be better than attempting to improve information. For less severe health or safety risks, improving the operation of the workmen's compensation system—to scale each employer's premiums to the actual experience in his plant—may lead to better results, less costly regulation, and greater worker welfare.

Regulation of product safety by various government agencies—such as the Consumer Product Safety Commission, the National Highway Traffic Administration, and the Food and Drug Administration—has generally led to reduced choice for the consumer. With regulators setting the trade-off between cost and safety, there is a tendency to approve expensive, low-risk combinations and to ban somewhat riskier, lower-cost products. Moreover, requirements for enormous recall campaigns, financed by the manufacturer whenever a particular model demonstrates a number of defects that can cause injury, must certainly lead manufacturers to the conservative strategy of offering high-cost, low-risk products.

There may be no simple solution to the problem of product safety. In an increasingly complex world, consumers are unable to research each product they buy. Nor can insurance contracts be written that specify different levels of producer liability according to the risk preference of the consumer. With millions of models of consumer durables on the market, such a system would require enormous transactions costs and research outlays. Nevertheless, some systematic analysis of the value of risk reduction to individual consumers should be undertaken to provide regulators with a measure of the benefits they propose to offer consumers.

There are at least four general approaches to improving social regulation that should be explored as soon as possible. At least, Congress could require that each agency attempt to quantify the benefits and costs of its major regulations, analyzing the costs of several alternative approaches to the problem in question. Specific legislative requirements for this analysis would help relieve the political pressure on agencies in setting standards under current statutes and would tend to force regulators toward a consistent approach across standards. At present, there is little in the governing statutes to prevent the administrator of EPA, for example, from promulgating point-source standards for two different industries that have very different costs of removing the same pollutant in the same geographical area. Consistently applied, cost-benefit analysis could at least point EPA in the right direction, but it would not necessarily improve regulation.

There is considerable interest within Congress for legislative review of regulations and even congressional vetoes of regulations, but it appears that congressional staffs are not equipped to handle a review of the economic impacts of all major regulations. A danger exists that only those regulations affecting powerful lobbying interests would receive a thorough review. If the Congressional Budget Office (CBO) and the Office of Management and Budget (OMB) were to provide such a review, a more systematic analysis might be expected. But a major problem remains: Should an agency's regulations be subject to legal challenge if the CBO-OMB review of the regulation is unfavorable? Or should Congress be entrusted with the power to reverse agencies? The experience with the National Environmental Policy Act of 1969 should be reviewed carefully before entangling regulation with one more basis for judicial review. Delay has its own costs.

The most obvious problem in social regulation is that there is no market check on the zealous or incompetent regulator, who may mandate costs for private producers with relative impunity over a rather wide range. If each agency were forced to estimate the annual compliance costs, with the assistance of CBO or OMB, a regulatory budget could be imposed by Congress. Such a budget would simply limit the annual cost of compliance for all regulations for each agency to a maximum amount specified in advance. Temporary excesses would be taken from succeeding years' budgets (within a certain range) and deficiencies added to them.

There are at least two advantages to the regulatory budget. First, it would require Congress to debate the magnitude of the prospective benefits of EPA or OSHA regulation since it could not set limits on mandated costs without some measure of benefits. Second, it would strongly induce regulators to examine cost-effectiveness and the cost-benefit trade-offs for each regulation. Adding to the cost of any given regulation would reduce the range of discretion available for setting other standards as tightly as the regulator might like. At present, there is no such trade-off; OSHA can set the noise standard as tightly as it wishes without fearing a limitation on its ability to maneuver over, say, the cotton-dust standard. Since society's resources are not unlimited, it would be useful to expose regulators to the concept of "opportunity cost."

Economists have long advocated the use of market incentives instead of detailed standards or regulations. Only when the transactions costs from marketlike charges are prohibitive does a technocratic standard-basis system appear superior. While there is some theoretical basis for using quantities rather than prices as the object of control, deviations from even the quantity regulations should be penalized by fees proportional to the degree of deviation, that is, a pollution tax.

Some marketlike devices are currently under study at EPA. The use of a market system to ration fluorocarbon emissions is one example. Establishing a market for emissions of criteria pollutants in "nondeterioration" areas is another. Finally, EPA already has a trade-off policy for trading emission increments among firms in certain areas that violate clean-air standards. Firms desiring to add to emissions must buy "offsets" or reductions in the same pollutant from existing sources. Moving in this direction will be a slow process, given the political resistance that will be encountered. Nevertheless, other agencies should be instructed to seek similar marketlike devices to reduce the cost of government regulation.

Traditional Regulation

It has become painfully obvious to economists that rate and entry-restricting regulation in markets that would otherwise be competitive is inefficient and contributes substantially to higher prices. If the trucking, airline, and coastal maritime industries were deregulated, between $5 billion and $10 billion in annual shipping costs would be saved. Airline deregulation is proceeding apace, but trucking deregulation poses serious problems of finding a political solution to the reduction in the value of operating certificates (capitalized monopoly profits) that would result. Since the Interstate Commerce Commission has succeeded in limiting entry and allowing rates to be set artificially high, deregulation would reduce the value of route certificates for existing carriers. If truckers are not to block any meaningful attempt at reform, deregulation must be phased in slowly or these certificates will have to be repurchased by the government.

In energy markets there are ominous signs that price regulation could generate economic waste without any consequent benefit to consumers. The fundamental rationale for crude oil price regulation is to deny owners of oil reserves in the United States the rents they might reap from the 1973–74 escalation in world oil prices. In addition, since 1954 the Federal Power Commission (now the Federal Energy Regulatory Commission) has regulated the wellhead price of natural gas in order to transfer rents from producers to consumers. The regulatory strategy for oil and that proposed for natural gas is to limit prices on "old" wells while setting market-clearing prices for "new" wells. The rents from old oil or natural gas are then transferred to consumers. In the case of natural gas, the transfer has been principally to household users through a priority system. In the case of oil, rents are transferred to all users of refined products by an "entitlement" system that averages the price of old and new oil for all refiners. Each refiner of old oil, obtained at the regulated, low price, must pay an "entitlement" to refiners of new oil. The payments are calculated by the Department of Energy by means of an "old oil ratio" so that all refiners theoretically have identical crude-oil acquisition prices, regardless of their mix of old and new oil.

Each system of energy price control is designed to reduce consumer costs at some social cost of economic inefficiency. This regulation has undoubtedly reduced exploitation of existing reserves. For instance, the decline rate on old oil wells has risen sharply. Regulating the field price of natural gas has reduced the development of new reserves. But now there are indications that the Department of Energy might add to these inefficiencies, offsetting any potential gains to consumers.

In natural gas regulation, rolled-in pricing of imported liquefied natural gas (LNG) or domestic synthetic natural gas (SNG) is a possibility. This would allow high-cost LNG or SNG to be averaged with the low, regulated price of interstate gas, raising the price to industrial consumers. In short, the potential consumer benefit from regulation would be diverted to various high-cost producers of synthetic fuels or to foreign gas producers. The inefficiency and perverse distributional effects of such a scheme are obvious.

The crude-oil entitlements pool, now totalling $15 billion a year, is already being used by the secretary of energy for a variety of discretionary purposes, such as lowering the cost of oil in the northeastern states. Ideas for using this entitlements pool to subsidize various projects in the energy field are now circulating in the Department of Energy. But any such discretionary use of entitlements reduces the entitlements for refiners of new oil, thus raising product prices to consumers. For instance, if a million barrels each of old and new oil were produced, each refiner of new oil would get one entitlement for every barrel refined. But if 10 percent of these entitlements were diverted to firms with schemes that the secretary of energy wished to subsidize, the refiners of new oil would get only nine-tenths of an entitlement per barrel refined. To equate old and new oil costs to refiners (provided that the old and new prices remained unchanged), the value of an entitlement would have to rise. The cost of all refined products would rise as a result, negating a portion of the prospective consumer benefits from regulation. Such a scheme, if utilized, would provide the secretary of energy with considerable power to subsidize projects without the public's knowledge. Therefore, if a case is to be made for restricting the price of oil and suffering the output loss that results, benefits must not be parceled out as off-budget subsidies to a variety of special interests.

Setting minimum wages is another form of traditional regulation. The Fair Labor Standards legislation, which sets minimum wages for most employment in the United States, reflects an attempt to increase wages of both those with limited skills and those with whom they might compete in various sectors of the economy. It would be a mistake to interpret the minimum wage as affecting only those who would earn less than $2.65 an hour at present. Many workers who might be displaced by other technologies using low-cost labor are also protected by minimum wages, and reduced competition from low-wage workers generally elevates the entire wage structure. What is particularly unfortunate is that the minimum wage law induces employers to substitute better educated, part-time teenagers and women for full-time teenagers from low-income families. Thus it has the effect of increasing the unemployment rate of teenagers from the most disadvantaged homes.

It is difficult to estimate the full impact of the minimum wage on the price level. A study by Edward Gramlich suggests that each 1 percent increase in the minimum wage raises the average wage by 0.032 percent. Therefore, the increase of 35 cents an hour in January 1978 to $2.65 an hour increased the wage bill by approximately 0.5 percent. Given that wages constitute approximately two-thirds of national income, the increase in the general price level caused by the 1978 minimum wage increase alone was between 0.20 and 0.33 percent.

If Congress wanted only to redistribute income to workers with the most limited skills, it would enact a wage-subsidy program as a substitute for the minimum wage. Workers could be certified as eligible for a subsidy by the Labor Department and either paid subsidies directly through tax rebates or subsidized through their employers. While such a program would run the usual risks of bureaucratic mismanagement, it would provide a direct and visible subsidy for the needy population. Moreover, it would not add to the price level 0.2 to 0.3 percent each year as the minimum wage is indexed to the consumer price index (CPI).

The financing of social security through the payroll tax has a sound basis and, unlike some other government policies discussed in this essay, is not motivated by a desire to conceal the cost of the program from the electorate. Because Congress wished to construct a retirement system with a strong resemblance to a self-sufficient insurance system, employers and employees contribute to the social security trust funds in proportion to a worker's income up to a statutory ceiling. Of course, rising income levels and general inflation have led to payments from the fund in excess of the value of the retiree's contributions, thus placing the funds in an actuarially unsound position. Increases in current contributions or general-revenue financing have become a necessity for the near future if the system is to maintain its rate of payment from the old-age survivors and disability funds.

To replenish the social security trust funds, Congress chose to increase both the payroll tax rate (for both employees and employers) and the ceiling on the taxable wage base. Since one-half of these increases is borne by employers, they add directly to labor costs. If employers were able to reduce employee wages immediately by the amount of the payroll tax increase, no price-enhancing effect would occur. However, given downward inflexibility of wages, payroll taxes must be seen as adding to unit-labor costs and therefore to prices in the short run.

Given the effect of payroll taxes paid by employers on the general price level, two alternatives exist for financing the social security system—employee taxes or general-revenue funding. If taxes were paid entirely by employees, the inflationary effect on unit labor costs would not occur unless wage demands immediately and exactly offset the employee taxes. Similarly, if general-revenue financing were utilized, there would be no price-level effects unless the taxes collected generally by the federal government—principally personal and corporate income taxes—were shifted forward to prices and wages. There is little evidence that this is true for personal income taxes, but some empirical estimates of substantial corporate tax shifting exist. Nevertheless, general-revenue financing would have less immediate price level effects.

There have been recurring proposals to shift the disability and health programs in the social security system to general-revenue financing. However, such a shift could cause significant problems. At present, eligibility for disability insurance depends on participation in the system, which is far from universal. Once general-revenue financing becomes accepted for disability or, perhaps, the old-age survivors' program, it will be difficult to tie eligibility for benefits to past contributions to the system, and it would likely become a universal program. If the scheduled increases in disability and health insurance contributions were shifted to general-revenue financing, the reduction in employer taxes would be nearly $15 billion in fiscal 1979. Thus employer costs would be reduced by nearly 1 percent of the domestic private product.

Conclusion

Throughout this essay are examples of legislative actions to benefit a relatively small group of people at the expense of the many. Most of these policies are extremely inefficient means of redistributing income. Creating or protecting jobs through foreign-trade protection may cost as much as $50,000 or $60,000 a job each year. The economic cost of crop-restriction programs in agriculture is substantial. Technocratic standards for protecting workers may cost up to $70,000 a worker each year.

Why does the electorate sanction this maze of government programs that generally reduce the standard of living? Why are there not more direct mechanisms for redistributing income from urban consumers to rural farmers, from workers in low-risk occupations to workers in high-risk jobs, and from consumers to workers and businesses competing with foreign firms? The answer lies in the nature of the representative democracy that has developed in the United States. Legislative committees are highly specialized, listening closely to groups with strong interests in a certain area but not hearing much from the general electorate, which has far less at stake in the issues before each committee. With growing specialization and a recent trend toward congressional dominance over the executive branch, congressional committees and subcommittees and their staffs are able to serve the interests of the few at the expense of the many with little difficulty. Only when the costs to the many become very large—as in the case of energy legislation—is there a countervailing pressure, but even this offsetting force may not work well enough to obtain a result that is efficient and therefore in the public interest.

In recent years, Congress has been made aware of its tendency to add to the price level. The House now requires an "inflationary impact statement" and the Senate a "regulatory analysis statement." These statements are supposed to detail the effects on the price level of any bill reported from committee, but they are the committee staffs' superficial, biased views of the proposed legislation. For instance, the following bills in 1977 and 1978 were claimed by the relevant committees to have little or no effect on the price level: the Emergency Agricultural Act of 1978, providing for large increases in setasides in order to raise prices and incomes for farmers; the Fair Labor Standards Amendments of 1977, raising the minimum wage; the Sugar Stabilization Act of 1978, raising the price of sugar through import tariffs; the Federal Mine Safety and Health Amendment Act of 1977, providing for extended and tighter regulation of mine safety; and the Black Lung Benefits Reform Act of 1977, requiring larger contributions by employers to insurance funds. Unlike the budget-cost estimates prepared by the Congressional Budget Office (CBO), these impact statements are generally very short and lack any supporting analysis.

If Congress were to attempt to reform its processes in order to reduce the tendency to legislate for special interest through the price level, it should require detailed impact statements for each major bill, to be prepared by CBO or by its contractors. Moreover, these statements should be released to the public and distributed widely before each committee marks up the bill. While this small step would not change the fundamental political dynamics of the legislative process, it might provide some resistance to the most egregious example of policies financed through the price level.

A number of reforms could reduce the tendency of policymakers in Congress and the executive branch to bury the cost of government programs in the price level. These reforms would assist in slowing down the advance in the price level while it was being implemented, but it would also tend to improve economic efficiency in the economy—a more important result.

A detailed estimate of the economic impact of new legislation to accompany every bill reported out of committee could be required. These estimates should be published separately by the CBO and distributed to the public. All major social regulatory agencies could be subjected to a "regulatory budget," limiting the total compliance costs that the agency may mandate in a given year to a level predetermined by Congress. Direct payments to farmers can be relied on to redistribute income to them; if necessary, the limitations on total payments to each farmer now contained in various farm programs could be repealed. Subsidies could replace the minimum wage; since the benefits of the minimum wage extend to workers far above the minimum wage level, the minimum wage would have to be phased out gradually, but there should be no general wage subsidy to overcome these political problems. Attempts to continue the entitlements program for crude-oil price regulation could be curbed; if the system is to be maintained, the authority of the secretary of energy to redirect entitlements at his own discretion should be removed. Any movement toward rolled-in pricing of imported synthetic natural gas or domestic synthetic natural gas could be opposed. The employer contribution to social security could be replaced by general-revenue financing for at least a portion of the program—perhaps the health and disability segments of it. Finally, some mechanism to alleviate the effects of sudden increases in imports on business—including direct payments—could be sought to allow for the repeal of section 201 of the Trade Act of 1974 and the antidumping law. Low-price imports should be accepted and not excluded.

If the inflation rate were as low as 1 or 2 percent a year, these policies would still merit strong consideration. With inflation accelerating to 8 percent in 1978, the case for placing them high on the national agenda is much more compelling.

Government Operations and Inflation

MARTIN J. BAILEY

The influence of the government on inflation, outside the realm of monetary and fiscal policy, is relatively small and is overwhelmed by the latter. This essay will examine the analytical and practical limits of this relationship to see how great the dominance is and place in perspective the comparative unimportance of the subject. Government operations, however, can indirectly add to pressures for inflationary monetary and fiscal policy. Governmental operations and structures are also extremely important in the realm of economic growth and well-being.

Inflation becomes a problem of serious concern to policymakers and to the public when it continues for several years. No one worries about isolated episodes of 1 or 2 percent increases in the price level. But continuing, substantial inflation has been a worldwide concern for more than ten years. It is in this context that one finds the overwhelming importance of monetary and fiscal policy.

In analyzing the sources of inflation, an identity is the best starting point: the real value of all the money in circulation, or its "purchasing power" over goods and services, equals the dollar amount of this stock of money divided by an index of the price level. The real value of the stock of money is an interesting quantity because both theory and experience indicate that it is the monetary quantity of interest to households and firms as they choose the disposition of their assets between liquid and income-earning forms. The definition of the real stock of money is not controversial. The proposition that "the real stock of money is the interesting quantity" is a practical statement of fact that is also relatively free of controversy, although one must bear in mind that it goes beyond the mere definition.

Now this definition directly implies, also as a definitional matter, that each change in the real stock of money consists of the change, if any, in the nominal stock adjusted for the change, if any, in the price level. For example, if the number of dollars in circulation increases by 10 percent while the price level rises by 6 percent, there is a net increase of 4 percent in the real stock of money. The percentage change in the real stock of money equals the percentage change in the nominal stock less the percentage change in the price level. The same truism may be stated in a different order. The percentage change in the price level equals the percentage change in the nominal (dollar) stock of money minus the percentage change in the real value of that stock.

Some definitions are more useful than others. This one is especially powerful because it shows the percentage change in the price level as the difference between two variables whose control is in specific hands, and whose behavior is straightforward.

The nominal stock of money is entirely controllable, to the extent they choose to do so, by the monetary authorities, particularly the Federal Reserve System. Its several instruments of control are not only sufficient but redundant; the purchase and sale of United States government securities on the open market, which the Federal Reserve regularly does, could be used to increase or decrease the stock of money by huge amounts, far beyond what is required for stable prices and a relatively stable economy. There may be a question about the will but not about the ability.

The second percentage change that defines the change in the price level, that in the real stock of money, results from decisions by households and firms, which choose how much of their total assets to hold in the form of money. They decide this in relation to their income and wealth, and as with other matters they behave consistently in terms of real quantities. Changes from time to time in the real stock of money that people are willing to hold have been found in extensive research to be systematic and predictable. For example, the real stock of money rises steadily over time as real income grows, if other influences remain unchanged. It has also found that the real stock of money varies inversely with the interest rate. Occasionally the real stock of money, determined by the public's willingness to hold it, appears to vary for other reasons, but generally such changes are statistical illusions. A recent example is the apparent sharp drop in balances held, for given real incomes and interest rates, in 1975 and 1976; it has now been discovered that a change in banking practices led to a major understatement of the true money supply. Research on this subject has established, as reliably as almost anything in economics, that there is a stable demand function for the real stock of money. That means that the percentage change of this stock is governed by a stable, predictable relationship.

The role of the interest rate in the demand for the real stock of money, as a practical matter, is of secondary importance except for the analysis of transitional and feedback relationships. In the short run it serves as a buffer when real income or the nominal stock of money changes. Either such change, among others, creates a temporary discrepancy between the real stock of money in existence and the amount the public is willing to hold in the long run. The public is then induced to accept the actual stock by a change in the interest rate. In due course there follows a change in the price level (and possibly also in real income) that tends to bring the real stock of money back into line with what the public is willing to hold at the long-term "normal" interest rate, allowing the interest rate to return to its normal value.

An inflation-interest feedback arises during cumulative inflation that the public has grown to expect. What is predictable about the interest rate, averaged over several years, is its real value—the net rate of return in real terms, after subtracting the expected rate of inflation. There are short-term fluctuations in the real interest rate, as just noted, but over long periods it remains quite stable. Therefore, when inflation is built into people's expectations, the nominal interest rate quoted in securities markets rises to include the rate of inflation, added to the real rate of interest. The higher nominal interest rate then reduces the real stock of money the public is willing to hold and thus drives up the price level still further. Hence it reinforces an established inflation.

Because of the stability of the real rate of interest, averaged over several years, the above types of changes in interest rates observed in securities markets have no independent effect on the real stock of money or on the price level. As a buffer and feedback variable, the interest rate moves around in response to other variables, while tending to return to its long-term stable real value. It can be disregarded in this discussion.

Hence, for policy analysis of long-term influences on the price level, one needs to look at only two variables—the nominal stock of money created by the authorities and the real stock as determined by real income. When the only lasting influence on the real stock of money is real income and when the authorities fix the quantity of money in nominal terms, no other variable can influence the price level except by influencing real income or by affecting how much nominal money the monetary authorities allow to exist in circulation. There is nothing very controversial about this statement, although it is often overlooked.

What does all this mean for such supposed influences on the price level as the wage-price spiral and the inflationary impact of costly government programs and regulations? It means that these "influences" have no influences unless they affect real income or unless they somehow affect the amount of nominal money the authorities allow in circulation. For example, wages and prices can continue upward on their own momentum for a time, without an increase in the nominal quantity of money, if in so doing they provoke or aggravate a recession—a reduction in real income. Similarly, the sharp rise in the price of imported oil in 1974 and the decline in the exchange value of the United States dollar since 1971 tended to raise the United States price level by reducing real income. However, these influences are small compared to changes in the nominal stock of money.

Table 1 shows the percentage changes in money, prices, and real income in two periods since World War II: 1950–65, when prices rose very little, and 1965–78, when prices rose substantially. In particular, from 1950 to 1965 the consumer price index (CPI) rose just under 2 percent a year, compounded, for a total rise of 31 percent. In contrast, from 1965 to 1978 the CPI rose at over 5.5 percent a year, compounded, for a total rise of 104 percent—the price level more than doubled. The real GNP rose 73 percent and 52 percent, respectively, in the two periods; the real stock of money the public was willing to hold rose 13 percent and 9 percent, respectively. Despite these low figures for the public's

TABLE 1

Percentage Changes in Money, Prices, and Real Income

Period	Consumer Price Index	Nominal Stock of Money (M_1)	Real Stock $\frac{M_1}{CPI}$ of Money	Real GNP
1950–65	31	47	13	73
1965–78	104	123	9	52

Note: 1965–78 figure adjusted for deposits omitted from M_1.

willingness to hold additions to the real stock of money, the authorities increased the nominal stock by 47 percent and 123 percent, respectively, in the two periods.

Because of the low rate of growth the public will accept in the real stock of money, that variable has been comparatively stable, swamped by the other changes. That means that, as a rule of thumb, one can state what amounts to an iron law of inflation: the price level will rise only if there is a substantial increase in the nominal stock of money. The higher the rate of growth of the nominal stock of money, the higher the rate of rise of the price level. The influence of other variables is so small as to be almost negligible.

The facts and the logic of this position are unassailable, and most economists, when pressed, accept them but object to their being stated this way. Many want to say that circumstances beyond their control force the monetary authorities to increase the quantity of money in circulation, or they advance other arguments of a similar character. None seriously denies, however, that the monetary authorities have the legal powers and the technical instruments available to change the stock of money in any way they desire. It is a question of will, not ability.

To understand the lack of will to limit the increase in the money supply, it is helpful to go back to the conventional economics of the 1950s, when the Phillips curve was an exciting new discovery. Its discovery suggested that if policymakers wanted to reduce unemployment, all they had to do was accept a modest amount of continuing inflation, such as 5 percent a year. This seemed a small price to pay for a permanent increase in output, they thought, and a permanent reduction in unemployment. A few economists argued that the gains would be only temporary, after which inflation would be permanent and output and employment would drop back to their normal growth trend lines. Now no one doubts that the latter group has been proved right by events. In recent years both high inflation and high unemployment have prevailed. Now when the idea of using monetary restriction to stem the inflation is considered, many economists and most policymakers fear a major increase in unemployment. Again, their fear reflects a too easy acceptance of the notion of a stable Phillips curve, stable now at an unpleasantly high level. They seem to suppose that a reduction in inflation by holding down the growth of the money supply (the only method that works) would lead to permanently high unemployment, at much higher levels than any recently experienced. This explains why the monetary analysis presented here is so unfashionable.

An especially clear and straightforward statement of the viewpoint metioned above was made by Arthur Okun:

> The government can reasonably control the course of total spending in the economy—GNP measured in dollars—via fiscal and monetary policy . . . . The critical question is how much of that . . . slowdown would show up as a desirable reduction of the inflation rate and how much as an undesirable reduction of output and real income. . . .
>
> We have clear recent evidence on the way slowdowns in total spending are split between reduced inflation and reduced production; and that evidence is jarring. It suggests that a five point slowdown in dollar GNP under present circumstances would cut the inflation rate by less than a percentage point and cut the growth of real output by more than four percentage points. In short, it would eliminate real growth and barely put a dent in the inflation rate.
>
> To cut today's inflation rate in half would require a recession deeper than the double-sized 1973–75 decline. . . . The long-run costs in business confidence and capital formation and in worker incentives and attitudes would be enormous.[1]

The "clear recent evidence" on the split between reduced inflation and reduced production is simply another version of the Phillips curve. In the 1950s and early 1960s the economists most in favor of high-pressure economic expansion urged that this presumably stable curve could be counted on to convert a modest rate of inflation, no more than 5 percent a year, into high output and low unemployment. In the late 1960s a grand social experiment with this idea took place by accident rather than design when Arthur Okun, as chairman of the Council of Economic Advisers, fought a creditable but failing rear-guard action against Lyndon B. Johnson's inflationary policies during the Vietnam war. The result of this experiment and the subsequent administrations' failure to reverse it are well known; the supposed Phillips curve has "shifted upward," unemployment and inflation have both been high. Okun and others, apparently not noticing how easily the curve shifted up, are utterly convinced that it cannot be brought down again the way it was pushed up—by monetary and fiscal policy.

The Impact of Government Operations

Although the principal factor in inflation is the nominal stock of money, various factors influence real income and can therefore affect the price level by changing the desired real stock of money. Several of the influences that seem to drive up the general price level directly do so in fact because they lower real incomes and therefore lower the real stock of money that the public is willing to

---

[1] *Washington Post*, August 28, 1978 (reprinted from *Capital Report*, American Security Bank, 1978).

hold. An example is the rise in the price of imported oil in 1973 and 1974. By reducing the quantities of oil and other goods the United States could afford to purchase abroad, this rise cut into the real standard of living and lowered the real GNP. Besides the permanent reduction of the real GNP below its previous long-term growth path implied by the rise in oil prices, it was further reduced temporarily in the economic recession that began in 1974 and reached bottom in 1975. The onset of recession is widely thought to have been induced by the oil price rise, and at least indirectly there is probably a connection. In any case, prices rose sharply in 1974 and 1975 while real income and the real stock of money declined. With the recession now nearly over, its transient association with a large price rise is also nearly over. The moderation of the inflation, other things being equal, contributes to recovery from the recession. These are comparatively pronounced, easily measured income effects related to the price level.

A less pronounced but similar real income effect is associated with overzealous and misguided government regulation of industry. In many instances the regulators have been subverted by the industry they are supposed to regulate and have assisted established firms in the industry in fending off competition and in raising prices against the consumer. (The traditional pre-1970 regulators almost all fell into this trap, and the more recent ones have often done so also.) Before the current reforms, airline regulation was an archetype, and it was also an outstanding case of induced waste. Route restrictions, combined with high fares and no limitation on the number of flights once a route was obtained, encouraged overinvestment by the airlines, dissipating what would otherwise be monopoly profits in high costs. The effect of this combination clearly reduces the real GNP through waste—empty seats in the aircraft—and so tends to raise the general price level. A wide variety of other regulatory activities have similar effects.

A curious case that is less clear-cut is environmental regulation, particularly the required pollution control devices on automobiles. These devices raise the prices of new automobiles and their maintenance costs. As in the case of airline regulation, they lower the real GNP, as now measured, and tend to raise the price level. However, they reduce air pollution, which up to a point is a benefit worth paying for. Therefore, with a more accurate measure of the real GNP, one that properly reflected the value of air quality, these devices might raise the real GNP and not raise prices. Undoubtedly they increase the amount the customer has to pay for an automobile. However, it is not a true price increase but an additional quality feature that is part of the real product. How, then, should price index statisticians handle this type of change?

There is definitely some merit in the reasoning that pollution controls improve the correctly measured real product and that their cost should not be considered to represent true price increases in final products. However, allowing a plausible and possibly meritorious change in the consumer price index for pollution controls would open the door to endless political tinkering with that index, as has clearly already happened with the politically loaded index of prices paid by farmers.

Nevertheless, many regulatory and other actions of the government lower the real GNP and therefore raise prices, other things being equal. In considering these actions, one should distinguish between two types of effects—those things that induce waste, reducing the real product in the private sector, and those things that involve waste within the government. Before addressing these, however, one should note a broad, gross impact effect of government spending that falls outside the scope of this essay. Whenever the federal government spends more for any purpose, it seldom resists the temptation to allow part of this spending to be financed by an increased deficit rather than by taxation. An increased deficit is likely to have a direct inflationary effect, through an interest rate effect on real balances. As a general rule, the monetary authority mistakenly tries to limit the rise in interest rates and does something even more inflationary; it finances part of the increased deficit by putting more money into circulation. But the broad, gross impacts of government spending are another subject.

The two types of effects of government operations that fall within the scope of this essay are induced waste in the private sector and direct waste in the government. The first tends to raise the price level as measured in conventional and official price indexes; other things being equal, the second does not.

Induced waste in the private sector takes several forms, of which the airline case already mentioned is one of the important ones. Another example, fundamentally similar but much different in appearance, is that of government transfer payments, such as welfare and unemployment insurance. Although the effects vary with the circumstances of the families receiving the payments, there is no doubt that the more generous these payments are, the larger the number of people who choose to remain unemployed or to stay out of the labor force entirely. A number of recent research papers have confirmed these effects. To the extent that fewer people seek or accept jobs, the real GNP is lower and the price level is higher. Another example is transfer payments to farmers, which, combined with acreage reduction requirements, reduce total output and induce inefficient use of land and other resources in farming. Higher farm prices, lower total output, and a higher general price level result.

Welfare payments to families with potential wage earners encourage withdrawals from the labor force, although the significance of this effect is still being studied. More definite is the effect of prolonged, generous unemployment insurance payments, which vary by state. Undoubtedly, this effect is significant. Also, the incentive effects on employers of the size of covered wages and of experience ratings have been found to be substantial, affecting their willingness to lay off workers and create high labor turnover. A third way that the government affects the labor market, if preliminary work now under further study holds up, is that relatively high, rigid wages in federal, state, and local government encourage workers to wait for government jobs and to remain unemployed while waiting. The cumulative result of all such incentive effects could come to several percentage points of lost real GNP, which, other things being equal, would mean a higher price level.

This increase of a few percentage points means little in comparison with the more than doubling of the price level since 1965. Moreover, some of these incentive effects were in place before 1965, or partially even before 1950. Their direct influence on the recent inflation has therefore been almost negligible. However, their indirect effect may have been considerable. Since 1950, the period of coverage and the percent of earnings covered by unemployment insurance have tended to increase. The added unemployment induced and encouraged by these tendencies reinforces rising job-search unemployment associated with the increased number of teenagers and women in the labor force. As a result, the amount of unemployment that must be accepted as the "natural" amount has risen by at least 1 percentage point—which is officially recognized—and may have risen by more. Within some groups of officials, and especially among supporters of an active fiscal policy in the Congress, such as sponsors of the Humphrey-Hawkins bill, this change is resisted or ignored. Ever since World War II and the passage of the Employment Act of 1946 the federal government has been committed to maintaining high employment. In practice this has meant responding with an active fiscal policy and with rapid increases in the stock of money in circulation whenever unemployment has risen much above 4 percent. Before 1965 that was not serious. However, the coincidence of inflationary policies during the Vietnam war and a rising level of normal unemployment has put subsequent administrations in the position of having to aim for an unsustainable low unemployment level and to try to wind down an inherited inflation at the same time. Under these circumstances, the attempt to decelerate inflation gave way completely in the early 1970s and is still of doubtful priority. Every fraction of a percent of unemployment induced by unwise transfer-payment policies adds to the pressures for continuing inflationary monetary and fiscal policy. Thus their indirect effect, by this path, can be quite large until the higher unemployment levels are widely recognized as either inevitable or as reducible only by including the right incentives in the tax-transfer systems.

Induced waste in the private sector thus has a small direct effect on the price level and a large indirect, political effect. Waste in the operations of the government, though it tends to lower the general standards of living, has neither of these effects on the price level. The taxing-spending operations of the government tie up the same amount of cash whether the money is well spent or wasted. Waste in government would raise the implied price index of real government services, if such an index were to be computed, but it has no effect on the price level as it is now measured. The consumer price index includes only private goods. The GNP deflator includes an index for the government sector, that is, an index of wages paid by government and of government purchases of private goods and services; it is an input price index, which is unaffected by how efficiently the inputs are used.

Further, misuse of government resources does not as a general rule add to unemployment or to political pressure for inflationary policies. To the extent that there is a backlash against waste, an incidental effect could be less inflationary fiscal and monetary policies.

Among other possible effects of government operations on the labor market, one seems important enough to mention. Changes in the composition of government spending shift demands for goods and services among industries and so shift employment among industries. These shifts increase labor turnover and, if there are lags in filling new jobs, tend to increase unemployment for a given size of government budget. Like the increases in unemployment discussed earlier, these generate political pressure for overreaction in monetary and fiscal policy.

For example, the cutback in defense spending in the last four years of the Vietnam war was replaced by the rapid growth of other government spending. Parallel with and slightly behind the cutback in defense was the cutback in the space program. Regardless of the merits of these cuts, the variable nature of these two programs has led to significant shifts in industrial activity and employment. Since 1969 the attendant unemployment reinforced the political pressures noted in connection with other increases in job-search unemployment. Hence, in such instances a change in defense spending, either up or down, can contribute indirectly to inflationary policies.

Effects on Growth and Standards of Living

There is a considerable risk of stunting the growth of and even reducing the standard of living implicit in the broad regulatory powers granted by some thirty acts passed since 1969. These acts place no upper limit on the costs that regulatory authorities can impose on the private sector and on state and local governments. The potential costs of literal compliance with present laws would be truly enormous.

An extreme example of the legislation of arbitrary objectives placed under control of a regulatory agency is the case of "zero discharge" of pollution into the inland waters of the United States by 1985. This objective is specifically mandated by the Federal Water Pollution Control Amendments of 1972. In setting this objective, Congress did not consider the possible costs or question whether the benefits of pure water are worth the cost. When the Environmental Protection Agency (EPA) surveyed the potential costs of meeting a set of interim objectives that it had adopted to be complied with by 1983, it was shocked to learn that these costs would come to an estimated $468 billion solely for cities and towns. The additional amount needed to stop agricultural runoffs of fertilizers, pesticides, and so on in all kinds of weather was not estimated and is probably incalculable. It may, in fact, be technically impossible to end all water pollution. Merely coming close to that objective would require an initial capital outlay greater than one year's entire GNP and would further require a continuing operating cost that would consume annually a substantial fraction of the national product.

Of course, it is politically impossible to spend these sums of money before 1983, or any other year soon. The EPA recognized this impossibility immediately and scaled down the "needs" to $150 billion; appropriations in the federal budget are running about $5 billion a year. That does not mean that the political process has found a wise or well-structured compromise but merely that in this case the most outrageous demands of the law are being quietly ignored. More-

66 | MARTIN J. BAILEY

over, it is not certain that there will be comparable restraint in other areas such as the regulation of suspected cancer-causing chemicals.

The law governing occupational health and safety regulation is virtually as extreme and ill-considered as the law on water pollution, and the cost implications, still only vaguely known, may well be as serious. When the Occupational Safety and Health Administration (OSHA) proposed its Coke Oven Emission Standard, the Council on Wage and Price Stability commented: "Our analysis concludes that, at a minimum, this standard would cost $4.5 million per life saved. . . . If we were to spend $4.5 million per cancer death in an attempt to save all lives lost to cancer, we would commit ourselves to an annual expenditure roughly equal to our entire gross national product."[2] Despite this analysis, OSHA adopted the standard essentially unchanged and has systematically ignored this type of consideration in other cases. Officially, OSHA suspects that between 1,500 and 2,000 chemical and other substances may cause cancer. Based on the costs of control mandated up to this point in final or proposed OSHA regulations, the cost of controlling all of them in work places will come to $400 billion per year. It must be presumed that these costs would increase with the growth of the economy.

In addition, OSHA is supposed to regulate other work place hazards, the Consumer Products Safety Commission regulates the design of consumer products, the Food and Drug Administration regulates foods and drugs, and so on. All these activities impose costs on the private sector and tend to lower the standard of living. The total costs are unknown, and the above estimates are tentative and will be revised when more data become available. Clearly, however, the potential impact is enormous.

By 1975 the running costs of pollution abatement by business had risen to almost $10 billion a year for all industries except mining; in addition, capital investment was running between $2.5 and $3.0 billion. This type of cost has risen rapidly since 1968. Costs of worker safety have also risen rapidly and were great enough by 1975 to reduce the rate of growth of total resource productivity by 0.36 percentage point, or by about one-sixth of the historic average growth rate. They have significantly cut into economic growth and with a continuation of recent trends could quickly stop all growth altogether.

In the minds of most people a slowdown or cessation of growth would seem to be inflationary. However, this need not be the case. There is no reason to expect an increase in normal unemployment from environmental, worker health and safety, and consumer product regulation, and hence no reason for such regulation to generate pressure for inflationary monetary and fiscal policy. The inflationary effect of slowing down the rate of growth is entirely conditional on what happens to monetary and fiscal policy, and in any case it is small. Thus the importance of growth effects lies in the balance of real costs against real benefits and not in any collateral effects on the price level.

[2] James C. Miller III, statement before OSHA on behalf of the Council on Wage and Price Stability, Washington, D.C., May 11, 1976.

Conclusion

Government operations have too small an effect on the general price level to be taken seriously. The right focus of attention is on monetary and fiscal policy and especially on the quantity of money in circulation. Government operations become significant when their effects, mainly through induced unemployment, generate overwhelming political pressures for monetary expansion and fiscal looseness. These induced effects have been considerable in the past ten years and seem to have played a large role in the inability of successive administrations to limit monetary expansion.

Improving the incentive effects of government operations so that they induce less unemployment would surely be desirable in any case, especially if it makes less inflationary monetary and fiscal policies easier to follow. However, the thing to remember is that such policies are essential and can be implemented regardless of any other policy.

Transfer Payments and Inflation

PHILIP SAUNDERS, JR.
JUDITH MARKLAND
BENJAMIN W. WURZBURGER

Transfer payments are a government mechanism for redistributing income or purchasing power. The recipient of a transfer payment qualifies purely on the basis of a political determination; the individual provides no goods or services in return, and when he or she does provide something, its fair market value is less than what the person is paid. Transfers differ from most government purchases of goods and services, of which the major items are wage payments to government employees and expenditures for military hardware. In addition to redistributing income, some transfers function as automatic stabilizers for the economy, providing increased income flows as wage and other income sources wane in an economic downturn. Unemployment benefits are the best example of these.

There are many government income redistribution vehicles: in-kind payments (such as surplus food distribution and Medicaid); reduction of taxes for selected groups by tax credits or deductions; support of business or employment of particular groups (farm price-support purchases and comprehensive employment training); provision of services to a specific group (legal services for the poor and Indian health services); and the provision of credit or insurance (Federal Housing Administration mortgage insurance, agricultural commodity loans, and student loans). In the broader sense, all of these are transfers. However, the standard government definition of transfers—the national income or account definition—is cash payments to individuals, such as social security, unemployment benefits, and government employee retirement benefits. These are of primary concern here.

In 1977, all government cash payment programs totaled $199 billion, or 10.5 percent of the GNP, and this massive figure would be substantially larger if a broader definition of transfers were used. In 1978, for example, William J. Lawrence and Stephen Leeds prepared for the Institute for Socioeconomic

Studies an inventory of federal income transfer programs for people whose incomes are defined as being relatively low or as having been reduced and tallied fiscal year 1977 expenditures, including administrative costs, of $248 billion by the federal government alone. Costs of the farm price-support program would add $4 billion to this figure, while state and local transfers, excluding federal grants in aid, would add some $10 to $15 billion more. Including other transfers via tax reductions—mostly to people who, in the main, have adequate income—would bring the total to over $300 billion, or about 16 percent of GNP.

The pattern of income redistribution depends on the means by which transfers are financed. Most social insurance programs are financed through payroll taxes. Federal programs (such as Aid to Families with Dependent Children, food stamps, tax credits, and taxable income exemptions) and government services (such as Head Start and community health centers funded through general revenues) are primarily financed through the personal income tax and corporate income taxes.

A major characteristic of the postwar economy has been the steady rise of the government's role. Total government expenditures—federal, state, and local—climbed from around 25 percent of GNP in 1950 to 32.9 percent in 1977. Although it is recognized that transfer payments in the narrow sense have expanded significantly in the last twenty-five years, it is less well understood that they account for almost all of the government's expansion as a proportion of GNP. Total government transfers to individuals grew from around 4 percent of GNP in the early 1950s to 10.5 percent in 1977 and in the same period climbed from about 15 to 32 percent of government spending.

The preponderant growth in transfers has come through expansion of social insurance programs, especially social security. Other major social insurance programs are unemployment compensation and federal civilian employee retirement. Social insurance payments, which now constitute 23.2 percent of all government expenditures, accounted for about 7 percent in the early 1950s. Social insurance benefits in 1977 were $132 billion, by far the largest category, representing 78 percent of federal transfers. As most social insurance benefits are paid from trust funds financed by payroll taxes, these taxes have climbed proportionally as a percentage of total tax receipts and of labor compensation. Taxes to pay for transfers, as well as for other government programs, have risen not only in absolute terms but also as a percentage of GNP, and tax receipts totaled one-third of GNP in 1977.

Taxes and Inflation

The critical issue in determining whether a tax is inflationary is whether the taxpayer passes on the cost of the tax—an individual by higher wages and a firm by higher prices. There is no direct inflationary impact if the taxpayer absorbs the cost of the tax. Employer payroll tax, personal taxes, and corporate income taxes will be considered in this light. The remarks made here are generally applicable regardless of whether the tax proceeds finance transfers or some other government expenditures.

Considerable evidence and professional opinion indicate that increases in the employer payroll tax are inflationary and that employers do not succeed in completely shifting the tax on to employees. The supporting evidence is based, for the most part, on traditional wage equations, in which the primary determinants of the wage rate are recent and past rates of inflation and various specifications of the unemployment rate, modified by the inclusion of the employer payroll tax as an additional explanatory variable. Estimates of how much of the tax is shifted to employees vary considerably, from zero in one case to 50 percent in another. It is presumed that the balance of the tax is shifted forward in higher prices. A rough average of the estimates indicates that about three-fourths of the tax increase becomes embedded in the nominal costs of employee compensation, and the remainder is shifted back to the employee. Hence a percentage point increase in the effective employer payroll tax lowers wages by 0.25 percent and raises labor costs by 0.75 percent.

History provides some idea of the magnitude of the impact of employer payroll tax increases on the inflation rate. Between 1957 and 1977 the effective social security tax rate, the ratio of employer contributions for all social insurance programs to total employee compensation, rose from 3.2 to 6.9 percent. Following the econometric finding that a 1 percent tax increase leads to a 0.75 percent increase in labor costs, the social security tax increases led to a 2.8 percent increase in wage costs over these two decades. On an annualized basis, this amounts to 0.14 percent a year.

While 0.14 percent is a small increment to the inflation rate, it is only the first round effect. Any ultimate impact depends on the extent of the wage-price spiral. There is rather general agreement that prices can be fully raised to reflect unit labor cost increases, but more debate exists on the effect of inflation on wages. The Wharton Quarterly Model (May 1978) estimates that a 1 percent increase in the price level leads to a 0.9 percent increase in wages. If this factor is applied, the 0.14 percent annual increase in prices calculated above ultimately becomes a 1.4 percent increase in the rate of inflation. A more conservative estimate of the response of wages to prices (say, 0.75 percent for every 1 percent initial increase in the rate of inflation) would ultimately lead to about a 0.5 percent increase in the rate of inflation. None of these numbers is firm, and the margin of error could be large in either direction. The analysis does indicate, however, that the potential—and even likely—impact of employer payroll taxes on inflation is not inconsequential.

Personal taxes include payroll, income, and capital gains taxes. Increases in personal taxes are inflationary if the taxpayers can obtain higher wages to offset the tax increases. It has been observed that money wages only seem to go in one direction—up and never down. Wages are not established in perfect markets but in markets that are highly influenced by politics and social behavior. The principle that money wages should not decline except in extreme circumstances seems to be generally accepted by both employers and employees.

A similar observation might be made about disposable personal income that is similarly inflexible downward. On a per capita basis, disposable personal income in the United States has declined only once in the last forty years. In large part, this upward trend results from the fact that wage rates have not declined, but the two are not directly related. The effective tax rate has not been constant but has been rising. It is reasonable that people attempt to defend not only their pre-tax income but their after-tax income as well.

Labor markets are imperfect, and in wage negotiations success depends in good part on the tenacity with which a party holds a particular point of view. Most contemporary wage negotiations focus on job security and on how many people are out of work (that is, the supply of labor), but they also concentrate on the cost of living, the standard of living, the ability of the employer to pass on the cost increase to his customers, relative wage differentials, and the notion of a "fair" rate of pay. In the dynamics of wage rate setting, a reduction in income imposed by increased taxes further stimulates wage demands.

In recent years, some governments have operated on the belief or hope that workers respond to take-home pay and would insist on less inflationary wage settlements if they received tax reductions. Great Britain's spring budget in 1977 contained proposed income tax reductions conditional on satisfactory agreement on a new pay policy. The Norwegian government made tax concessions in both 1975 and 1977 in connection with wage settlements. Sweden reduced income taxes in 1975 and 1976 as a part of wage settlements but then perversely offset the tax loss by increasing employer payroll taxes. Tax-based incomes policy proposals made in recent years are predicated on the notion that workers will trade wages for tax relief.

The empirical findings on this theory are inconclusive. Tests have been performed, sometimes using employee payroll taxes and at other times using employee payroll taxes and personal income taxes combined. George Perry of the Brookings Institution examined United States payroll taxes in the 1953–68 period and found that approximately 40 percent of the increase in employees' contributions was passed on to employers in the short run in the form of higher wages. In the postwar United Kingdom, real take-home pay was a statistically significant determinant of wage increases, although the effect was small. For example, a 10 percent decrease in take-home pay, or an extra 10 percent on the effective tax rate, would lead to only a 1 percent increase in money wages. It is not surprising, however, that a relationship between taxes and wages was found in the United Kingdom, whereas it has not been found consistently in the United States. The fact that British unions have more power at the bargaining table and more voice in government policy than their American counterparts may be the explanation.

The theory that taxes are in some part passed on in the higher wages is probably sound, even for the United States. Given the sophistication of union bargainers and the tendency of workers to look only at the bottom line of the pay slip, it would be irrational to expect taxes not to affect wage increases.

However, the effect is probably so small that it gets lost in most statistical analyses. To the extent there has been an impact on inflation in the United States from higher personal taxes, it would be largely traceable to transfers because they have accounted for the greak bulk of the increase in government expenditures.

Economic theory implies that, in the short run, corporations bear the full burden of the corporate income tax and that the tax is therefore noninflationary. As for the long-run impact, the question depends on a still unresolved issue—the sensitivity of saving to the net rate of return. According to the common finding that aggregate saving is independent of interest rates, the corporate income tax is noninflationary in the long run. Standard microeconomic theory implies that a tax on an inelastic factor of production will be totally borne by the suppliers of that factor. Thus, in the short run, where the capital stock cannot be adjusted, a tax on corporate income will be totally borne by capital, and corporations will absorb the corporate tax revenues out of profits. An increase in the corporate income tax will not result in a price increase.

In the long run, if aggregate saving responded sympathetically to the net after-tax rate of return, an interesting sequence would result. An increase in corporate taxes would lower the net rate of return, which in turn lowers savings and investment, which then lowers the capital stock in the long run, which finally lowers productivity and raises prices. Thus corporate taxes would be inflationary in the long run. It is therefore necessary to examine whether the net rate of return exerts any impact on the aggregate consumption-saving decision.

Some studies have failed to find any impact of the interest rate on private savings. Others have reported positive elasticities of saving with respect to the interest rate, while still others have reported negative elasticities. Many of these studies used inadequate measures of the rate of return, failing to adjust appropriately for both taxes and inflation. One of the most recent studies paid special attention to the correct measure of the net rate of return variable and found that private savings would fall significantly if the net rate of return were to fall. Here, too, the implication is that the corporate income tax is inflationary in the long run.

The jury is still out on the saving/rate of return issue. Effective corporate income tax rates are no higher now than they were in the 1950s. Even if the rate of return—and hence corporate tax rates—does affect savings, past inflation cannot be attributed to rising corporate tax rates. Of course, if government expenditures continue to grow as a percent of GNP, the story on corporate tax rates may be different in the future.

Transfers and Government Deficits

To the extent that tax revenue increases do not cover increased government expenditures (which can be traced largely to increased transfers), the increased expenditures lead to deficits. One would expect tax revenues to increase even faster than dollar incomes since tax rates increase with incomes. Tax receipts have increased but not as fast as expenditures, rising from 25 percent of GNP in the early 1950s to 32 percent in 1977. This was a rise of 7 percent in the GNP share while the expenditure share rose 8 percent. The gap has varied over time but has widened most recently since 1973.

So far, expenditures and taxes of all levels of government have been considered. At the federal level, the history is similar. Federal transfer payments, including grants-in-aid to state and local governments to be used for transfer payments, have grown to $186 billion in 1977, an increase since the early 1950s from 15 percent to about 44 percent of federal expenditures and from 3 percent to 10 percent of GNP. Over the same time span total federal expenditures rose to $423 billion, or from 20.0 percent to 22.4 percent of GNP, far less proportionately than the increase in transfers that have even squeezed out other programs in relative terms.

The growth of transfers in excess of normal growth in revenues implies the need for tax increases. Payroll taxes to finance the social insurance benefits have indeed risen; however, general revenue taxes have not kept pace with other expenditures. Effective tax rates have climbed in the last fifteen years as inflation has pushed individuals into higher tax brackets and Congress has attempted to moderate this effect by legislating tax rate reductions. Changes in federal tax receipts attributable to tax changes over the fiscal years 1969–77 cumulated to an estimated -$5.8 billion. The result of expanded program coverage, coupled with only gradual increases in effective personal tax rates, has been the increased federal deficits. The deficit increased from $1.5 billion in 1950 to over $7 billion a decade later and soared in 1976 to $66.4 billion.

Since a deficit is a residual figure, whether it occurs because expenses are too great or revenues too meager can be argued endlessly. Similarly, it can be argued that expenditures are too high because one program has grown too much or another was insufficiently cut. These theoretical arguments have been vacuous in political terms. Tax increases have been unpopular, and program cuts (which, other than transfers, would have been mainly in payroll) have eluded the most determined reformers, efficiency experts, and fiscal conservatives. Without program cuts or sufficient growth in revenues, the incremental programs inevitably lead to deficits. Transfers are easy to legislate because they buy votes and are frequently phased over time to disguise the fiscal consequences. The public and its elected representatives have preferred to buy now and hope that someone else will pay later.

Transfers lead to deficits because they invariably cost more than expected. This is true partly because the political temptation to distribute largesse from the public coffers is more than most congressmen can withstand. The problem has been exacerbated by the method of appropriating money. Historically, the executive branch has developed program estimates that, though sometimes inaccurate, were fitted into a single budget and fiscal policy. But Congress voted programs piecemeal, and the inevitable result has been more than the budget comprehended and the revenues could match. A second cause of transfer program overspending is that these "entitlement" programs are not contracted for specifically with the limits of voted appropriations. Congress sets criteria that tell who is to receive a particular kind of transfer; by meeting the criteria, the individual receives the transfer.

The budget history of the United States amply documents the fact that the cost of all major federal income transfer programs to individuals has been underestimated. In 1977, a fairly representative year, the aggregate underestimate was $4.3 billion; in the 1965–77 period, the cumulative difference was $55.6 billion. These figures are significant as an indication of the government's persistent tendency to spend more than is initially announced. The old-age, survivors, disability and health insurance program, Medicare, and railroad retirement underestimates are relevant not to historical budget deficits but to the problem of coping with the substantially increased old age expenditures expected in the future. These programs, as well as unemployment insurance, are funded from payroll taxes which, on the average, have covered the expenditures. Directly related to budget deficits so far have been only those underestimates on programs funded from general revenues: $2.7 billion in 1977 and $34.1 billion cumulative for 1965–77. Underestimates on programs primarily funded from general revenues have varied over the last twelve years from around zero to over 100 percent of the federal deficit; on average, overruns have accounted for about 20 percent of each year's deficit and about 13 percent of the cumulative deficit. A large but highly variable portion of the underestimates is due to inaccurate estimates of the cost of ongoing transfer programs rather than costs triggered by new legislation. In 1974, for example, underestimates were $1.8 billion and over 38 percent of the federal deficit; the following year underestimates totaled $8.3 billion and over 18 percent of the federal deficit.

A significant change may have occurred with the Congressional Budget Act of 1974, which sets deadlines for budget proposals and requires the passage of two concurrent resolutions, the second of which sets a floor on revenues and a ceiling on expenditures. The act's main purpose is to force Congress to deal with expenditures and revenues on a coordinated basis. In fiscal 1977, the first full year under this new system, the results were fairly encouraging. The estimates for ongoing programs were above the actual expenditures. Total overruns, relative to executive branch estimates, in the general revenue funded programs of $2.7 billion were as low as they have been since 1973. Congress voted program increases, so the $2.7 billion may not have been overruns within the framework of the concurrent resolutions. Only time will tell whether the new congressional procedures will achieve control over legislated expansion of programs in excess of revenues. The misestimation part of the problem will probably linger and is potentially serious because of the massive rise in transfer programs expected under existing legislation.

Another aspect of the transfer programs that exacerbates inflation is that many, by being indexed to prices, provide another feedback loop in the inflationary spiral. Combined with inflation, indexation increases program costs and produces either higher taxes or bigger deficits with the inflationary consequences. Even on nonindexed programs, Congress tends not only to legislate benefit increases to keep up with inflation but to provide increases in real benefits as well. Either way, offsetting the effects of inflation on transfer payments exacerbates the inflationary spiral. A further effect of the cost of living increases is the comparison effect on wage earners. People who see recipients of transfer payments keeping up with inflation feel that they should also keep up, and the only way is by demanding wage increases.

The inflationary impact of federal government deficits is a matter of degree and circumstance. Deficits financing government expenditures in an economy operating at or near full capacity will lead to excess demand and inflation. Deficits in a slack economy have less, perhaps even negligible, inflationary impact. In any economy not continually below full capacity, deficits in some years will theoretically be balanced by surpluses in other years, and the inflationary impact will be minimal. But the reality is that surpluses have been few and far between. Even surpluses on the full-employment basis have been infrequent since the mid-1960s. The long-run impact has been inflationary— probably significantly so.

Monetarists argue that federal deficits are irrelevant because only the money supply matters in the long run. This may be true in economic theory, but here again the Federal Reserve response to political realities and the public desire for orderly credit markets tend to ensure that credit is available when the Treasury is borrowing. The deficits lead to more credit; regardless of theory, the end result is much the same.

The Role of Social Security

Given the rising importance of social insurance contributions—especially social security—in total tax receipts, it is worthwhile to examine their impact on the economy as a whole and especially on inflation. In addition to the direct inflationary effect of the employer payroll tax, there is evidently a direct link between social security and inflation through the impact on private saving. It is a major tenet of the life-cycle theory of consumption that individuals save during working years to support consumption during their retirement. One implication is that social security and private pensions reduce saving during working years. In the case of social security, which is not funded, any such reduction in saving would reduce total private saving and therefore capital accumulation. Some of the early studies in this area concluded that private pensions led to an increase in personal saving, especially when pensions were vested and income and age levels were taken into account. These conclusions are explained by a "recognition effect"—an individual enrolled in a private pension plan is forced to assess the importance of saving for his retirement.

Martin Feldstein attributes these early findings to the earlier retirement age made possible by pensions and notes that both pensions and social security reduce savings by substituting for household assets at retirement and also increase savings by lengthening the retirement period over which assets will be needed. The net savings effect depends on the relative strength of the two forces. Feldstein specifically tests for the effect of social security wealth on savings by using the life-cycle consumption function, which relates consumer expenditure to permanent income, the stock of household assets in the traditional sense, and social security wealth. The latter is estimated both on a gross basis—as the present value of the retirement benefits that could be claimed by those in the labor force or those retired in a particular year—and on a net basis, the net of the present value of social security taxes to be paid. Using time-series data, Feldstein concluded that, on both a gross and a net basis and at various discount rates, social security lowers personal savings by at least 50 percent and probably more. A minor portion of this effect occurs as payroll taxation lowers disposable income, thus reducing saving directly. A 50 percent reduction in personal saving implies a 38 percent reduction in total private saving, since personal saving over the long term has averaged about three-fourths of the total and since there is no offsetting gain in public saving. Feldstein estimates that the negative impact of social security on personal saving is likely to rise over time as the earlier retirement effects of the system weaken along with their effect of raising saving.

Others disagree about the magnitude of Feldstein's conclusions. Alicia H. Munnell, for example, has also done extensive work on the impact of retirement benefits on life-cycle saving, using both cross-sectional and time-series approaches. She concludes that social security has a significant negative impact on personal saving but that Feldstein's work seriously overstates the magnitude of the effect. Her work would imply a reduction of $3.6 billion in 1969 saving compared to Feldstein's $51.2 billion based on his 1974 study; however, Feldstein's 1978 work reestablishes a large negative impact on saving from social security.

One may conclude that social security does significantly reduce personal saving, although the magnitude of this impact is still a matter of controversy. Evidence from surveys of those recently retired indicates saving at about the same level as in the 1940s, but the real question is what would have been saved without social security, given recent higher income levels. The real effect is probably somewhere between Munnell's and Feldstein's conclusions, but both agree that the negative impact of social security on private saving will increase over time.

The reduction in saving and therefore in capital accumulation reduces productivity and thereby diminishes real output. One can estimate the magnitude of the impact by splitting the difference between Feldstein's and Munnell's findings and assuming a 22 percent reduction in saving and the savings rate. This implies a long-run reduction of 22 percent in the capital-output ratio, 30 percent in the capital stock, and 7 percent in output below what they would have been without social security.

It takes a long time for the social security programs to grow, for their impact to be felt, and for adjustments to occur in the capital stock. If the adjustment process takes forty years, growth in real GNP will probably be reduced by about 0.175 percent a year below what it would otherwise have been. Reduction in output would have increased the growth rate in unit labor costs by 0.175 percent. With cost markup pricing by firms, price increases can be conservatively estimated at 0.15 percent higher than they would be otherwise. Including the wage-price spiral impact, the rate of inflation ultimately increases by about 0.5 to 1.5 percent. As with the employer payroll tax, it can be held that social security, by substituting for personal saving, makes an uncertain but not inconsequential contribution to the rate of inflation.

The Future Outlook

The above evidence indicates that much of the growth in government spending has been due to the expansion of transfers, primarily of social security. Since the percentage of older people in the population is projected to rise rapidly during the next fifty to sixty years, the expansion is likely to continue and place significant strain on the economy. This projected increase is dramatic. The group aged sixty-five and over is projected to rise from about 10.5 percent of the population in 1975 to more than 18.5 percent in 2035, if birth rates are held at the replacement level of 2.1 children per woman. Compared to 1945 when the proportion of those sixty-five and over to the population as a whole was only 7.5 percent, the increase is even more dramatic. This significant aging of the population will place enormous strain on unfunded retirement systems such as social security, which is financed solely on a pay-as-you-go basis. As the number of social security beneficiaries increases from 19.7 per hundred workers in 1977 to 22.3 in 1990 and to 36.7 in 2050, the load that any single worker bears will increase greatly.

This burden translates into a sizable increase in payroll tax rates. Estimates of the social security expenditures and tax income as a percentage of the effective taxable payroll are projected to rise from 12.6 percent in 1977 to 17.9 percent in 2025—a 43 percent increase in the tax rates. It should be stressed that the additional tax burden in these projections results from the shifting age composition of the population, not from any effort to increase real social security retirement benefits, which of course might be made. In fact, replacement ratios (the proportion of benefits received to previous earnings) for retired beneficiaries are projected to decline to 1985 and then to remain constant.

Social security in no sense represents the full burden that the retired will place on the proportionally smaller work force in the future. Most federal, state, and local employee retirement funds are only partially funded, if at all. Relatively little attention has been given to the potential cost of the government employee pension funds. Indeed, one of the reasons that detailed projections are omitted is the paucity of hard and comparable data. The best, in fact the only, extensive work in this area has been done by Alicia H. Munnell and Ann M. Connolly. Their estimates imply that, although benefit payments of state and local, civil service, and military retirement systems combined were only 1.4 percent of GNP in 1975, they will increase by a factor of about 5 in real terms between 1975 and 2000. In other words, they will grow at almost 7 percent a year in real terms—twice as fast as the real GNP can reasonably be expected to grow. In another measure of the problem, Munnell and Connolly estimated that unfunded liabilities for state and local, civil service, and military retirement systems totaled $629 billion in 1975.

The nonretirement transfer programs could also present a problem. Under the existing legislation in 1975, the Congressional Budget Office projected transfer expenditures for the year 2000 and found the projected expenditures on veterans' benefits, supplemental security income, Aid to Families with Dependent Children, Medicaid, and food stamps would be no higher than 1975 expenditures as a percent of GNP. Of course, program legislation has changed frequently in the past. Indeed, the major problem in relying on any of these projections is that Congress and other political bodies may increase benefits. The history of liberality with public funds, together with the consistent underestimates of costs, indicates that the expenditures may well turn out to be larger than the projected sums.

Potential reductions in the costs of supporting the young may offset the increasing retirement costs caused by an aging population. The elderly are projected to increase from 19.2 percent of the working age population (twenty to sixty-four) in 1975 to 31.0 percent in 2025. This increase will be offset by a decline in juveniles as a percentage of the working age population from 64.1 to 48.2 percent. As a result, the overall dependency ratio—the ratio of nonworking age to working age population—will remain about 80 percent. Based on work done by Timothy D. Hogan, calculations have been made for the potential long-term effect on selected government programs for elderly and young people resulting from these demographic shifts and projected increases in social security coverage; it is estimated that social security and old age related programs may rise from 3.2 percent in 1977 to 5.5 percent of net national product in 2025. However, youth related programs should decline in relative importance, so the combined effect is a rise from 9.1 percent to 10.2 percent of the net national product.

These estimates are presented as an academic illustration, not as a forecast. The relevant point is not the specific percentages but the idea that the smaller population of young people could free resources to support older people. The above analysis deals strictly with government spending and ignores private costs.

Of course, an academic exercise rarely provides an accurate forecast of future events. Birthrates of AFDC mothers are unlikely to drop in line with those of the population as a whole; school expenditures seem to function like price increases, being much stickier in a downward direction than when being raised. A major problem is that education is provided by the state and local governments. Any national savings, under current arrangements, must come from a myriad of state and local decisions. Some progress appears to have been made in that elementary and secondary school expenditures have fallen from 5.1 percent of net national product in 1970 to 4.85 percent currently.

Nevertheless, the above exercise indicates only potential savings to offset higher future expenditures on the elderly—savings which are not likely to be realized without substantial, determined efforts on the part of the taxpayers.

One factor that will greatly influence the future size of the social security burden is the retirement age. The presence of social security and private pension systems has steadily and significantly reduced the participation of older members of the population in the labor force. An unfunded retirement system suffers doubly from a trend toward earlier retirement, which increases the number of beneficiaries while simultaneously reducing the number of workers to support the system. Lowering the retirement age in 1985 would raise taxes proportionately more than they would be lowered by a corresponding increase in the retirement age, although a five-year shift in retirement either way would dramatically affect tax rates. The proportionate cost of early retirement rises dramatically as the population is projected to age.

One obvious way to reduce the future burden of social security taxes is to encourage later retirement. Recent congressional legislation prohibiting mandatory retirement before the age of seventy may promote this trend. It is also probable that as fewer young people enter the labor force more older people will continue working. Unfortunately, the current social security benefit structure encourages retirement at age sixty-two and penalizes those who retire after age sixty-five. Until this is changed, there is an institutionalized economic incentive for early retirement that not only makes the social security system more costly but raises the cost of private pension systems as well.

The 1975 Social Security Advisory Council report recommended that serious consideration be given to extending the retirement age. It suggested, for example, increasing the retirement age by one month every six months from 2005 to 2023. This would raise retirement and early retirement ages three years each by 2023 and reduce the tax rate 1.5 percentage points from 2025 to 2050. Another suggestion was to raise the delayed retirement credit, which now increases benefits only 1 percent for each year retirement is delayed. Norway currently increases benefits 9 percent for every year that retirement is delayed between sixty-seven and seventy.

The phenomenon of an aging population is not peculiar to the United States. In fact, most major European countries will face rapidly aging populations in the 1980s and 1990s. High birthrates before World War I were followed by decades of war and depression and then more rapid declines in birthrates than were experienced in the Western Hemisphere.

Relative social security tax burdens are substantially greater elsewhere than in the United States. In 1975 social security contributions, as a share of the gross domestic product, were 60 to 100 percent higher in France, Germany, and Italy than in the United States. In 1973 the old-age employee payroll tax rate was almost 15 percent in the Netherlands and about 9 percent in Germany, Norway, and Austria. Although it is hazardous to compare programs and coverages across countries, each of these tax rates is higher than that projected for the United States beyond 1990, while combined employer-employee old-age payroll taxes in seven Organization for Economic Cooperation and Development countries were higher in 1973 than the 15.3 percent payroll tax rate projected for the United States beyond 1990. Despite these financing burdens, most countries have had little luck in reducing the payroll burden, partly as a result of the greater political power of the retired as they increase as a proportion of the population.

Whether this experience is transferable to the United States is hard to say. It is doubtful that the populace would tolerate a level of taxation as high as that in some European countries merely to transfer income from one group to another. Even if they would, higher taxes are not a solution to the pension problem.

An interesting aspect of the international experience is that high payroll tax burdens are found in countries with low inflation experiences (Germany and Austria) and very high inflation experiences (Italy, Norway, and Sweden). Clearly, inflation is caused by much more than taxes. In addition, a taxpayer's response to a tax seems to depend very much on the political and social environment and on observation consistent with the different econometric findings in the United States and in the United Kingdom referred to earlier.

Several conclusions may be drawn from this analysis. Transfers have been the major source of growth in government expenditures and a major contributor to payroll tax increases, the federal government deficits, and thereby, presumably, to inflation. The social security system has contributed to inflation through its negative impact on savings and through the employer payroll tax. Financing of transfers through personal taxes, including the employee payroll taxes, is probably inflationary to a small degree, but the evidence does not conclusively support that contention. Since demographic shifts will substantially increase the cost of the retirement systems under existing law over the next fifty years, the inflationary impact of transfers is likely to increase unless changes are made.

The government should restructure the social security system in order to produce later retirement by gradually delaying the earliest age at which retirement benefits are payable and by changing the benefit scales to encourage later retirement. It should reevaluate the acceptability of rising tax rates and inflation, reexamine the social security income replacement rate to determine what level of retirement income is justifiable, and reassess the benefit and eligibility criteria for nonretirement transfers. As the juvenile proportion of the population declines, government programs for juveniles—particularly education expenditures—should be systematically reduced in order to free resources. The new congressional budgeting procedures should be continued and strengthened to ensure coordination between expenditures and revenues. Finally, the government should develop more reliable information and projections on the civil service, military, and state and local employee retirement systems.

Works Cited

Boskin, Michael J. "Taxation, Savings and the Rate of Interest." *Journal of Political Economy* 86 (1978): S 3-27.

Congressional Budget Office. *Growth of Government Spending for Income Assistance: A Matter of Choice.* Washington, D.C.: Government Printing Office, 1975.

Feldstein, Martin. "Social Security Induced Retirement and Aggregate Capital Accumulation." *Journal of Political Economy* 82 (1974): 905-26.

Henry, S.G.B.; Sawyer, M.C.; and Smith, P. "Models of Inflation in the United Kingdom: An Evaluation." *National Institute Economic Review*, no. 77 (1976): 60-71.

Hogan, Timothy D. "The Implications of Population Stationarity for the Social Security System." *Social Science Quarterly* 55 (1974): 151-58.

Lawrence, William J., and Leeds, Stephen. *An Inventory of Federal Income Transfer Programs.* White Plains, N.Y.: The Institute for Socioeconomic Studies, 1978.

Munnell, Alicia H. *The Future of Social Security.* Washington, D.C.: The Brookings Institution, 1977.

Munnell, Alicia H., and Connolly, Ann M. "Funding Government Pensions: State-Local, Civil Service and Military." In *Funding Pensions: Issues and Implications for Financial Markets.* Boston: Federal Reserve Bank, 1976.

Perry, George L. "Changing Labor Markets and Inflation." In *Brookings Papers on Economic Activity*, no. 3 (1970): 411-31.

Schnabel, Constance, and Schnabel, Morton, "The Short-Run Incidence of Payroll Taxes." Paper delivered at the Annual Meeting of the Eastern Economic Association, April 1978.

Health Care

MORTON D. MILLER

The American health care industry is the nation's third largest industry after agriculture and defense, employing almost 5 million persons. It includes some 350,000 active physicians and over 7,000 hospitals. Hospitals alone employ some 3.2 million persons. The industry has responded admirably to the incentives provided for its growth, and, except for some problems of availability and accessibility, it is widely acknowledged as the best in the world. Unfortunately, its costs are high and increasing at a distressing rate.

Health care inflation has escalated since the passage of Medicare and Medicaid in 1965, and it has become the paramount concern of almost everyone involved with health matters. The magnitude of the problem can be seen from the fact that the percentage of the gross national product (GNP) devoted to health care grew from 4.5 percent ($12 billion) in 1950 to 8.8 percent ($183 billion) in 1978 and is projected to be 9.7 percent ($323 billion) by 1983. At the current rate of inflation in this area, expenditures almost double every seven years.

From a more parochial perspective, one should be reminded that during the Great Depression a more than adequate health insurance policy paid $5 a day for hospital room and board and $25 for ancillary services. Today, insurers often pay 80 percent of charges, will limit an individual's overall liability to no more than $1,000 in any one year, and will readily undertake to pay benefits without limit. Many believe that the growth of such comprehensive insurance protection has undermined the cost consciousness of the consumer and the providers of health care.

The vast majority of Americans now have protection against the cost of health care from one source or another through either public or private programs. From its beginning during the Great Depression and its expansion through federally granted tax advantages, health insurance has grown in the United States to the point where nine out of ten individuals under age sixty-five have private health insurance, and three out of four Americans in this age group, or 144 million persons, have significant coverage against catastrophic medical expenses. After taking into account the impact of government-sponsored programs, such as Medicare, Medicaid, and the Veterans Administration system, as well as private plans, it is estimated that some 90 percent of the total population have some protection against the cost of medical expenses. It is further estimated that over three-quarters of the population have coverage that could be considered adequate.

The impact of such extensive insurance coverage on the behavior of different types of providers becomes apparent when one examines their sources of revenue. For example, hospitals receive 90 percent or more of their revenues from a third party, that is, a source other than the individual on whose behalf the expense was incurred. For physicians, the proportion is 61 percent, and for dental services, for which insurance is still in the developing stage, it has already risen to 19 percent.

With such extensive third-party payments for medical and dental care, rapid inflation has become of increasing concern to those who finance these payments, primarily employers and all three levels of government as well as individuals responsible for their own insurance or care. Considering the way health care is organized and financed and the implicit and often conflicting incentives within the sector, health care inflation is a natural result. There are many facets to the problem, and in a real sense everyone is to blame.

Factors Promoting Inflation

The laws of supply and demand do not operate in the health care sector to moderate prices and the consumption of services to any significant extent. With third parties paying so much of the cost, price is not perceived by the consumer to be a critical factor in his decision-making. Additionally, to a large extent the physician controls the nature and volume of the services rendered. Furthermore, in keeping with the Hippocratic tradition, the physician views the care of the patient as his primary responsibility regardless of the cost. Under the circumstances, it is hardly surprising that prices are rising excessively as services increase in volume, thus driving total expenditures to levels unacceptable for many people. It should be mentioned at this point that rising health care costs are not peculiar to the United States but are prevalent throughout the Western world.

Technological advances have further added to inflation in the health care industry. Not many years ago sick people went to a hospital to die, whereas today they expect to receive treatment that will lead to their recovery. Many of the early medical advances—such as immunization, antibiotics, and the development of sanitary water supplies—had a low unit cost and were relatively simple to introduce. These early advances significantly reduced morbidity and mortality due to infectious diseases like pneumonia, tuberculosis, and diphtheria. The control of infectious disease has been called the first epidemiologic revolution. More recent advances in medical science, stimulated by benevolent philanthropy and generous government support for research and development, have been neither simple, inexpensive, nor easy to introduce. In fact, they have tended to add to, rather than replace, the need for capital investment and at the same time have required additional and often specialized personnel. For instance, coronary care units, renal dialysis, hip and other joint replacement operations, and new types of diagnostic equipment, such as CAT (computer assisted tomography) scanners, are expensive, capital intensive, and highly sophisticated to the point of requiring trained professionals to utilize them properly. Furthermore, the complexity of much of the new technology has added significantly to the potential for mishap in the course of treatment and to the cost to providers of malpractice insurance.

Admittedly, new technology offers a significant opportunity for prolonging or improving the quality of life, but a significant price is associated with each advance. The cumulative effect of the strengthened capacity of medicine and its widespread introduction is a substantial increase in the cost of the care provided. In the last analysis, each new technical breakthrough should be cost-benefit effective, but no formal mechanism exists for determining whether it is. Doubts are being raised with respect to some practices, most notably the expensive coronary bypass operation now being widely performed.

The population of the United States is gradually growing older. Some 22.4 million Americans are over sixty-five. By 2000, it is estimated that some 31.8 million will be over sixty-five, and by 2030 this group will increase to 55.0 million. In 1976, approximately $1,500 was spent on health care for each individual over age sixty-five, compared to $547 for those between nineteen and sixty-four and $250 for those under nineteen. Therefore, as the population ages, one can expect that the proportion of the GNP devoted to health care will increase accordingly.

Subsumed in the fact of an aging population are difficult ethical and moral issues that will have to be carefully considered. To what extent should physicians attempt to prolong the life of older Americans? In that connection, much of the high technology introduced in recent years, though costly, is of marginal value. Some nations have already begun to face these issues. For example, under its national health insurance system, the United Kingdom limits renal dialysis to those under the age of fifty whose remaining productive life could make the treatment worthwhile.

It is estimated that the United States has some 100,000 more hospital beds than are needed and that the supply of physicians is more than adequate for current needs. Yet the number of hospitals, medical schools, and physician graduates continues to increase. More medical specialists, particularly surgeons, are being produced than are needed but not enough family or primary care practitioners. Also, the facilities and physicians tend to be concentrated in the affluent urban and suburban areas rather than the rural and inner city areas where the need is greater.

Since the cost of maintaining a staffed but unfilled bed is almost as great as that of an occupied bed, the incentive for the administrator, whose goal is to maximize revenues, is to apply both overt and covert pressure on the admitting physicians to fill any unoccupied beds. Empty beds appear to be the only rational explanation for the practice of admitting patients on a Friday for procedures not to be performed until Monday or holding patients until Monday when they could have been released the previous Friday. Obviously, the net result is to increase the revenues flowing to the institution and to add to the cost of health care.

An oversupply of physicians, particularly specialists, is reflected in an increased utilization of physician and ancillary services. Several studies have shown a direct correlation between the number of surgical procedures performed per thousand persons in a given geographic area and the number of surgeons in the same area. Other studies indicate that, contrary to expectations, the fees charged by specialists tend to be higher in areas with a high concentration of specialists. Various explanations have been offered for this nonmarket phenomenon, the key one being the principle of targeted incomes. A physician apparently establishes an income level that he or she would like to achieve and then proceeds to generate services to provide it. It has been estimated that, in addition to his fees, on the average each physician authorizes or arranges for services that cost $250,000 to $300,000 a year.

The regulation of health care is another source of inflation. While much of it is beneficial, this regulation has become overburdening and counterproductive from a cost standpoint. The Hospital Association of New York State has estimated that some 25 percent of the costs of its member-hospitals is directly attributable to regulation. While one should be willing to pay the cost of ensuring that hospitals are safe places for people to receive care, that the funds entrusted to hospitals are appropriately spent, and that the care provided is of the highest quality, one must question whether regulation by some 161 different federal, state, and local agencies is the best way to achieve these goals. The duplication of costs is significant since each agency requires that reports be filed on its own forms, that data be kept in a way that is unique to the given agency, and that the hospital comply with all of its edicts, even though they may contradict those of some other agency.

Other areas of the health care sector are faced with a similar regulatory maze. The cost of complying with the morass of drug regulations has seriously interfered with the development and introduction of new drugs. The pharmaceutical manufacturers have responded by reducing their investment in research and development, thereby lessening the likelihood of developing new drugs that could have a beneficial effect on both the health of the nation and the cost of health care.

Anti-inflation Measures

There is no single or simple solution that will slow the rapid rise in health care costs. Actions that could help abate the inflation in the health care sector fall into four general categories: the way providers are paid, the way the cost of health care is shared, the way the industry is organized, and the way individuals behave.

For the most part, providers of health care are paid on the basis of fees per unit of service or their retrospective costs. By increasing the utilization or the base cost of their services, providers are generally able to realize their desired income levels or needed revenue flows. Tighter controls over their actions could be accomplished in several ways. The choice of the preferred mechanism depends largely on one's belief concerning the proper role of government and the understanding one has of the motivation of the providers.

Some feel that it is necessary for the government, particularly the federal government, to expand its purview by regulation in order to control provider behavior. The most far-reaching of such proposals is embodied in Senator Edward M. Kennedy's national health insurance proposal. It would establish a national budget for health care expenditures each year to be allocated on a regional or state basis in accordance with some objective formula. The providers within each defined area, working in conjunction with the government, would decide how their budget allowance was to be expended. Such a proposal assumes that a national budget can in fact be established, that a rational apportionment by geographic area and among different types of services can be made, and that the individual in need of treatment would bear little or no responsibility for paying for his care.

A more moderate approach is the one advanced by the Carter administration. The administration focused on hospital costs, which alone account for some 40 percent of the total health care expenditures and which have been increasing at a rate significantly above that of health care as a whole. The proposal would have placed a ceiling on increases in net hospital revenues equal to one and a half times the GNP deflator and a separate ceiling on capital expenditures equal to $2.5 billion per annum, a figure approximately one-half of the average of capital expenditures for the last five years. The proposal failed to pass in the Ninety-fifth Congress.

A variant of the president's proposal contemplates the determination of hospital budgets and rate charges on a prospective basis each year by a commission set up specifically for that purpose by enactment in each state. Such a process has the advantage of being able to account more readily for local differences and the needs of specific institutions while still requiring that each hospital stay within a predetermined budget.

State prospective hospital budget review and rate approval has been very successful in the states that have tried it. One of the keys to its success is that all payers reimburse a given hospital at the same or comparable rates for similar services. In most states where that is not the case, Medicare, Medicaid, and Blue Cross pay the hospitals something less than cost on behalf of their beneficiaries with the result that charge-paying individuals as a group must make up the difference between the actual cost and the lesser reimbursed cost. The difference between charges and reimbursed cost can be as much as 50 percent. By establishing parity levels among payers, the states that have state prospective budget review and rate approval programs are able to prevent the hospitals from shifting their costs from one class of payer to another and thereby avoid the impact of revenue controls.

Another approach would involve the negotiation of rates and standards. Under this approach, the third-party purchasers of care would band together for the purpose of negotiating both the rates of reimbursement and the standards of care with the providers. The negotiations would be carried out separately with the hospitals, with the physicians, and perhaps ultimately with other types of providers.

The providers would have to agree not to make any charges exceeding the negotiated rates and not to seek to collect the value of any unreimbursed care from their patients. They would also have to propose and agree to the standards of care against which their performance would be judged. Without such standards, providers could easily add to their revenues simply by increasing the number of their services whether or not they were needed.

Such negotiation would place on the purchasers of care the burden of ensuring the introduction of more effective management into the delivery of care. It would also require that the purchasers of care develop a system for the collection, transmission, and analysis of patient care and claims data in a uniform and coordinated manner. Such a system would allow the purchasers to monitor the providers' adherence to the negotiated rates and standards of care and would act as the basis for future negotiations. A specific exemption from the antitrust laws for this purpose would be required in order for the process of negotiation to be tried. A proposal for such an exemption is before Congress and the Federal Trade Commission.

There has been much debate over whether the patient's sharing the cost of services is an effective means of restraining increases in the cost of care. Some believe any payment required of a patient constitutes a barrier to his obtaining necessary care. Others are convinced that modest coinsurance and deductible mechanisms can be constructed in such a way as to remind the consumer of his responsibility for the extent of services rendered without deterring him from seeking necessary care. This view is broadly held within the insurance industry.

Apart from coinsurance and deductibles, a great deal can be done to make the individual aware that in the long run he is paying for his health care, whether directly or through a third party. Under the current tax treatment of health insurance premiums, employer costs are fully tax deductible and partially deductible for individuals. One hundred percent employer deductibility provides an incentive for workers to seek to have their employer-paid insurance cover as high a proportion of their medical expenses as possible. From the workers' point of view, a dollar in benefit costs is worth two dollars in wages.

It is time to rethink the tax treatment of health insurance premiums. The government should continue to allow individuals and corporations to deduct 100 percent of premiums for tax purposes, but only up to some level such as $1,000 a year per family, which is the current average cost of a comprehensive group (health insurance) program. Any employer-paid portion of the total premium in excess of the cap would then become imputed income to the employee on whose behalf it had been paid. Such a change in tax treatment would tend to make employees much more conscious of the costs incurred on their behalf, reduce the employee incentive for adoption of first dollar coverage, and provide a positive incentive for the employee to consider the price of medical care.

The organizational structure of the health care industry has developed without much concern for its efficiency or the optimization of its resources. In many respects, it is still a cottage industry despite the fact that it has become enormously more complex and interrelated because of tremendous technological strides. There have been, and will continue to be, numerous attempts to rationalize the organizational structure of this industry.

From a legislative standpoint, these attempts have taken the form of health-planning legislation charging locally sponsored organizations with the responsibility of establishing short- and long-term plans for the delivery of health care. Such plans attempt to integrate ambulatory and in-patient care into some rational distribution along with primary and tertiary care and to avoid unnecessarily duplicating services or facilities. The mechanism used for implementing these plans is a certificate-of-need process that requires a hospital to receive approval from its local health planning agency for any capital expenditure over $150,000. Without such approval, Medicare and Medicaid will not reimburse the hospital for its share of the capital costs incurred in constructing the unapproved facility.

Another approach for introducing greater rationality into the health care system that has been given legislative support is the development of alternative health care delivery systems. Such systems are symbolized by the health maintenance organizations (HMOs) through which a broad range of physican and hospital services is guaranteed in return for periodic fixed payments by or on behalf of those enrolled in the plan. The most prominent of such systems are the Kaiser-Permanente Health Care Plans, which have been in existence for about forty years. They have the advantage of being able to manage the total health care needs of the individual in an efficient manner. Encouraging the development of health maintenance or similar organizations and financially supporting their formation continues to be a major thrust of the Department of Health, Education, and Welfare. In an attempt to introduce some degree of overall management into the fee-for-service system along the lines common to alternative health care delivery systems, professional standard review organizations were established by law to review the appropriateness, the necessity, and the cost of the care received by federal beneficiaries.

An interesting alternative to the highly regulated approach taken by recent legislation can be found in Minneapolis-St. Paul. In the last ten years, some six health maintenance organizations in the Twin Cities have competed with one another for subscribers. Such competition has markedly reduced the escalation of health care costs in the area and has improved the utilization of existing resources. The competition has also forced the physicians and hospitals not involved with the HMOs to examine the ways that they organize their services. The lesson of Minneapolis-St. Paul is that, given time and a significant enough concentration of alternative health care delivery modules, market forces can be introduced into the health care sector, lower cost levels achieved, and the need for burdensome regulation lessened.

Increasingly it is recognized that each individual can and must play a role in maintaining his own health. The health care system has been predicated too long on the premise that once people become ill, physicians and others would make them well. Preventive medicine has not been emphasized, in part because physicians did not know how to prevent many of the illnesses. People have been led to believe that the miracles of modern medicine were such that almost any problem, given time and enough money, could be cured.

With the control of infectious disease through immunization and antibiotics, a significant improvement in morbidity and mortality took place. The diseases most prevalent today are chronic ailments that generally do not appear until later in life, and often do not have a single identifiable cause. Many chronic diseases are in part self-induced. They are often the product of overeating, poor diets, smoking, lack of exercise, and the abuse of alcohol and other substances.

In the last five years considerable attention has been given to reformulating the role and responsibility of the individual in maintaining his own health. Some believe that the nation has embarked on a second epidemiologic revolution—focused on the behavior of the individual and the control of disease through a greater awareness and understanding of life-styles that are likely to be conducive to good health. The way to bring about this revolution is through the continued development and support of health education programs designed for children, adults, and senior citizens alike. Fortunately, health education programs are already making their mark and are currently enjoying rapid growth and increased academic, government, and business involvement.

The private sector, including health insurers, has been in the forefront of these developments. Corporate contributions of funds and personnel helped establish the National Center for Health Education in 1976. A not-for-profit organization devoted to stimulating health education initiatives in the private sector, the center has several major efforts under way. One will help local school systems introduce new health education curricula that emphasize parental participation. A second will design health education materials for employers to use. A third will support community-based involvement in health education through a series of eight regional forums for local citizen organizations. Moreover, the Department of Health, Education, and Welfare is launching a major initiative designed to provide the public with health information in more effective ways and to promote health in the work setting.

A recent survey conducted by Louis Harris for the Pacific Mutual Insurance Company clearly showed that more and more Americans are attempting to exercise regularly, have improved their diets, and recognize the hazards of smoking and alcohol. Health education offers significant promise of turning this new sensitivity into action by helping individuals to realize the consequences to themselves and their families of the choices they make.

It would be in the interest of the public to initiate certain actions at once. The certificate-of-need and health planning programs should be employed on a wider basis so as to restrain further capital expansion and eliminate redundant beds and facilities. Preadmissions testing should be vigorously encouraged to eliminate costly duplication of laboratory testing in hospitals. Experiments with second-opinion surgery should be expanded so its effectiveness in eliminating unnecessary surgery can be determined. More care should be provided in ambulatory settings and additional ambulatory surgical centers should be developed for routine and minor surgery. Health insurance benefit plans should be redesigned so that they provide more incentive for ambulatory and preventive care as well as cost consciousness on the part of the insured and their physicians. Activities such as professional standards review should be extended beyond Medicare and Medicaid so as to encompass all patients. Additional incentives for the development of managed systems for the delivery of care should be provided so as further to enhance competition among providers. Incentives for states to establish hospital prospective budget review and rate approval commissions that comply with federally promulgated guidelines should be included in any cost containment programs enacted by Congress. Efforts directed toward disease prevention and health education should be expanded. Finally, purchasers of care should be actively supported in their efforts to secure a limited exemption from the antitrust laws so they can jointly negotiate rates of reimbursement and standards of care with providers in the interest of cost containment.

The War Industry

KENNETH E. BOULDING

It is difficult to assess the impact of any particular segment of society or the economy on the process of inflation, because inflation is the property of the whole society. It is the result of an enormously complex set of interacting decisions that set off an endless chain of further decisions. The very success in the measurement of the aggregates of society, such as the gross national product (GNP), the consumer price index (CPI), and various measures of inflation, often obscures the reality that society consists of a vast structure of "minute particulars," in the words of William Blake, that the real world is a process by which these minute particulars continually act and interact on each other. One tends to think of inflation as a rise in the price level, that is, in some number representing an aggregate index of prices. The price level, however, is a construct of the human mind. The reality is the price of a particular item purchased by a particular person at a particular store at a particular time and the hundreds of billions of such purchases that constitute the reality of the economy.

Inflation is the rise of some statistical average or aggregate of particular prices over time. Measures of it, such as the consumer price index, the wholesale price index, and the GNP deflator, are much more imperfect than many people realize, particularly over long periods of time, simply because of the constant change in the nature of commodities and the nature of the commodity mix. What, for instance, was the price of a particular color television set in 1929? The question is absurd because the commodity did not exist. Nevertheless, the tendency is blithely to aggregate the prices in 1929 with those in 1979. The change in the quality of commodities, including labor, is very hard to estimate, and this makes all measures of inflation subject to a noticeable but indeterminate error. Nevertheless, if the price index in 1979 is about four times what it was in 1929, something has surely happened; the error is certainly not of that order of magnitude.

The process of inflation, therefore, consists of a rise in the price of certain commodities without a compensating decline in the price of others. Included, of course, is the price of particular kinds of human services (wages) in the general set of prices. Prices and wages, however, do not rise or fall without human decisions. The question should be asked, therefore, which framework of human decisions leads to a rise or a fall in prices and which changes in this framework lead to an excess of one over the other. The answer is clear in general but not always in detail. Prices are determined either unilaterally (retail prices usually by the seller) or by bargaining, either individual or collective, between the seller and the buyer. A price-maker will raise a price or lower it if the movement is felt to be to his or her advantage. Sellers are limited in the prices they can ask by the willingness of buyers to buy, as expressed by demand. A rise in this willingness (expressed by a shift in the demand curve to the right), where the buyers are willing to buy more at each price or the same amount at a higher price, raises the incentive for the sellers to raise the price. In the case of labor, it is frequently the buyer who quotes a wage, though over some 25 percent of the labor market wages are determined by collective bargaining between employers and unions. Even the individual buyer of labor, however, is limited in the range of wages offered by the potential supply of labor, and fear of a labor shortage will raise the wage offered.

The Money Supply

A persistent tendency for prices and wages to rise in money terms must be due to a persistent increase in money demand. This can only happen for two reasons: either a persistent increase in the total stock of money or a persistent decline in the demand for money itself, as expressed by the proportion of assets that people wish to hold in this form. Money, it should be noted, is a rather vague concept. Assets possess different degrees of liquidity. They are ranged in the order of their liquidity, and everything beyond a certain point is considered money. Where the line is drawn, however, is rather arbitrary, and one always has to look for changes in the liquidity of different assets and the willingness of people to hold them. It is clear, however, that persistent and long-run inflation can only come from a persistent long-run increase in the total stock of money. A decline in the demand for money cannot go on for very long. It may have had some impact on the present situation, particularly the development of credit cards and other instruments of easy credit. One could even imagine a society without any money at all; all transactions would be recorded in a central computer that simply changes the number representing people's total assets. Even under these circumstances, however, without physical money, people would still distinguish among various kinds of assets and inflation would persist if assets regarded as liquid continually increased.

The relationship between the money stock, or at least one measure of it (M_1), and the CPI since 1929 indicates that this has been the age of inflation. Since 1940 there have only been two years in which the CPI fell. Much more alarming, the United States seems to have had accelerating inflation since 1970. A constant rate of inflation is something that society can adjust to fairly easily once it is generally recognized. An accelerating inflation must inevitably lead to hyperinflation and some sort of collapse. It is a little odd that since about 1964 the CPI has lagged behind the money supply, suggesting that the willingness to hold money of the type M_1 has increased. This is very surprising in light of the inflation itself, which is a tax on the holding of money and a fairly severe one, and in light of the increased use of credit cards and a variety of liquid assets. This puzzle seems inexplicable. There are, incidentally, other puzzles in monetary statistics. Per capita holdings of actual cash in 1978, for instance, seem absurdly large—roughly $400. In view of the fact that a large majority of people in this country almost certainly have less than $100 cash in their wallets and pockets, a small number of people must hold very large amounts of cash. It is hard not to believe that the purposes of this are somewhat clandestine and that monetary statistics have certain ominous overtones.

The next question is that of the sources of the increased money stock. It has two principal sources. By far the most important one is the government deficit. This deficit must appear as an increase in the financial assets of the public, either in the form of government securities, cash, or bank deposits. The willingness of the public to hold government securities is limited. Deficits in excess of this willingness tend to be monetized, that is, to appear as government securities in the assets of the banking system, which result in expansion of the bank deposits in the possession of private citizens. Even in the absence of a government deficit, the banking system is capable of expanding the money stock by increasing its loans and investments and creating deposits. But in the absence of continually expanding reserves its capacity to do this is limited, and expansion of reserves comes primarily from the federal budget deficit.

To show the relationship between the federal government deficit and the CPI, it is useful to divide the last fifty years or so into four periods. The first period is from 1929 to 1940, the Great Depression and partial recovery from it, where the overall budget deficit was quite small, not even large enough to offset the enormous deflationary course of the Great Depression. The second period is that of World War II, with a very large deficit, a suppressed inflation during the war that made itself felt mainly after the war, up until about 1948. Then followed a period of moderate deficits and moderate inflation from 1948 to about 1969. Finally, from 1969 on, there have been large deficits, again resulting in accelerated and perhaps accelerating inflation. The first period might be called the "depressed 1930s"; the second, "World War II"; the third, the "long boom"; and the fourth, the "growing crisis."

Military Expenditures

The gross relationship of the war industry to these four periods is shown in figure 1. In the period of the "depressed 1930s" the war industry was negligible. Almost all of the budget deficits and the inflation of the second period were related to the war industry and World War II. In the third period, the "long boom," the Korean war created both a budget deficit and a slightly accelerated inflation but on a relatively small scale compared with World War II. After the Korean war, the deficits were not closely related to the war industry, except for the Vietnam war. These deficits were much smaller than those of the Korean war, though qualitatively they may have had a much larger impact. They do seem to have accelerated inflation somewhat. In the 1970s, however, the relationship changed. The war industry continually declined as a proportion of GNP. It cannot be blamed for the increasing deficit, and it is hard to blame it for the increased rate of inflation.

Some international comparisons further support the view that in the 1970s any relationship between the proportion of GNP devoted to military expenditures and the rate of inflation is extremely tenuous. In 1975 indeed the United States had a lower rate of inflation than five countries—Japan, West Germany, Italy, France, and Canada—with a smaller proportion of their GNP in military expenditures. Before 1970, it is probably safe to say that inflation was primarily a war-related phenomenon. After 1970, inflation became what might almost be called a "normal characteristic" of the total society and was hardly related at all to the size of the war industry. This is not to say, of course, that a major increase in the war industry in another war would not also increase inflation. Indeed, under present circumstances it would make hyperinflation an even more likely accompaniment of war than it has been in the past. That is one of the increasing costs of war, and it is not much in the public consciousness. If there is a third world war, the hyperinflation that was characteristic, say, of Germany in 1923 or Hungary in 1946 could well be completely universal, because it is clear that in the 1970s the normal defenses against inflation have become much weaker, even though they have not entirely disappeared.

There remains a nagging question as to whether the war industry does not make a disproportionate contribution to the structural causes of inflation, and these must now be examined. If the primary, immediate cause of long-run inflation is the persistent tendency for governments to run deficits, one must inquire why this is so. These deficits are a result of decisions taken in the complex interactions of the political process. Every decision, even when it is a decision not to do something, is the result of some set of images of the future, or "agendas." These are ordered in the mind of the decision-maker—best, second best, and so on—according to a value system, and the decision-maker presumably chooses what is thought to be the best. The persistence of government deficits and of inflation suggests, therefore, that the other alternatives are perceived, even perhaps unconsciously, in some sense to be worse. One must look, therefore, for these perceived alternatives and ask why they are perceived to be worse.

Two broad answers might tentatively be given to this question; the first rather obvious, the second more subtle. The obvious answer is that there are only two ways to reduce budget deficits. One is to increase government receipts through increased taxes. The other is to diminish government expenditures, which means to diminish government purchases of goods and services or government transfer payments. If either of these is perceived as politically unacceptable and likely to get the decision-maker defeated in the next election, then

FIGURE 1

*Federal Purchases of Goods and Services for National Defense
(as a percentage of GNP) and the Consumer Price Index (base year 1967), 1929-77*

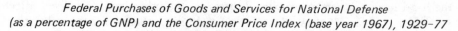

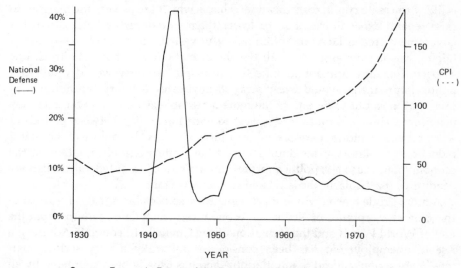

YEAR

Source: Economic Report of the President, 1970 and 1978.

inflation may easily be perceived as the least of three evils, the other two being increased taxes or diminished public expenditures. In the 1970s in the United States—and perhaps to a smaller extent in some other countries—a "tax revolt," more at the local than at the federal level, suggests that increasing taxes will be so unpopular politically that it will lead to political defeat of politicians associated with this policy.

A subtle problem related to the war industry is that most nonmilitary government expenditures in the United States are made by state and local government, and a large part of federal expenditures is to the military. Little solid data exist on this matter, but the hypothesis seems plausible that the taxpayer feels helpless about federal taxes and that much of his or her frustration is transferred to the state and local level. This may help explain the pressures that have built up to California's passage of Proposition 13 and resulted in the failure of school taxes and school bonds at the local level and also perhaps the financial crises of cities like New York and Cleveland. If that is so, then the military expenditures of the federal government may be indirectly responsible for a good deal of tax resistance at the local level, simply because the military and indeed the federal government are perceived as remote and rather alien, whereas the citizen feels he or she can really do something about government at the local level.

The diminution of public expenditures is likely to be resisted almost as much as an increase in taxes. Taxes affect nearly everybody, and what affects everybody is so widely distributed that it is hard to organize any opposition to it. That is perhaps another reason why the opposition to taxes appears only at the local level. Government expenditures, on the other hand, intensely affect particular people. A cut in particular expenditures, whether for the military or for other purposes, affects individual persons in individual localities and hence is likely to create counterorganization. That is why it seems very much easier to raise federal expenditures than to lower them, for once they are raised, the government creates large and often powerful vested interests in favor of maintaining existing budgets. With all the rhetoric about zero-based budgets, one suspects that any attempt to take this principle seriously would result in a political uproar that would sweep away its advocates. Military expenditures indeed may turn out to be one of the more adjustable aspects of government expenditures, simply because it is subject to wide fluctuation between periods of war and peace and is therefore used to large changes. It could well be that a reduction of military expenditures would have much less of an effect on the economy and cause less political protest than a reduction of federal civilian expenditures, particularly those related to social welfare.

A more subtle reason why budget deficits are so popular is that, at least since the general acceptance of Keynesian economics, which dates perhaps from the end of World War II and the formation of the Council of Economic Advisers, a rise in unemployment has been considered politically a very serious matter—more serious indeed than inflation—and has usually been countered by an expansion of the budget deficit. This relates to the well-known "Phillips curve dilemma"—that the reduction of unemployment can only be obtained at the cost of an increase in the rate of inflation. If this is so, then an increase in unemployment beyond some politically acceptable level is always likely to result in inflation, simply because of the measures taken to offset the unemployment. There is some difference among the political parties in the United States—the Democrats are more afraid of unemployment and the Republicans more afraid of inflation—but it is a fairly small difference. There now seems to be some indication that the Phillips curve is moving upwards and to the right, that is, each level of employment now requires a higher rate of inflation to support it. If true, it is indeed ominous.

Why, then, is there a Phillips curve, and if it is rising, what is causing it? This forces one back to the question as to whether price- and wage-makers raise prices and wages because they perceive an existing increase in demand or whether they anticipate an increased demand in the future, which may then be generated by government deficits and a further increase in the money stock. This problem of "cost-push" versus "demand-pull" inflation is difficult to solve. One could postulate a system in which any increase in prices and wages would be followed by enough increase in the money stock to justify them. Such a system would make hyperinflation a certainty, for there would not be any limits at all. Traditionally, however, the limiting factor has been unemployment, depression, and unsold stocks, which have not then produced an offsetting increase in the money stock. If this limit has become unacceptable, then one would have to ask whether any other limit would be acceptable; and, if not, then perhaps hyperinflation is inevitable—a very depressing conclusion. Inflation occurs when everyone wants more than there is. The dynamics of the price system enables people to try to claim more than there is through increased money incomes. If money incomes exceed what is available from real incomes, then the price level must rise to offset the increase.

It is interesting to ask whether the war industry plays a special role in the tendency toward cost-push, that is, whether the restraints on the rise in the prices of its inputs—wages and materials—are less than they are in other sectors of the economy. If so, the war industry may play an unusually large role in inflation in proportion to its size, through the autonomous increase in wages and prices that lead to unemployment in the absence of budget deficits and further inflation. Unfortunately, a satisfactory answer to this question would require far more research than it has been possible to do. The hypothesis has at least a certain plausibility in that the war industry operates to a considerable extent on a cost-plus basis. Costs, therefore, are expected to be recovered, and hence it is reasonable to form the hypothesis that the resistance to increases in prices and wages will be less in the war industry than it is in many other areas of the economy.

Unfortunately, there seems to be no research on this question, in spite of all the work that has been done on the economics of the war industry. Research would have to be done on a comparative basis and would have to be part of a general study of what might be called "autonomous" increases in prices and wages, for the significance of the war industry in this regard is evident only in the setting of the rest of the economy. Table 1 shows the percentage of the labor force that is subject to having its wages determined by collective bargaining, which is somewhat larger in a small part of the war industry than it is in the economy at large. This evidence certainly gives some support to the hypothesis that the war industry is disproportionately a source of cost-push, but in the absence of much more detailed study it cannot be taken as definitive.

A further problem is a widespread belief, particularly among the older

TABLE 1

Comparison of Douty and Freeman-Medoff Estimates of the Extent of
Unionization of Production Workers in United States Manufacturing Industries

Industry Groups	Extent of Collective Bargaining Coverage (percent)		Extent of Union Membership (percent)
	Douty (1958)	Freeman-Medoff (1968–72)	Freeman-Medoff (1973–75)
All manufacturing	67	61	49
Ordnance and accessories	84	79	64

Source: Richard B. Freeman and James L. Medoff, "New Estimates of Private Sector Unionism in the United States," *Industrial and Labor Relations Review* 32 (January 1979):173.

generation, that an expansion of the war industry diminishes unemployment. There is no doubt that World War II reduced unemployment and brought the United States out of the Great Depression. But, during the great disarmament of 1945–46, more than 30 percent of the economy was transferred from the war industry into civilian industry without unemployment rising above 4 percent. This experience suggests that, given the right environment, the war industry is extraordinarily adaptable and adjustable and can be reduced easily with beneficial economic consequences. In the early 1960s a fairly sharp reduction in the war industry was accompanied by a substantial reduction in unemployment, mainly because state and local governments expanded to take up the slack. By contrast, the period immediately following the Vietnam war produced an increase in unemployment associated with a decline in the war industry. It is clear, therefore, that the belief that the war industry produces employment is an illusion and that in fact changes in the war industry can be accomplished relatively easily, particularly if they are offset successfully by changes in other elements of the system.

The Structure of Financial Markets

Another aspect of the inflation problem to which the war industry may relate (though again it would take a great deal of research to identify its quantitative importance) is the structure of financial markets, particularly the relation between interest and profit. This problem has been surprisingly neglected in the literature for almost fifty years, although it was extensively discussed in the decades before 1930. The problem can be simply stated: an employer exchanges money (pays wages) for a real asset (the product of the work). By paying wages, the employer sacrifices interest that the money could have earned on bonds or notes. In return, he will make a profit if the value of the real asset, determined by its ultimate sales price, is greater than its costs in labor, materials, and other inputs. Employment, therefore, involves a sacrifice of interest in the hope of a profit. If the economic situation is such that the potential profit is not greater than the interest that could be earned, then the labor market economy is in serious trouble. This was the case in 1932 and 1933, when profits were negative, interest rose to 13 percent of the national income, and virtually anybody who hired employees was certain to be worse off than he would have been if he had purchased bonds or made loans. It is surprising that there was any employment at all in these years. It was only habit and the need for continuing existing organizations that prevented unemployment from rising far more than the 25 percent that it reached.

In the 1970s there are ominous signs that the United States may be edging toward a similar position. In the 1950s and even the early 1960s, real interest rates were astonishingly low, perhaps because the financial community had not realized that there was a long-run inflation. Now, of course, they have caught on to this fact. Nominal interest rates have risen to the point where real interest is positive, and interest is absorbing an increasingly larger proportion of the national income. The rise in the Phillips curve may be closely related to the increase in interest relative to profit. As hiring employees becomes increasingly unprofitable, more and more inflation is perhaps needed to give people the illusion that it is profitable.

The alarming implications of this phenomenon can be realized by asking, What would happen if the United States stopped the inflation tomorrow by a Draconian policy of federal budget surpluses, either by increased taxes or diminished expenditures, and by restrictive monetary policy? The result would undoubtedly be a spectacular economic collapse and a major depression, simply because real rates of interest would then be so high that no economy could stand it, and profit would be completely eroded. The real rate of interest is roughly equal to the nominal rate minus the rate of inflation. With nominal rates of interest now on the order of 6 to 12 percent and even higher, these would become the real rates of interest if inflation suddenly ceased, and profit would likely become negative again, although other adjustments in the economy might restore it.

Any cessation of the inflation, therefore, would either have to come about slowly because of the time structure of interest contracts, or the nominal rate of interest would have to be adjusted in all existing contracts. That would not be impossible. A law could be passed stating that all rates of interest on all existing contracts were halved, and there is indeed something of a precedent for this in the abrogation of the gold clause in the 1930s. Government intervention in the financial system, however, is rare, probably for good reasons, and it is something that the United States has not considered and is unprepared for.

Whether the war industry has any role in this problem is unclear. It is an unstable industry, depending as it does on the uncertainties and vagaries of the international system. Historically it is by far the most unstable part of the American economy. Even though the cost-plus arrangements diminish the risks, it is at least possible that its pressures on the capital market push up interest rates. This is somewhat parallel to the hypothesis that its cost-plus aspects give it a disproportionate role in the cost-push aspects of inflation. Again, however, an appraisal of the role that the war industry occupies in the total picture would require an extensive research program that included the whole economy.

The rise in the war industry since World War II—and it was certainly a result of World War II—from an almost negligible element in the American economy to an important sector that has averaged about 7 percent in the last thirty years is a very striking structural change. As long as it was believed, as perhaps it was generally through the period of the "long boom," that the war industry contributed to full employment, it was not perceived as an economic burden. The 1970s, however, brought a real structural change in the political process, with much larger demands on government for civilian expenditures, and especially for redistributions. Under these circumstances, the war industry is seen as an active competitor with civilian expenditures, particularly when there is strong resistance to increasing taxes. This is seen in the budget for FY 1979, where President Carter's proposed increase in military expenditures is clearly perceived to be at the cost of expenditures for human welfare. If military expenditures are perceived as effective in protecting national security, they may be acceptable. Increasingly, however, civilians have become alienated from the military and perceive themselves to be merely hostages in a situation over which they have no control and which will inevitably lead to almost total disaster. Under these circumstances, the pressure for disarmament will unquestionably rise and military expenditures will increasingly be perceived not only as a burden in the sense that they reduce welfare expenditures but also in the sense that they do not provide the security that they are supposed to. Anything except war that is subject to an increasing perception of cost and a diminishing perception of benefit would seem to have a doubtful future.

The author wishes to express his gratitude to Guy M. Burgess for his assistance in the preparation of this essay.

The Labor Force

JAMES W. KUHN

Simultaneous inflation and high unemployment, or stagflation, is a new economic phenomenon in the United States. The recessions of 1954, 1957, and 1960 halted their preceding inflations, but the recessions of 1966–67, 1969–70, and 1973–75 only briefly checked rising prices and allowed inflation to continue even when excess demand had disappeared. Until fifty years ago, prices were remarkably flexible, falling even more than they rose; in three-quarters of the years from 1800 through 1929 prices either fell or remained stable. While war expenditures and occasional notorious speculative booms sometimes pushed prices to very high levels, they did not stay there long. As a consequence, the Bureau of Labor Statistics reported that the consumer price index (CPI) in 1929 stood no higher than it had in 1800. In all but one of the thirty years after the Civil War inflation of 1864, prices remained stable or fell—a remarkable and unmatched record. Given the changing structure of the economy and the newly mobilized political forces of recent decades, that record will not be duplicated.

Since 1939 the yearly CPI has declined only twice—1949 and 1955—and no longer falls or even stabilizes during recessions. Particularly surprising has been the persistent and high rate of inflation from 1975 to 1978, which has averaged over 7 percent in a slack economy where the unemployment rate has also averaged over 7 percent. Moreover, the continuing inflation during the upswing from the recession does not appear to be fueled by particular price increases or by any special conditions. Over the last three years it has been general, affecting all sectors in much the same way. The prices of food, fuel, and imports that had spurted upward in 1973–74 have not climbed significantly faster than the general rate since then. Apparently, forces more fundamental and influences more widespread are encouraging a general price rise and preventing downward pressures from coming into play.

The history of price indicators suggests that those forces have been slowly growing since the early 1940s, making price declines or even price stability more unlikely. Robert L. Heilbroner suggested that today's inflation is "ultimately rooted in the basic changes" made in the economy "to forestall another, possibly fatal" Great Depression.[1] John Kenneth Galbraith argued that these forces of change can be easily identified: "Corporations and organized groups have the power to shove up prices and produce inflation."[2]

The Changing Structure of the American Economy

Identifying the changes in the economy that give power to corporations and organized labor groups to push up prices and wages, however, is not as easy as it first appears. If such power has grown with the downward rigidity of price declines and the enhanced propensity of prices to rise, whatever the state of the economy, it should show a similar increase and enhancement over recent years and, in addition, should reveal its particular effectiveness during the past three years. A capacity to raise prices is not easy to prove, but data are available on characteristics that one might reasonably expect to correlate with power, such as relative size of employment or share of gross national product (GNP). Unfortunately, such data do not unambiguously indicate that big business and big labor have markedly increased their power, standing, or influence in the economy in recent years.

While organized labor claims more members today than ever before (over 22 million), its share of the labor force has steadily declined. In 1956 almost 28 percent held membership, whereas only 22 percent held membership in 1978. Unions have been able to hold their own in heavy industry only because employment in this sector has hardly risen in a decade. During the same period, moreover, this sector has shrunk in relation to the economy as a whole. Manufacturing employment comprised more than a third of the labor force in 1950 but less than a quarter in 1978; because the proportion of production workers in manufacturing has steadily fallen, the union's opportunity to increase membership has been further limited, and industrial unions have not been very successful in organizing white-collar, nonproduction workers.

Union membership has grown sufficiently among government workers to offset some of the relative decline in the manufacturing industries; one result is that the largest union in the AFL-CIO is the American Federation of State, County, and Municipal Employees. The American Federation of Teachers has also risen swiftly over the last twenty years to rank among the ten biggest unions. Thus, if unions' power to influence the economy has markedly increased in recent years, it has done so despite a shifting and relatively declining membership base.

The decline of union membership parallels the eroding share of total employment in manufacturing industries where most large business corporations have established themselves. Measuring the industrial sector by its employment

---

[1] *New York Times*, December 22, 1978.
[2] Ibid., January 12, 1978.

may, however, understate its power; traditionally, it has been the economy's most innovative and productive sector, increasing its efficiency by turning out ever greater outputs with more capital and fewer employees. Yet, if one measures economic influence of manufacturing by relative shares of GNP rather than by employment shares, the picture is not changed much; manufacturing contributes about the same, or slightly less, to GNP today than in earlier years, and the long-term trend tilts slightly downward. Certainly there is no evidence that the industrial sector, as a whole, has increased its relative weight in the economy.

Within manufacturing there nevertheless appears to be a definite trend in the concentration of power and influence among the largest firms. Employees in the *Fortune* 500 largest industrial firms accounted for almost 60 percent of all manufacturing workers in 1963, but fifteen years later they employed over 78 percent. The larger the firm, the greater the concentration. The five largest firms accounted for nearly one in eleven manufacturing workers in 1963, and by 1977 for more than one in eight. Where the 500 largest industrial firms reported just over half of all manufacturing sales in 1955 and 73 percent in 1970, by 1975 they accounted for over 87 percent. The largest industrial firms also report an increasing share of manufacturing assets (over 80 percent) and, of course, a large portion of profits—more than three-quarters in 1975. An increasing number of these firms have become conglomerates that carry on a variety of productive activities. While they loom larger and larger as business entities, they do not necessarily exercise more economic power within the diverse markets they serve.

Though their sector of the economy has not grown in recent years and indeed may have shrunk, the largest industrial firms control a larger portion of it than ever before. Their concentration has continued apace through the recent period of chronic inflation and high unemployment. Possibly this continued concentration has increased the ability of large corporations to maintain and even push up their prices and has enabled the unions with whom they bargain to increase wages despite recession unemployment. However, inflation has been so widespread throughout the economy that it appears to be fed by many forces, not only the growing concentration of business within manufacturing.

Whatever influence large industrial corporations have on wages and prices within their sector, it can be decisive in the economy only if it increases its range and effects on the other, expanding parts of the economy. Two of them— trade (both wholesale and retail) and services (medical and health, educational, professional, repair, religious, entertainment and recreational, lodgings, and so forth)—have become increasingly important employers and economic contributors. These two sectors, with their many small firms and high degree of competition, have increased their share of wage and salary workers from just under a third in 1950 to over 41 percent in 1978 and have also steadily increased their contribution to GNP, accounting for just under 30 percent. The small average size of business firms in these sectors and their competitive markets may reduce their economic influence below that suggested by their size. That their influence has diminished over the last decade, however, does not seem likely.

If the large, oligopolistic industrial firms and their associated unions are to be identified as the prime causes of the continuing inflation, then one needs to assume that their growing concentration has enhanced their economic and employment base. If such an offsetting has actually taken place, one has to explain how and why the growing, competitive sectors such as services and trade should exert relatively less and less influence even as they increase their employment base and maintain or increase their share of GNP. The changes in relative size and influence among sectors have not clearly shifted the economic balance between the small decentralized firms and big centralized business.

In two areas, however, certain changes have tended to make both prices and wages less flexible than during the early 1960s—the gradual decline of agriculture and the growth of government. The farm sector has been made up of small units selling in competitive markets with flexible prices and wages; the state, local, and federal governments do not ordinarily sell their services, but taxes to cover the "price" of government hardly show the flexibility of farm prices. Of all earnings, government-set wages are among the least responsive to unemployment and recession. If more and more Americans are employed in the public sector, wages could become more inflexible.

The number of persons in the labor force who work in agriculture has decreased from one out of eight in 1950 to one of twenty-eight in 1978. Agriculture's contribution to GNP has also declined—though not so dramatically as its number of workers—from 5.5 percent in 1950 to 2.9 percent in 1978. The fact that most of the declines in both employment and the share of GNP took place before 1970 suggests that the shift away from agriculture has been gradual; it is not a new force that suddenly manifested itself in the 1970s. The shift to government has also come gradually; the number of wage and salary workers employed by all government increased from 13 percent in 1950 to over 19 percent in 1975. Governments increased their expenditures as a share of GNP by a similar amount, from 13.5 percent in 1950 to 22.1 percent in 1975.

While governments, as employers, are not highly responsive to unemployment, they have recently responded to public discontent. Expenditures, which as a share of GNP reached a peak in 1968, have declined by 10 percent; the share of workers, which was 19.1 percent in 1975, has decreased by more than 1 percentage point. If governments had continued to hire employees at the rate they had for many years up to 1975, they would have provided jobs for nearly 900,000 more persons in 1978 than they actually did. Had those looking unsuccessfully for jobs declined by an equal number, the unemployment rate would have fallen to around 5 percent. Thus the nation's continuing high unemployment is perhaps due in no small part to the swift decline in new government-created jobs. Had government workers' wage increases been held down (or even eliminated) and government jobs increased, the economy would be in better condition than it is.

This conclusion seems warranted: the gradual decline of agriculture's competitive economic influence (with its generally flexible wages and prices) and the simultaneous rise of governments as large employers have introduced an increasing degree of wage rigidity in the labor market. That rigidity may well have raised the economy's threshold of responsiveness to unemployment and made it more susceptible to any unleashed inflationary forces.

The general shift from blue- to white-collar jobs has probably also raised the threshold, while creating even more opposition to any anti-inflation policy that raises unemployment. Although employers have traditionally been less willing to lay off white-collar employees than blue-collar workers, this tradition has been so eroded over the last twenty years that the white-collar share of unemployment is rising faster than its share of employment. White-collar workers today are more subject, and blue-collar workers are less subject, to the pain and costs of unemployment than ever before. In 1958, blue-collar workers absorbed over 57 percent of all unemployment, whereas in 1977, when the unemployment rate was higher, they accounted for 39 percent; their share of the unemployment had decreased three times faster than their share of employment. The white-collar share of unemployment rose from 18 to 29 percent, more than three and a half times faster than the white-collar share of employment. Thus the extension of unemployment to occupations that had been relatively immune has no doubt increased opposition to policies that use unemployment to mediate economic activities.

As a result of the widening impact of unemployment, employees are less inclined to accept recession as a consequence of any anti-inflation policy. Insofar as the economy has shown increased stability, manifesting fewer and narrower swings, all participants—workers, producers, and sellers—now suffer lighter penalties for keeping up prices and wages than in former times. In 1978, Martin Neil Baily pointed out that economic variability appears to have lessened significantly after 1946, when the federal government made stabilization a matter of explicit government policy. Changes in the rate of growth of real GNP were smaller in the 1960s and 1970s than in the 1950s and much smaller than in earlier periods.[3]

An important contribution to the stability of the last two decades has been the multiple government programs designed to maintain incomes for the elderly the unemployed, the handicapped, and the poor. The federal government greatly expanded its transfer payments and grants-in-aid during the 1960s. In 1963 a third of all federal expenditures went to transfer payments and grants-in-aid to states; fifteen years later these two categories accounted for 57 percent of federal expenditures, or nearly $260 billion—one-eighth of the GNP.

(Transfer payments)have become an important and an enlarging source of personal income. Since 1967 they have been the second largest source, surpassed only by wages and salaries. Twenty years ago they supplied a little less than $1 out of $14 of personal income; in 1978, $1 out of $7.50. The largest part of transfer payments comes in the form of old-age survivors, disability, and health insurance benefits (OASDHI), and it has escalated dramatically

[3] Martin Neil Baily, "Stabilization Policy and Private Economic Behavior," *Brookings Papers on Economic Activity*, no. 1 (1978), pp. 11–60.

since 1970; in 1958, OASDHI was but a third of all transfers, and in 1978 it was more than half. This large, assured, and growing flow of income to the retired and elderly should help stabilize the economy, since the recipients undoubtedly spend most of it on current consumption for items such as nondurables and services. In fact, personal consumption expenditures for these two kinds of purchases have varied less and stabilized more in recent years than earlier. Accordingly, producers and sellers who serve consumer markets have probably found conditions more favorable to maintaining or raising prices and wages than in the postwar periods.

Other influences may also contribute to the recent stability of spending. Among the most important is the marked increase in the number and share of young adults aged twenty to thirty-four. In 1977 they constituted over one-quarter of the population, a sharp gain over 1960 when they accounted for less than 19 percent. Since they are forming families and establishing households, their propensity to spend is relatively high compared with older groups. Moreover, since young adults' share of the population will be maintained for another few years, the economy will feel the consumption effects well into the 1980s, with consequent demand presures that increase prices.

Changing demographics of the labor force may also have allowed inflation to flourish. The changing age mix, for example, has tended to lower productivity gains because young and inexperienced workers do not match the output of experienced workers. In 1960 less than 17 percent of the civilian labor force was between sixteen and twenty-four years of age; in 1977 over 24 percent, almost one out of four, were in that age group. Such a change affects productivity only marginally, however; the kind and amount of capital investment and technological improvements are probably more important.

While other factors—research and development, allocation of resources, economies of scale, and stricter legal requirements—have contributed to the lagging growth of productivity, they can be changed far more easily than demographics. Nonetheless, the nation must give careful attention to all factors, for the record clearly indicates that productivity's slowdown over the past decade has seriously hampered all efforts to stem inflation.

From 1968 to 1978, the rate of change in output per manhour has averaged less than half that from 1947 to 1968. Such a dramatic change suggests the need for careful examination of the structure of the nation's productive institutions, as well as the procedures that workers, producers, buyers, and sellers have adapted to conduct their economic affairs. One can guess that, in disparate ways, all have reshaped their institutions and procedures to protect themselves against inflation. In the process of adaptation, all have impaired the nation's capacity to make productivity gains and to combat inflation. It is imperative, therefore, to explore the sundry ways Americans have adjusted to inflation.

How Americans Adjust to Inflation

Recent opinion surveys indicate that Americans have passed a new judgment on inflation's permanency. As recently as the 1974–75 inflation, when the price level increased at a double-digit rate, nearly two of three persons rejected the statement that inflation had become "one of the facts of life and was here to stay." By the summer of 1978, however, 90 percent of those surveyed agreed that inflation could be expected to continue. Since voters obviously believe that continuing inflation is a serious problem, the president and others are trying to make political capital out of programs to combat it. But surveys reveal that the electorate's skepticism has been intensified by the voters' perceptions that government itself, not business or labor, is the major culprit.

Doubting the government's ability to stop inflation, Americans understandably search for ways to protect themselves. To the degree they are successful, they will be less ready to bear the costs of anti-inflationary policies. The president will therefore find little room for maneuver; policies that squeeze aid to cities, welfare programs, and farm subsidies or that threaten to provoke a rise in unemployment (particularly among minorities and women) will be politically unattractive. Already the politicans are preparing to make much of the losses inflicted by administration policies aimed at reducing price rises.

Most business leaders agree with Tilford Gaines, who wrote in November 1978 that "everyone by now should be able to agree that inflation is the most serious, most dangerous, most debilitating" economic illness.[4] But many Americans do not agree, and their numbers are increasing. Since neither economists nor any other experts have explained clearly and specifically the costs and losses of inflation, the public's view is understandable.

Unless those concerned with anti-inflation policy understand who gets hurt and how they get hurt, they are not likely to fashion the political coalitions necessary to support a sustained attack on inflation. Common sense says that inflation imposes different costs, some quite general that affect all people and income groups and others that affect particular persons with exposed assets and income. Sir John Hicks and Arthur Okun have described the first kind of general injury. Hicks said, "Any system of prices [and wages] . . . is bound to work more easily if it is allowed to acquire, to some degee, the sanction of custom. . . . This, I believe, is the true reason why inflation is damaging. . . . In conditions of inflation [arrangements] continually need refixing, so that issues which had seemed closed have to be reopened."[5] Okun, explaining the injury in more detail, pointed out why the public feels it more keenly than economists in general: "Thus, the welfare costs usually attributed to inflation. . . should be viewed in a broader context as disturbances to a set of institutions that economize on information, prediction, and transaction costs, through continuing buyer-seller relationships. Inflation does fool people . . . [particularly] by depriving them of a way of economic life in which they need not depend heavily on the formulation of costly and uncertain point-estimate expectations. . . . It explains why most Americans dislike inflation so much more intensely than does most of the economics profession."[6]

---

[4] Tilford Gaines, *Economic Report*, November, 1978, Manufacturers Hanover Trust.
[5] Sir John Hicks, *The Crises in Keynesian Economics* (New York: Basic Books, 1974), p. 79.
[6] Arthur Okun, "Inflation: Its Mechanics and Welfare Costs," *Brookings Papers on Economic Activity*, no. 2 (1975), p. 359.

Hicks and Okun emphasized that everyone—buyers and sellers, workers and employers, producers and consumers, corporations and individuals—relies on the dollar as a yardstick for calculating fair standards for markups and wage differentials. A depreciating dollar disturbs valuable sets of relationships and disrupts regular patterns of ties and transaction. Since these disturbing, disrupting effects are so widespread and diffused, they produce general dissatisfaction but do not seem to provoke sharp enough political reaction on which to build an anti-inflationary program. Rather, each group strives to protect its most important source of income, maintaining its relationship to the changing yardstick usually through some form of indexed or escalating income, to keep pace with rising prices.

Mobilizing political support for anti-inflationary pressures becomes more difficult as groups gain index protection. Mobilization is further complicated by the degree of differences among groups in successfully protecting themselves against inflation. Those who suffer few losses need not cooperate in cutting the losses of others.

Wealthy individuals have always denounced inflation more loudly and with more passion than the poor, and they still do. This explains why the Repubican party has usually been more anti-inflationist than the Democratic party, with its labor, minority, and poor constituencies. It was not surprising, therefore, to see many leading corporate managers pledging support for the Carter administration's anti-inflation efforts in 1978—even at the possible cost of an economic slowdown and lower profits—while the usual Democratic-party interest groups opposed the administration's programs. With few exceptions union leaders were opposed because they feared that guidelines would cut workers' real wages and barely affect producers' prices. Spokespersons of minorities and welfare groups also fear income cuts.

Joseph J. Minarik of the Brookings Institution has attempted to measure the effects of inflation on the rich and the poor. His preliminary findings help explain the political lineup on the Carter economic proposals. Minarik pointed out that, in general, "labor income keeps up with prices while transfer payments and property income tend to lag, especially when balance sheet effects (in the case of property income) are taken into account. On the expenditure side, households could be said to benefit from inflation in that rents lag behind the general price level and home mortgages payments are fixed. But household real income is reduced by income taxes faster than money incomes."[7] To discover how inflation specifically affects different income groups, he surveyed a population sample of household tax returns from the Internal Revenue Service. The sample provided an accurate cross-section of the population, with income and expense data, that allowed calculation of the effects of inflation over time. Minarik used two measures of income. The first included a narrowly defined, current flow of money to households, such as wages, salaries, business income, interest dividends, rents, royalties, pension benefits, government

[7] Joseph J. Minarik, "Who Wins, Who Loses from Inflation," *The Brookings Bulletin* 15 (Summer 1978): 7.

cash transfers, and private cash benefits, all before taxes. The second measure of income was a broadly defined, current flow of money and accrued value. It included the first kind of money income and also income in kind, such as employer-financed employees benefits and government in-kind transfers, the depreciation of the cash value of bonds, the lagging of corporate retained earnings, and the appreciation of home values. The second measure also made appropriate adjustments for local, state, and federal taxes.

Minarik found that the effects of inflation on commonly recognized, narrowly defined, current income are those that most people sense: the poor get poorer and the rich get richer. Low incomes fall behind price rises, mainly because welfare payments lag behind inflation. Middle incomes remain about the same since wages and salaries on average keep up with prices and home-owners benefit from contractually fixed mortgage payments. At upper income levels, the rich receive higher interest payments.

Testing the effects of inflation on the second measure of income shows significantly different costs and benefits to the rich and the poor than using the first narrower measure of income. The poorest 10 percent are only slightly affected; as debtors and receivers of in-kind income they gain about as much as inflation takes. The lower middle-income households (the third of households just below medium income) lose at a rate equal to the rate of inflation mostly because few own homes that appreciate in value, and the elderly lose because their few liquid and cash assets decline in value. The upper middle class (from medium income to the top 20 percent) keeps up with inflation. For those with annual incomes from $20,000 to $200,000 inflation losses run ahead of the inflation rate. A rise of 2 percentage points in the rate of inflation reduces real income for families with money incomes of $40,000 to $60,000 by 4 to 6 percent a year; the same rate of inflation imposes a 10 percent cut in the real income of a family with a $100,000 income, and a 17 percent cut for one with an income twice as high. At higher income levels the few who are very rich find ways to shelter their incomes, offsetting some of the inflationary losses. Even with a $1 million income, however, an inflationary increase of 2 percentage points will impose a loss of 5 percent.

The elderly lose at all income levels. Rising prices erode their assets such as bonds and other cash savings. Although their social security payments move up with inflation, their private pensions are usually fixed. In general, the higher the elderly's income, the larger the cut inflicted by inflation.

Net debtors gain the most from inflation. The significant point to note is that the federal government—with about 18 percent of total debts, public and private—is among the largest debtors. Householders, through mortgages and consumer credit, account for more than a quarter, and corporations account for 42 percent. The big change has been the rise in corporate debt as business managers adjust to long-term and continuing high rates of inflation. Most of the creditors who lose are relatively well-to-do, although an unknown but probably increasing share comes from pension funds of upper middle-class workers.

Winners and losers are thus found throughout the population. The poor who receive only monetary welfare payments and who own no house lose in inflation. They were particularly hurt by the rapid rise of food prices in 1973 and fuel prices in 1974. Both exceeded the rise in other prices by a substantial margin. Since then, as already noted, the prices of most goods and services have moved more or less together. The elderly lose through fixed income pensions and through their savings in bonds or other such assets. Middle-class households, the net debtors who own their homes and receive most of their income from wages or salaries, suffer least and may even gain slightly. The rich lose because so much of their income is earned from bonds and other liquid assets and because progressive personal income taxes rise faster than nominal income.

Those hurt most by inflation have urged general public policies to combat it but have even more urgently pushed for procedures and programs to mitigate inflation's adverse effects on themselves. Political efforts and economic activity aimed at helping particular groups have enjoyed more success than any general inflation remedies; each interest group has pushed its own program and sought its own shelters. The result is a piecemeal institutionalization of inflation that protects some and hurts others.

Congress formally indexed social security payments in 1975 so that they rise automatically with inflation for 34.5 million Americans. It also indexed supplemental security income that goes to 4.3 million elderly poor and disabled persons; the Food Stamp Program, which provides benefits to nearly 20 million people, is also indexed. Payments made under the Aid to Families with Dependent Children (AFDC) program are not indexed and have lagged behind inflation over the last five years.

Wages and salaries in government and in the high-wage concentrated industries (durable manufacturing, transportation, public utilities, and communications) have generally kept up with inflation. It is important to note that the proportion of workers covered by cost-of-living adjustment formulas has increased from 25 percent in 1967–69 to 60 percent in 1976–78. Around 6 million workers enjoy this added protection against inflation, and another 3 to 4 million federal government workers and smaller numbers of nonunion workers also receive regular increases in line with general price rises. If the family members as well as wage earners or payment recipients are included, approximately one-half to two-thirds of all Americans have at least part of their income indexed; possibly as much as a fifth of personal income is now tied to the inflation rate and increases in close step with it. Since the pain of inflation is softened, it is easy to complain and difficult to accept anti-inflation actions.

Business firms, too, are increasingly indexing their prices to keep revenues in line with inflation. Many utility companies adjust rates automatically as fuel costs change; office building leases usually include escalator provisions to cover rising utility bills, real estate taxes, and labor costs. Escalator clauses are also common in long-term commercial construction, defense procurement, and capital goods contracts.

Conclusion

Americans have two excellent reasons for being less than enthusiastic about stopping inflation. First, many have already adjusted or are in the process of adjusting to its pressures and loses. Second, the costs in lost output and unemployment of restraining aggregate demand are very high. Those who strongly believe in returning to a stable price economy will have to offer less costly attacks on inflation. Since broad-effect policies—such as restriction of the money supply and reduction of aggregate demand—are neither politically feasible nor economically efficient, more specifically directed, effectively targeted policies need to be sought and pursued.

Each proposal to control inflation affects an interest that is perceived by members of particular groups as vital to their well-being. For example, consumer groups and their legislative representatives fight measures that would allow incremental costing of imported liquid and synthetic natural gas. Such costing would raise gas users' prices, though it would benefit fuel users in general. Truckers and unionized drivers fear deregulation of their industry, though the efficiencies to be gained by the economy are substantial. Labor union leaders resist all proposals significantly to change the minimum wage, seeing in them an attack on labor in general.

The controversy over the minimum wage illustrates the costs and benefits of government regulation as well as the difficulties in securing changes. Economists have long been suspicious of minimum wage legislation as too open and brash an interference in the market's wage determination. On theoretical grounds they have predicted gains for employed workers who enjoyed the higher, mandated wage; theory suggested, though, that many other workers would lose, particularly those whose labor was not worth the minimum and who thereby lost jobs or were denied work. Empirical studies through the 1970s have confirmed the theorists' warnings; teenagers appear to bear the larger part of the loss. The minimum wage almost surely decreases opportunities for teenagers to secure full-time work, pushing them into part-time work where the minimum wage does not apply. They suffer less steady work and lower earnings than they might otherwise expect, and, in addition, many receive less on-the-job training and poorer preparation for adult work than they need.

Such studies do not persuade proponents of the minimum wage, among whom union leaders are most prominent. First, unionists view the studies skeptically. Second, relatively few teenagers join unions, and union leaders speak first of all for their employed members who do receive some benefit from the minimum wage. Further, union leaders have supported the minimum wage since 1937 when both William Green of the AFL and John L. Lewis of the CIO, who agreed on little else, supported President Roosevelt's original bill. For labor officials to contemplate major changes in the present legislation, to decrease coverage, or to lower the rate would be a repudiation of their history and traditions; low-wage unionists in textiles, garments, and other low-wage industries would complain of a breach of faith.

Certainly if business groups focus on the minimum wage as an important contributor to inflation while ignoring or downplaying other influences, such as indirect subsidies through price supports and wasteful industry regulation, labor's fears will be enlarged. They will see an attack on them under the guise of an anti-inflation campaign. Thus, the political costs of removing or replacing the minimum wage are apt to be high and, even if eventually successful, unlikely to be timely.

This survey of structural changes in the economy that have helped to entrench inflation over the last generation, as well as the inadequacy of proposals advanced to reverse them, has presented a bleak scene for inflation fighters. If Americans really want price stability, they will have to work more assiduously to get it than they did to secure safeguards against depression and economic decline. Or they may learn to live more easily with continuous inflation by changing enough of the economy to slow its rise and by taking special care to protect the poor and aged from its destructive effects. The problem developed over a long period, and it will not be solved quickly.

Inflation and Economic Policy

EDGAR R. FIEDLER

Until recently, unemployment was the primary economic fear of the American people. The specter, a product of the Great Depression, was that of the desperate family breadwinner unable to find a job month after month, year after year, while his wife and children remained destitute. Today it is known that in most cases unemployment comes in spells of relatively moderate duration and that its hardships are usually alleviated by a variety of income maintenance programs. About half the time there is a second wage earner within the family itself. To a considerable extent, the mass fear of joblessness has faded. But inflation has taken its place, both as the central economic issue and as a national anxiety. No one feels capable of coping with inflation, and no one can find an acceptable way of controlling it.

Inflation would be less troublesome if its nature and its causes were better understood. Not even the experts understand it thoroughly. By far the most common confusion is the tendency to equate inflation with price increases of individual items. People note one or two specific prices, such as homes or gold or hospital fees, and erroneously conclude that all prices are going up and at roughly the same rate as those selected items.

In fact, many prices go up in times of no inflation, and some prices go down during highly inflationary periods. Examples of declining prices in the face of rampant inflation include ballpoint pens, color television sets, antibiotics, and most recently computers, calculators, and digital watches.

The diversity of prices in the face of inflation was one of the striking lessons of the 1971 wage-price freeze. During September of that year, when the wholesale price index showed some increases for individual items, an investigation was undertaken to find out if some sellers were violating the freeze regulations. The explanation was found in the provision of the Economic Stabilization Act of 1970, the legal basis for the freeze, that prohibited any price from being controlled below its May 1970 level. When the wholesale price index was examined in detail it was discovered that out of the 1,600 specific nonfarm commodities priced for that index, some 400 had declined between May 1970 and August 1971.

Despite the 5 percent rise in the industrial wholesale price index over those fifteen months, about one-fourth of the individual prices had decreased. That is a striking result and an important lesson about the nature of inflation. Although it is true that many more prices go up than down during periods of inflation, the widespread failure to appreciate the diversity of prices leads to wrong diagnoses of inflation (e.g., that the greed of businessmen or unions or a spurt of demand from abroad is to blame) and to wrong prescriptions (e.g., direct controls or export restrictions). Indeed, what movements of individual prices really indicate is their microeconomic role: the item-by-item allocation of production and consumption. Individual price changes are the economic signals that tell consumers what is plentiful and what is scarce and tell producers about consumer preferences. In short, prices are the primary mechanism for reconciling supply and demand for every commodity and service throughout the economy. Again, however, that does not explain much about inflation.

The Nature of Inflation

Inflation is a macro process rather than a micro process. A general phenomenon, it is pervasive and comprehensive. It is not limited to certain products or industries or geographic areas. The aggregative nature of inflation is demonstrated by the way it is defined arithmetically; it is the change in all prices, on average. Thus inflation is measured by the most comprehensive price series, the consumer price index and the GNP deflator.

The way these price indexes are calculated is indicative of the nature of inflation. To compute a price index, the statisticians add up the prices of all the items in a comprehensive "market basket" of goods and services (each item weighted according to its sales volume) and compare the total with the total for the same market basket in a base period. In other words, how much money does this standard list of items cost now compared with the base period? What this suggests, of course, is that money has something to do with inflation—or, more specifically, the amount of money per unit of output. Indeed, many state categorically that money is "everything." This is the message of the classic definition of inflation: "too much money chasing too few goods." The monetarist school of economics goes still farther, claiming that inflation is always a monetary phenomenon.

The monetarists have assembled an impressive amount of evidence in support of their position—evidence covering many countries and many years, in some cases a century or two. According to Milton Friedman, "There has never been a long, continued period of substantial inflation which has not been accompanied by a more rapid increase in the quantity of money than in output. There has never been a rapid increase in the quantity of money relative to output that has not been accompanied by inflation. . . . All cases show the same relationship. Prices dance to the tune of what happens to the quantity of money per unit of output."[1]

---

[1] Milton Friedman, "Is Inflation a Curable Disease?" (Alex C. Walker Memorial Lecture, Pittsburgh, December 5, 1974).

To many people, the monetarist case is persuasive. Yet it has obviously not settled the raucous controversy that continues to rage about the nature of inflation—and even less, the controversy about causes and cures, to which this essay will turn later. One reason is the time aspect of the monetarist analysis. A key phrase in the above Friedman quotation is "long, continued period." The monetarist proposition is virtually unchallengeable in the long run (say, a half-decade or more). However, in the short term (a few months, a year, or sometimes two years) the relationship between money, supply, and inflation is not as well defined.

In the long run, the relationship between money and inflation is extremely close, and thus any diagnosis or prescription that does not take into account the monetary dimension is not worth considering. For shorter periods, however, other factors are involved. On an annual basis, some two-fifths of the variation in the rate of inflation is not associated with monetary fluctuations. Thus, when the inflation rate accelerates from 5 to 7 percent, as it did from 1976 to 1977, one would expect almost a percentage point of that change to be associated with factors other than money. That is too large a variance to ignore, as the monetarist approach often seems to do.

This difference in the explanatory power of money over varying time horizons is an important part of the discord that so often marks debates about inflation Those who stress the monetarist approach almost always consider the long run, while those who stress other factors usually consider a much shorter period. Typically, neither group makes its time horizon explicit. As a result, the parties in the debate often talk past one another. Too often, the result is wasted effort.

Because of differences associated with the time horizon, it is useful to analyze inflation in three dimensions. The first, underlying or built-in inflation, operates over the long run. It can also be labeled the monetary dimension.

The second is related to the business cycle, which exerts a major influence on the inflation rate over the intermediate term. When the economy has been expanding for a few years, the nation's productive capacity comes to be fully utilized, sellers' markets become the general rule, and inflation accelerates. Alternatively, during recessions, when workers and machines are unemployed or underemployed and markets are weak, the rate of inflation subsides.

This cyclical pattern is essentially the Phillips curve. The original relationship, as formulated by British economist A. W. Phillips in the 1950s based on almost one hundred years of data for the United Kingdom, showed an inverse relationship between unemployment and the rate of change in wages. More often an alternative version of the curve is used, in which prices are substituted for wages. That is, the unemployment rate is set off against the rate of change in prices—essentially the same relationship as the original, because wage changes and price changes are nearly parallel. (The essential difference between the two series lies in their trend rates of growth; on average, wages rise faster than prices owing to increases in productivity.)

A decade ago, the Phillips relationship was widely accepted and was often used as a tool for policy analysis. Some unwanted inflation had to be accepted if unemployment were to be reduced. The economic events of the 1970s, however, appeared to invalidate the Phillips curve. The United States economy, like the economies of other industrial nations, experienced both high unemployment and high inflation simultaneously, or stagflation (a combination of stagnation and inflation). In particular, when high unemployment did not provide a cure for high inflation, many policy analysts wanted to discard the Phillips relationship altogether and deal with each of the two major economic problems without regard to the effect of one on the other.

But to abandon the Phillips curve altogether would be a serious mistake. There is a short-term relationship between inflation and unemployment—a relationship that cannot be ignored in the analysis of inflation and economic policy. In fact, the Phillips curve can be revalidated by a minor refinement. The error in the original version was its implicit assumption that the average rate of inflation across the full business cycle (and, indeed, across many cycles) would be zero, or at least very low. If that condition holds, it is almost certainly true that low unemployment is coupled with high inflation and high unemployment with no inflation or perhaps even deflation. This was the experience in the United States, for example, between the Korean and Vietnam wars. During that period inflation averaged 1.5 percent, with a high of 3.3 percent (in 1957, at the end of the mid-1950s boom) and a low of −0.6 percent (the recession year of 1954), and the Phillips curve seemed to be a useful representation of the real world.

Since the mid-1960s, however, the original Phillips relationship has gone awry. In effect, the economy has adapted to a continuing high rate of inflation. The Phillips curve can be resurrected, however, by simply changing the price side of the relationship to the *rate of change* in the inflation rate. The true relationship between unemployment and price movements is not the presence or absence of inflation but whether it accelerates or decelerates.

The three forms of the Phillips relationship are illustrated in figure 1. The original version is shown at the left. The center diagram represents the more common formulation, in which the inflation rate is substituted for the rate of change in wages. Although no scale is shown, the zero line in the middle panel would be above that in the first diagram by the trend rate of productivity growth, that is, by 2 or 3 percentage points. At the right is the current version, representing the adaptation of the economy to an ongoing inflation. The important change is that the vertical scale in the right diagram is the rate of change in the inflation rate instead of the inflation rate itself.

This adaptation is the explanation of stagflation. The economic policies of the past decade and a half have produced a continuing, built-in rate of inflation of approximately 6 to 7 percent, and when inflation has built up that much momentum it will continue for some time almost irrespective of the level of unemployment. That is, the institutional structure of the economy accommodates itself to the ongoing inflation. In particular, consumers, workers, investors, and business managers all come to expect that inflation will continue. However, there is still a cyclical dimension to inflation. Although high unemployment does not stop inflation, it does slow it down, as it did in the United States in

FIGURE 1

The Phillips Curve in Three Versions

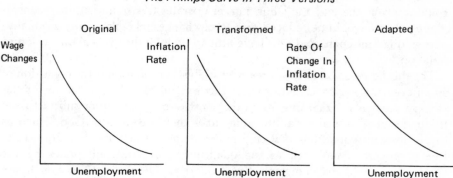

1975. Moreover, a low rate of unemployment will bring about a new acceleration of the inflation rate, as is happening in 1978.

A change has taken place in the unemployment-inflation trade-off since the mid-1950s—the increase in the so-called natural or noninflationary rate of unemployment, that is, the level of unemployment that generates no pressures toward either an acceleration or deceleration in the underlying rate of inflation and thus produces a stable inflation rate. This change in the noninflationary unemployment rate has come about for two reasons—a shift in the composition of the labor force and a reduction in the degree of economic hardship associated with a given level of total unemployment. First, there has been a great influx of married women and young people, a considerable number of them part-time workers, into the labor force. These groups often have requirements for specialized working conditions, such as a convenient location and flexible hours, and they can often afford to take more time looking for the right job. Thus they change jobs more often and spend more time between jobs than the family breadwinner. As a result they always have above-average unemployment rates. Statistically, this change in labor-force composition toward higher unemployment groups will bring about a higher total unemployment rate even though the rate for each separate group does not increase. Second, the unemployed today are subject to less economic pain than used to be the case, because of the development of more generous income-maintenance programs, the greater prevalence of families with two wage earners, the increased availability of savings, and other reasons. Consequently, most people who lose their jobs today are under less pressure to accept the first offer they get regardless of the pay and working conditions. These changes do not make joblessness a preferred status—excpet occasionally when the tax system has a particularly perverse effect—but they do make unemployment more tolerable than it was some years ago. The net effect is to increase the "natural" rate of unemployment. In terms of the diagrams, the Phillips curve has shifted to the right.

As this shift suggests, nothing is permanent or fixed about the level of the natural rate of inflation. Indeed, the demographics of the 1980s are likely to reduce the noninflationary unemployment rate (shift the Phillips curve to the left) by roughly half a percentage point. If training programs or other means could improve the way the labor market operates, the noninflationary unemployment rate would be reduced. But these changes take place only gradually, over a long time span, and thus have little to do with the cyclical dimension of inflation.

The third dimension in this three-way analysis of inflation is the collection of specific events—often called "special factors" or "supply shocks" or "inflationary accidents"—that operate in the short term to add to or subtract from the underlying rate of inflation. Sometimes they are "acts of God," such as severe weather conditions that ruin major crops. Sometimes they are acts of foreign governments, such as the quadrupling of crude oil prices by the Organization of Petroleum Exporting Countries (OPEC) in 1973. Sometimes they are acts of the United States government, such as minimum wage hikes, wage and price controls, and costly safety regulations.

Special factors always prevail in great numbers. Most of them, however, are small in their overall effect, and most of the time they offset one another—some add to inflationary pressures but some work the other way, with the net balance in most years averaging out positive, but not far from zero. Occasionally, however, these events affect an important sector of the economy intensely enough to affect the overall price level significantly.

The classic instance occurred during the early 1970s, when disastrous crop failures caused food prices to explode, OPEC pushed up energy prices in a massive way, simultaneous economic booms in every industrial country created especially severe demands in internationally traded commodities, and the devaluation of the dollar and the end of direct price and wage controls released inflationary pressures that had been suppressed earlier. The result was a dramatic acceleration of the overall rate of inflation to double-digit levels in 1973 and 1974. What would normally have been a period of about 6 percent inflation (based on the underlying and cyclical dimensions of the problem) suddenly jumped to a rate twice that high.

There are three key points to understand about these special inflationary factors. First, while they are always present in many forms, they rarely have a noticeable effect on the comprehensive price indexes. Other occasions when this took place include the suppressing impact of price and wage controls in 1972, the especially moderate behavior of food prices in 1955 and 1976, and the commodity price explosion that accompanied the outbreak of the Korean war in 1950. In the other postwar years, the omnipresent special factors simply did not carry enough weight to cause a conspicuous displacement of the rate of inflation.

The second point is that many of the important special factors do not represent inflation in the usual sense of having more or less parallel influence on both the price and cost sides of inflation. That is, they do not push up nominal incomes but leave the real magnitudes for the economy as a whole essentially unaltered (which, except for some cyclical effects, is what inflation usually does). Instead, such events transferred real income from workers to other economic units. The food price explosion transferred real income to farmers. The fourfold increase in crude oil prices transferred real income to owners of energy resources. The devaluation of the dollar transferred real income to the United States's trading partners abroad. When these developments take place, therefore, the real income of consumers suffers an absolute drop—in contrast to the normal inflationary process.

A third point to understand about the influence of special factors is its one-shot nature. These inflationary accidents raise the price of one specific group of commodities over a short period only once. Under normal circumstances, these influences do not become part of the general inflationary process; they do not get built into the underlying inflation rate. Their effect on the general price indexes is a passing one; for a year or two they contribute a large increment (or decrement) to the measured rate of inflation, but thereafter their influence phases out of the system, leaving it with whatever inflation rate is dictated by the monetary (underlying) and cyclical dimensions. Special-factor inflation does get built into the underlying inflation rate to the extent that there is formal price-wage indexing through cost-of-living-adjustment (COLA) clauses in union contracts, as well as in a few other ways. However, COLA clauses exist only for less than 10 percent of the work force, so the impact of special-factor inflation on the underlying rate is small.

The Causes of Inflation

The three dimensions of inflation discussed above are causes of inflation, but only in a proximate sense. It is not enough to know that monetary growth, cyclical expansion, and various special factors are involved in the inflation process. One also needs to know why these events take place: why there always seem to be more inflationary than deflationary accidents, why economic cycles produce more inflation acceleration than deceleration, and why, in the American system, too much money is created much more often than too little.

In one respect, at least, the last of those three questions is the most intriguing. In the United States, unlike many other nations, control of the supply of money rests with the Federal Reserve System, which has a degree of independence. The Federal Reserve governors and bank presidents who exercise that control are, more often than not, conservative. Yet, for some four decades, these generally conservative central bankers have presided over a monetary growth much faster than the growth of output and thus have helped cause a substantial inflation. How can one account for such behavior?

There are three interrelated answers. The first is the simple fact that Federal Reserve officials have the same multiple goals as other Americans, and the pursuit of these goals often leads to excessive money creation and thus to inflation. The second reason is congressional pressure on the Federal Reserve, pressure that is almost invariably in the direction of lower interest rates and more money. Because the Federal Reserve System is a "creature of Congress" and subject to fairly close congressional oversight, it is sensitive to the wishes of Congress, especially those of key committee chairmen. The concern is that if its opinion is treated too lightly, Congress will legislate new rules that will create much more permanent damage to the economy than would a partial acquiescence to their immediate wishes. The result is a compromise in the much-remarked independence of the Federal Reserve and the addition of a fairly constant inflationary bias to monetary policy.

The most specific reason for inflationary monetary policy is that the Federal Reserve often finds itself caught by the "deficit dilemma." Any time the economy is at or close to full utilization and the budget is in substantial deficit (including the credit requirements of off-budget agencies and the demands generated by federally guaranteed credit programs), it becomes difficult, if not impossible, for the Federal Reserve System to keep the growth of money within noninflationary bounds. The reason is that the Federal Reserve System, in addition to its responsibility for the quality of money, also has a responsibility to prevent credit crises and the severely contractional consequences that, in the United States's pre-Federal Reserve history, always followed such crises. Indeed, the Federal Reserve System was established as a direct response to the crisis of 1907. Obviously, the Federal Reserve System takes this responsibility very seriously, and whenever the financial markets appear to be headed for chaos (that is, when no lenders can be found at any reasonable interest rate to meet what would normally be considered legitimate demands for credit), the Federal Reserve is obligated to be a lender of last resort and supply the funds necessary to prevent disintegration of the credit markets.

This kind of situation arises when a large federal deficit must be financed at the same time credit demands from other sectors of the economy are already absorbing the available supply of savings. The federal government is always a premier borrower, so when the Treasury comes into the markets to finance a deficit it is always able to find willing lenders. But this creates a shortfall toward the end of the line of borrowers, thereby excluding some homebuilders or small businesses or municipalities (that would normally be legitimate borrowers) from the credit markets. As a result, a "credit crisis" threatens, and the Federal Reserve must step in as a lender of last resort. When it does, it creates new money and, consequently, inflation.

In short, in the face of a large federal deficit, the Federal Reserve is caught between its responsibility to limit the growth of money and its responsibility to act as a lender of last resort. Since the debilitating consequences of excessive money creation are neither so immediate nor so well understood as those of a credit crisis, the latter responsibility always takes precedence. The clearest example of this type of conflict took place in 1966 when the Federal Reserve recognized the mounting inflationary threat represented by the large deficit (a result of the Vietnam war and the Great Society programs) at a time when the economy was already at full capacity. For a while, the Federal Reserve took a strong stand against those inflationary pressures, constricting the growth of money and allowing interest rates to rise sharply. Their efforts faltered during the credit crunch of late September and early October 1966. At that point the financial markets began to collapse, especially the market for low-grade municipal securities where the spread between bid and asked quotations widened dramatically (to as much as 10 percent). The Federal Reserve was forced to meet this mounting crisis by supplying additional funds to the banking system, thereby abandoning the effort to prevent inflation from accelerating.

This episode illustrates the limits of the Federal Reserve's ability to prevent inflation in the face of large federal deficits. It also demonstrates the illusory character of two similar and somewhat prevalent beliefs. One of these ideas is that Federal Reserve officials with enough courage to persevere with stringent anti-inflationary policies can contain inflation. As already indicated, the Federal Reserve is not nearly as independent as it is often thought to be.

The second misconception is that the twin economic policy objectives of reasonably full employment and a gradual reduction in the inflation rate can be achieved simultaneously by running large deficits in the federal budget while gradually reducing the rate of monetary growth. This misconception, like the first, belies the conflict between fiscal and monetary policies; when fighting inflation, the two must be made to work together. The difficulty of this lies in the Federal Reserve's overriding responsibility as a lender of last resort. The fact is that the Federal Reserve is no different from any other organization that simultaneously pursues multiple, sometimes conflicting, objectives. It is rarely possible to favor one objective to the exclusion of all others.

In view of the close relationship between fiscal and monetary policies, it is appropriate to change the monetary dimension of inflation to the monetary-fiscal dimension. Nevertheless, this is still a proximate cause of inflation. The basic questions remain: Why so many large deficits? Why such rapid monetary growth? Why so much inflationary acceleration from cyclical expansions? Why so many inflationary accidents?

The root causes are mostly social and political.[2] There are occasional exceptions to this rule—for example, the short-term pressures brought on by "acts of God," such as crop failures—but by and large the sources of inflation are to be found in the way social attitudes interact with governing processes in the United States. Over the past fifty years, the American people have undergone two fundamental shifts in attitudes. First, they have adopted many new and extremely ambitious social objectives. Second, they have decided these objectives should be pursued through collective means.

The American political system, however, has not been adequate to the task. The demands of the political system far exceeded the economy's ability to produce. No systematic means existed for setting priorities, and there was no orderly political mechanism to reconcile the economic conflict between too much demand and too few resources. Inevitably, the result was inflation.

The way inflation arises out of these new social objectives and the inability of

[2] This concept is derived from the extensive writings of Albert T. Sommers. However, he should not be held responsible for this particular exposition and interpretation of the concept.

the system to deal with them in an orderly fashion are summarized in the following outline of the causes and consequences. In addition, it demonstrates the links between the root causes of inflation and the proximate causes discussed earlier.

One of the earliest and largest of the social goals to be adopted was the national commitment to full employment. The Great Depression changed the American attitude about unemployment. No longer was a worker's unemployment simply a matter of laziness and a lack of ambition. It became, rather, a failure of the national economy for which the federal government had to take responsibility. The government had to provide either public service jobs or income to the unemployed; more important, it had to prevent the unemployment in the first place. Over time the standards of performance have grown more exacting, and today even minirecessions are politically taboo.

The full-employment commitment is only one part of a broader social commitment to provide individuals and their families with security against almost all the hazards of economic life: social security to provide income during retirement, disability insurance and workmen's compensation to insure against injury, relief programs to alleviate the damage from natural disasters, and so on. The government is called on at every turn; it has become not only the lender and employer of last resort but also the charity of last resort—and even the family of last resort.

In the 1960s this trend toward more government-provided security took a further leap toward egalitarianism. This move was not total—that is, there was no intention to level all incomes to the average—but the objective called for much more redistribution than already existed. Accordingly, programs to aid the poor and disadvantaged proliferated—not only increasing the cash support levels of traditional welfare programs but also providing goods and services directly, such as food stamps, public housing, medical care, transportation, and legal services. In addition, the minimum wage was increased and the tax system moved in the direction of greater progressivity.

Major government regulatory programs were adopted to achieve a variety of specific objectives, such as clear air, clean water, equal opportunity, and occupational safety. Other restraints—on plant siting, transportation of hazardous materials, waste disposal, nuclear power, and price controls on energy—were extended and tightened, pushing operating costs up.

Further contributing to inflation are the shortcomings of the political system. The most obvious source of inflation in government is the practice of many politicians to buy votes with spending programs and tax cuts. Some do it quite consciously, others out of ignorance, and still others unintentionally. What could be more natural for a politician than to stress what he wants government to give to the people and to ignore, or at least deemphasize, what is to be taken away? Surely it is as human for politicians to pursue their self-interest (reelection) this way as it is for workers to seek higher pay and business people higher profits. The key difference is that workers and business people are subject to the discipline of either competition or regulation or both, whereas in politics the only competition is to see who can make the most grandiose promises. Of course, vote-buying politicians can get by with this only because there is a vote-selling public ready to believe it can gain from the transaction. Thus political irresponsibility, if that is not too strong a term, is found on both sides of the ballot box. One aspect of this phenomenon is the broad-scale granting of government benefits, such as across-the-board tax cuts. Another is legislation and other actions that favor a particular special-interest group. In effect, actions of the latter type are invariably a battle over income shares. While this fact is often understood, the politicians regularly behave as though the conflict does not exist. Benefits will be granted to one group, but nothing will be taken from the rest of society. Reconciling this inconsistency is left to inflation.

A second political shortcoming is the myopia and impatience of the American people, who want simple, costless, instant solutions to every problem, no matter how deep-seated and complex. As a result, politicians turn repeatedly to expediencies and choose policies that provide short-run gratification rather than long-term discipline. Arnold Weber once summed this up with the quip, "An economist's lag is a politician's nightmare." A more cynical version is, "To a politician, the long term is the time between now and the next election."

Several other things contribute to the inflationary bias of government. One is the tendency of the decision-making processes in government to falter whenever difficult and controversial issues arise, such as raising taxes, cutting spending, and agreeing on an energy policy. Decisions are sometimes postponed for years, because no mechanism exists in government to force a change. Another problem is the ignorance of both the politicians and the people about some of the most basic economic relationships. Still another is to be found in the shortcomings of the economics profession—for example, its limited understanding of the economic impact of policy actions, which severely restrict the capacity to fine tune the economy.

The ambitious social goals of America coupled with the shortcomings of its political system create inflation in several ways. The most obvious is through large deficits. Every spending and transfer program needed to meet the new commitments of government pushes the budget toward a deficit. The pursuit of self-interest by politicians and voters has the same effect. There is a constant tendency to overestimate the resources available to the government and to the economy as a whole. The society's collective reach exceeds its grasp.

The same things that encourage a deficit also spur the monetary authorities to create money faster than the growth of the economy. Occasionally this is forced on them by budget deficits, as in 1966, but generally it is simply their effort to achieve good economic performance, reinforced by pressures from Congress. Whatever the reason, the point is that Federal Reserve officials are neither wholly independent nor apolitical. They are fully aware of the social objectives of the American people and often share their objectives.

The tendency for both voters and politicians to choose short-run gratification and to postpone the necessary disciplines also works toward excessive monetary growth and big deficits. Excuses can always be found to defer balancing the budget, and the temptation to pursue short-run gratification is reinforced by the fact that when stimulative governmental policies are adopted, the economic advantages come first, whereas the negative effects do not come until later. When a stimulus is applied, the initial response of the economy is faster growth, low unemployment, rising real incomes, and improved profits. Before long, however, the feeling of well-being reverses, and when the stimulus has been excessive, the aftereffects are all painful: incomes and profits are squeezed, inflation accelerates, interest rates soar, and growth turns into recession. Yet, because the economic advantages come first, the government often travels this inflationary route.

The government's commitments to economic security and the egalitarian trend also exacerbate inflation by altering the risk-reward relationships of economic life. When the hazards of a free-market system are reduced and nonperformance is rewarded more than it is penalized, an inflationary bias is created. The flattening of the risk-reward trade-off encourages increases in costs and prices during the expansion phase of the business cycle and discourages cuts during cyclical setbacks.

Another proinflationary effect of these trends is the way they encourage consumption at the expense of saving and investment. In general, the long-run growth of government spending relative to total economic output tends to crowd out new investment. At the same time, specific programs like social security reduce the incentive for individuals to save and invest. A tax-and-transfer system that redistributes income from those who typically save and invest a high proportion of their income to those who are typically spenders also suppresses the total amount of new investment. The social and political trends of recent years, therefore, have been decidedly against growth. Similarly, because they enhance demand (consumption) while restricting supply (investment), these programs also tend to be inflationary.

Finally, the imposition of government regulations—both the old-fashioned kind like control of utility and transportation charges and the new ones like environmental cleanup and safety—adds billions of dollars directly to production and distribution costs every year. In the long run, these costs are passed on to consumers in the form of higher prices. In part, these higher costs and prices are worthwhile, because they result in cleaner air, fewer injuries, and so on. But it is also clear that the way the government formulates its regulations imposes enormous waste and gross inefficiency. The empty back-hauls of trucks operating under the Interstate Commerce Commission's regulation and the wasteful use of natural gas in intrastate markets because of interstate price controls are two of the most egregious examples. There is an urgent need for the application of rigorous cost-benefit analysis to the entire regulatory apparatus.[3]

---

[3] See Charles Schultze, *The Public Use of Private Interest* (Washington, D. C.: The Brookings Institution, 1977).

The Inflationary Process

Based on this analysis of the root causes of inflation and their interaction with the proximate causes, the inflationary process can be synopsized. In the long run, the rate of inflation depends on the social attitudes of the American people and the way their attitudes interact with the political process. In recent decades the growing demands for economic security, egalitarianism, a clean environment, and so on, coupled with political irresponsibility and shortsightedness, have created an addiction to large deficits, excessive monetary growth, cyclical overzealousness, inflationary accidents, and specific regulatory additions to costs. These, in turn, produce an underlying or built-in inflation. The chief characteristic of the underlying rate of inflation is its powerful momentum. The institutional nature of the price-wage process in the American economy makes the underlying inflation rate sluggish in its response to changes in economic conditions and thus difficult to dislodge.

At any given time, the observed rate of inflation depends on the underlying rate combined with cyclical pressures and special factors. Crop failures, devaluations, and other specific increases in prices and costs add to (or, infrequently, subtract from) the rate of inflation temporarily, but normally do not get built into the underlying rate. The business cycle also causes the inflation rate to accelerate or decelerate. The direction and force of cyclical pressures depend on the rate of resource utilization, that is, aggregate demand relative to aggregate production capacity. The three key zones of resource utilization are full-capacity operations which cause inflation to accelerate, near-capacity operations which mean stable inflation rates, and low-capacity operations which produce decelerating inflation. Under present conditions, the stable-inflation-rate zone may be in the range of 6 to 7 percent unemployment. In addition, however, the inflationary effect of the rate of resource utilization depends on the direction in which it is moving as well as its level. That is, unemployment at 6 percent in a decisively improving trend would probably be adding to inflationary pressures, but a stable 6 percent unemployment rate (stable for a year, say) may not be inflationary at all.

The impact of most anti-inflation policies depends on which zone of resource utilization the economy is in. To bring down the rate of inflation, policy must reduce economic activity to the point where the economy is in the zone of low-capacity operations. In other words, there is no magic connection between policy and inflation and no costless way to reduce inflation.

Policy Alternatives

The proximate causes of inflation are easily identified: the monetary-fiscal dimension, the cyclical dimension, and a variety of special factors. However, the social attitudes and their interaction with the governing process—the root causes of inflation—are much more complex and much more intractable to correction. Thus the question remains, What can be done to cope with inflation?

Unfortunately, there are no simple or quick solutions. The list of policy alternatives is by now a familiar one.

The first is still talked about by some people: make rapid economic growth and low unemployment the dominant policy priority and let the inflationary chips fall where they may. That is, they would simply ignore inflation. Although this is often discussed as a viable alternative, in fact it is not, at least not for long. As described earlier, a strong demand stimulus would quickly push the economy to full-capacity operations and generate an acceleration of inflation. In turn, this would soon bring about a cutback in spending and thus a new recession that would defeat the initial objectives of the policy. Because of this tendency to self-destruct, a policy decision to disregard inflation entirely is really no policy option at all, except in the very short run. Equally important, as recent public opinion polls have reconfirmed, the American people obviously have a much greater distaste for inflation now than they did earlier, so there is no political inclination to choose this policy alternative.

Another possibility represents the middle ground, a strategy that would take a strong stance against any acceleration of inflation, but at the same time it would make no effort to roll back the ongoing 6 to 7 percent inflation. As long as inflation stayed close to that range, policy would hold in a neutral stance. However, if a strong business cycle expansion threatened to propel inflation permanently above the 6 to 7 percent rate, policy would move sharply into restraint to ensure that any acceleration of the price advance was only temporary. Alternatively, in the down-phase of the business cycle, policy would turn stimulative as the main priority shifted to preventing a prolonged period of high unemployment.

In effect, this strategy would accept the average inflation rate of the past few years as a continuing fact of life, and it implicitly argues that in the long run the economy can operate satisfactorily in such inflationary conditions. In many ways the economy has already adjusted to a continuing rapid inflation, sometimes through formal contractual arrangements, but more often through ad hoc accommodations. There are, however, some very important gaps in the adjustment process. Pension benefits paid by private pension systems do not escalate with the general price level, which is a serious problem for retirees whose livelihood depends entirely or largely on their pensions. The system of taxing personal income is distorted in several important ways by inflation, for which only a few ad hoc, partial adjustments have been made. Accounting practices and business taxation are other areas where adjustment to inflation remains to be completed.

Despite the serious gaps that remain in the process of adapting to inflation, the economy can probably operate satisfactorily over the long term with a fairly steady 6 to 7 percent inflation rate, if such an option is chosen. The economy will do better in almost every way if a significantly slower rate of inflation or, still more desirable, no inflation at all, can be achieved. If necessary, however, a continuing rapid but fairly steady inflation seems viable.

The third alternative is the traditional prescription for eliminating inflation from the economic system: to pursue balanced budgets and restrictive monetary policies until excess capacity is created in both the labor and product markets. In effect, this strategy would put the economy into the recession phase of the business cycle and keep it there as long as it takes to squeeze the rate of inflation down to a desired level. But depressing the economy imposes enormous costs: high unemployment, foregone growth and investment, and lost profits. Furthermore, these costs may have increased in recent decades (despite the many programs designed to soften the blows) so that the economic pain inflicted by an effort to slow down inflation through general economic weakness may be greater today that it was two or three decades ago.

To keep enough slack in the economy to bring about a gradual reduction in inflation would require an unemployment rate significantly above the "natural" rate—perhaps 7.5 percent. To put a significant dent in the present rate of inflation would require that this 7.5 percent unemployment rate (along with the slower growth and depressed profits that go with it) be sustained for a long time—some estimates of the time needed to cut the present inflation rate in half go as high as six years.[4]

That is, quite obviously, a staggering cost—an additional million to a million and a half unemployed persons for about five years. The disadvantaged groups that always have above-average unemployment rates would bear a relatively large share of that cost. In addition, the depressed profits and foregone investment would have an even longer lasting effect on the advance of productivity, slowing the growth of the economy by a small but not insignificant margin for many years to come. Another cost is the losses that would accrue, as the inflation rate declined, to long-term debtors who were obligated to pay interest rates that incorporate an expectation of higher inflation. In effect, those debtors would not have the inflation they counted on to help them pay the interest on the loans. One has to question whether the American people would absorb the cost involved in such a severe policy course.

Beyond those direct costs is a major risk to the economic system. Americans value their system not only for its long record of economic growth and for a relatively wide sharing of the benefits of that progress but also for the freedoms it provides them. Over the past few decades, the trend toward more government intervention has been eroding those freedoms, but by and large Americans still have a predominantly private-decision economy. However, if after the economic trauma of the past decade the performance of the economy were to be further impaired for a number of years, the patience of the American people would be severely tested. It is not unreasonable to fear that sustained high unemployment and slow growth might result in a wholesale reshaping of the economic system through a major increase in government control of business

---

[4] For a slightly less pessimistic argument, see William Fellner, "The Core of the Controversy about Reducing Inflation: An Introductory Analysis," in *Contemporary Economic Problems*, ed. William Fellner (Washington, D.C.: American Enterprise Institute, 1978), pp. 1–12, and Phillip Cagan, "The Reduction of Inflation by Slack Demand," in ibid., pp. 13–45.

decisions. This risk must also be counted as part of the cost of sustained fiscal and monetary stringency.

A fourth policy option is some form of direct intervention by government into the price-and-wage-setting process within individual product and labor markets. The possibilities range from the comprehensive, mandatory controls undertaken during the period 1971–74 to mild forms of voluntary guidelines. The newest variant, currently under discussion, is tax-based incomes policies (TIP), an effort to use the tax system to induce more moderate increases in wages and prices. All such policies except TIP have been tried on many occasions here and in other countries, and what impact they have had, if any, on the overall inflation rate has been either very small or very temporary, i.e., a few months to two years. There is little or no evidence that incomes policies have contributed to a lasting cure for the price disease. Further, in many cases, direct intervention in the price-wage process has been used as a smokescreen to mask the impact of government actions that in the end made inflation worse rather than better.

The notion that usually underlies price and wage controls is that large corporations and large unions have considerable discretion in determining their prices and wages. They are perceived as having considerable power over the markets and as being almost immune to the forces of competition. Yet the evidence is not consistent with that theory except for the short run and for minor industries and a few small unions. Rather, competition seems to exert a powerful and pervasive force in the marketplace, which seems to reject the concept of cost-push inflation. Nevertheless, at any given time the precise size of many price and wage decisions surely involves what might be called a "zone of indeterminancy." That is, in the short run, some limited discretion exists. If outside intervention could push each price change and each wage settlement toward the bottom of that zone, it would make a modest contribution to the anti-inflation effort.

In theory, then, it seems possible that an incomes policy short of full-fledged controls, if properly applied, might help reduce the rate of inflation. This would, however, be a very delicate undertaking. Any suppression of prices or wages significantly below market-clearing levels would create a variety of economic distortions, including a loss of popular support for the program. The restraint on the price side would have to be closely balanced, industry by industry, with the restraint on the wage side. Furthermore, it would be necessary to coordinate the direct intervention rather precisely with fiscal and monetary policy to avoid the development of demand-pull inflation. Given the present state of the art, precise coordination of these policies appears to be beyond the capabilities of government administrators and professional economists. The complexity of the economy and thus the demands, in terms of management skills, are too great. To achieve success, the program would require too sensitive a touch on too many policy levers. In addition, any incomes policy has significant costs in lost freedoms.

Finally, it seems doubtful that public support for such a program can be gained from either business or, more important, labor. The politically powerful labor unions are at present adamantly opposed to any practical form of compulsory incomes policies for three reasons. First, rightly or wrongly, they feel that they were shortchanged in 1971–74 and would be victimized again. Second, they feel that compliance with wage guidelines would automatically be enforced by employers but that government would not be effective in enforcing the price guidelines. Third, any direct intervention by the government in the collective bargaining process tends to leave the leaders of unions without a function; the support of the rank and file depends on a perception that their officers are gaining something more for them than they could get themselves. When the government is determining wage levels, it is difficult for union leaders to sustain this belief. The opposition of organized labor and other groups is another of the serious costs generated by direct price-wage intervention.

A final anti-inflation policy alternative is a comprehensive endeavor to reduce costs, increase efficiency, and enhance competition in both the product and the labor markets. One element of this policy would be tax reform that curbs consumption by encouraging more saving and investment. For example, replacement-cost depreciation could be permitted. Income taxes could be replaced in part by a national sales tax. A larger investment tax credit could be introduced. The corporate tax rate could be cut. For individuals, the tax laws could be changed to eliminate the distortions inflation has created in the taxation of interest income and capital gains.

A second part of this policy would be a diligent examination of all current regulatory efforts to determine the cost-benefit ratio for each and to remove any that do not meet a reasonable standard. Fairly complete deregulation would be in order in some areas—the transportation system, for example. In other cases, some regulations might be modified to reduce the costs they impose.

The third element of this policy would be a campaign to break down the structural and institutional obstacles that keep prices and costs from falling. Instead of undertaking direct intervention by government into particular markets, an effort would be made to remove the barriers to efficiency and competition that have been put there by past government actions. The opportunities for increasing efficiency and reducing costs by removing barriers of this sort are much more extensive than might be suspected. Import restrictions now in place could be removed. Further increases in the minimum wage could be postponed, and a separate lower minimum wage for teenagers could be introduced. Enforcement of the antitrust laws could be intensified. The Davis-Bacon Act, which maintains high wage rates on government construction, could be modified. The unemployment insurance system could be changed to make it less of a disincentive to work. The monopoly of the postal service could be ended. Restrictive licensing practices could be eased. Building codes could be modernized. More timber could be harvested from federal lands.

Unfortunately, every action of this sort would be highly controversial. These laws and practices did not come into being frivolously, and there would be strong political opposition to their dismantlement. Accordingly, although this is the kind of policy alternative that is highly appealing for its effect on economic growth as well as its anti-inflationary implications, it is not an easy policy to put in place.

Conclusion

The brief description of alternative anti-inflation policies in the preceding section makes it abundantly clear that there are no easy choices, at least none likely to have much effect. Whichever choices are made, two things are certain. One is the enormous cost of any of these policy alternatives. The other is that significant results can be achieved only over a period of probably five to ten years.

The following recommendations, which are offered meekly, without a sense of confidence, attempt to take into account the complexity of the American economic system, the great doubt about how thoroughly inflation is understood, and the enormous difficulties of implementing economic policy in the American governmental system.

The recommendation offered most easily is to undertake the three-part pro-competitive policy outlined above. In doing so, however, caution is necessary in judging the extent to which this policy would reduce the rate of inflation. Most of the impact of the increased investment, reduced regulatory waste, and improved efficiency that would come out of this program would be in the direction of speeding up the growth of productivity and thus total economic growth. The effect on inflation would probably be quite modest. Nevertheless, because the economic costs are small, this policy is worth adopting as part of a comprehensive anti-inflation effort, even though the anti-inflation contribution that might reasonably be expected is also small.

Second, it is recommended that all forms of direct price-wage intervention be avoided. Although it is conceptually possible that an incomes policy with some compulsory elements could mitigate inflationary pressures slightly, the chances seem remote that the necessary ideal conditions and the required delicate mangement of the program could be attained and sustained. Even if everything went well, the anti-inflation contribution would be very small. Moreover, if anything went wrong, the costs in the form of lost productivity and lost freedoms would be substantial. Therefore, it is better to avoid direct intervention altogether.

The third recommendation, offered very reluctantly, is not to undertake a program of sustained fiscal and monetary stringency. This policy is the only one that, if rigorously pursued, could be counted on to reduce inflation to a manageable rate. But as desirable a goal as that is, the costs would be too great—too much unemployment, too much lost growth, all for too many years. The risk would be so great that the American people might conclude (after, say, three or four years of such a policy had achieved only a partial moderation in the inflation rate) that the poor performance of their economic system called for a large new injection of government control and a corresponding reduction of private decision-making. The substantial benefits of a low inflation rate are still not worth these costs.

The primary recommendation, therefore, is that the American people learn to live with the present built-in 6 to 7 percent inflation and attempt to keep it from accelerating further. As indicated earlier, this policy is not costless. While the economy has already come a long way toward adjusting to high, ongoing inflation, there are several important gaps in the process—such as fixed pension-benefit levels—and many smaller ones. Although it will take a long time, the economy should continue and complete the adjustment process. Accordingly, this policy alternative seems to be the least objectionable of the available choices.

Many will regard this recommendation as a surrender to inflation. In part, that is true. But it is not a surrender to an endless acceleration of the inflation rate. What needs emphasis here is that preventing a further increase in the rate of inflation is an enormously difficult task. The root causes of inflation, as presented in this analysis, are social and political in nature. Although something of a change has occurred in the social attitudes of the American people in the past few years, it is by no means a complete change. The full-employment commitment has been modified only slightly. The trend toward ever more government-provided security and toward additional government intervention of all kinds continues, though at a slower pace. Accordingly, it is still doubtful that the American political system will be able to muster the policy discipline—in the budget, in monetary policy, and in the regulatory area—necessary to keep inflation from accelerating still further. Even under this alternative, economic policy faces an extremely formidable challenge.

Monetary and Fiscal Policies

EDWARD M. GRAMLICH

Inflation is one of the most difficult problems that modern industrial economies have to solve. During the past fifteen years, countless proposals were advanced dealing with the problem—some of which were tried and found wanting, others not tried but still found wanting, and others that are yet to judged. One of the most puzzling aspects of inflation is that the economics profession still does not understand exactly how serious a problem it is.

This essay reviews the various causes of inflation—excess demand, cost-push or expectations, and autonomous shocks—and discusses these causes in the manner of the orthodox thought of the economics profession. It then describes, in these terms, the present inflation in the United States. Although this essay is concerned principally with monetary and fiscal policies, it digresses to consider the role of these basic instruments of stabilization policy in bringing about inflation. Finally, it discusses various cures for inflation.

The number of potential cures discussed is fairly large, but the promise of each one is rather limited. No new panacea will be proposed here—inflation is too fundamentally rooted in the character of modern day economics for that. Nor will the essay propose measures to try to stop inflation abruptly, because all known measures for bringing down the inflation rate simply have too serious costs if used in an extreme dosage. But it will propose a relatively eclectic strategy for dealing with inflation over a long horizon. It is not an original strategy, but it could be effective if the nation would only use it.

The classical bromide has it that inflation represents "too much money chasing too few goods." In more technical parlance, one can label this "excess demand inflation." Whatever is motivating aggregate demand—monetary or fiscal policy, investment, exports, or the stock market—is generating more demand for goods and services than the productive side of the economy can supply, and this excess demand makes it easy for sellers of goods to raise product prices and sellers of labor (workers) to raise wages. The result is excess demand inflation.

According to who is discussing the excess demand inflation, monetary or fiscal policy is usually, and appropriately, singled out for special approbation for the simple reason that they should be regulating aggregate demand so that excess demands do not result; excess demand inflation is *prima facie* evidence that these policies have not worked well.

The standard classroom way of discussing excess demand inflation is to draw the famous Phillips curve indicating the trade-off between unemployment and inflation. The former is *prima facie* evidence of deficient demand and the latter of excess demand. For the moment it will have to be assumed that inflation is not expected by anybody so that the curve will cross the horizontal axis, and then one can talk about this horizontal intercept of the Phillips curve, labeled in figure 1 as U*. Conservative economists call this the "natural" rate of

FIGURE 1

The Phillips Trade-off Between Unemployment and Inflation
When No Inflation is Expected

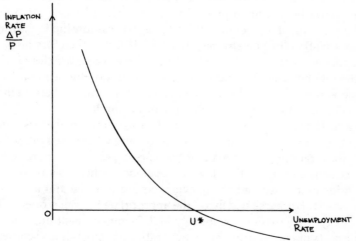

unemployment; liberal economists call it the "nonaccelerating inflation" rate of unemployment.

The conservative appellation derives from the fact that once expectations are added to the system, U* becomes the economy's long-run equilibrium position, through a process that is explained below. The more cumbersome terminology adopted by liberals has two rationales. First, U* is natural only from a macroeconomic perspective—not from a social perspective. From that perspective U* can be high indeed, and no good liberal wants to divert attention from the seriousness of the unemployment problem by calling it natural. Second, the reason U* is "natural" is that it causes inflation to accelerate. Going from U* leftward on the Phillips curve does exactly that, in both conservative and liberal models, and calling U^* the nonaccelerating point is more precise terminology. Finally, this terminological debate is just that, for all the vehemence with which liberals and conservatives debate inflation; noneconomists would be bemused to note that the underlying economic models of both schools are similar. Whether one is conservative or liberal, U^* acts as a target for monetary-fiscal policies. When the economy is guided to a position to the right of U^*, by highly restrictive monetary-fiscal policies or by neutral policies when private demands are weak, there will be excess capacity, sellers will lower prices, labor will bid down wages, unemployment will be low, and rates of inflation will be negative. When to the left of U^*, everything is reversed. One can then identify the kind of excess demand inflation by observing whether actual unemployment (U) is less or greater than U^*. If it is less, there is excess demand inflation; if greater, there is not.

If conservatives and liberals agree on this model of excess demand inflation, as they basically can, one might wonder why there is any debate between them about excess demand inflation. There are four reasons.

Measurement of U^*. Unfortunately the natural or nonacceleration unemployment rate cannot be measured precisely, like the rate of acceleration of falling bodies. Particularly when the underlying trade-off relationship is shifting greatly, it becomes difficult to determine just what U^* is and therefore just what the target for monetary-fiscal policy should be. Three recent articles on the topic pegged this rate between 5.5 and 6.0 percent, with no obvious political biases being demonstrated, but it is logical to suspect that liberals will err on the side of lowering U^* and conservatives on the side of raising it.

Relative costs and benefits of deviations. In a world where there is a short-run trade-off between unemployment and inflation and where the Phillips relationship is shifting rapidly, policymaking becomes a good deal more judgmental and subjective than might at first seem apparent. If there has been excess demand inflation in the past and all policymakers are agreed that it must be rooted out, they may still disagree widely on the appropriate interim strategy. To form such a strategy, the costs of temporarily high unemployment must be weighed against the costs of temporarily more rapid inflation. Liberals and conservatives typically see these costs very differently, with the former group more worried about the social cost of unemployment and the latter about the stability of the dollar.

Speed limits. There is another quite separate question regarding the time horizon over which deviations should be eliminated, a good illustration of which arose in the 1975 recession. Then the unemployment rate rose almost 4 percentage points to a peak level of 9 percent. Virtually all observers agreed that aggregate demand was deficient, that U exceeded U^*, and that monetary-fiscal policies should be geared to arresting the recession and lowering unemployment. But there was disagreement about how fast unemployment should be lowered—by 0.5, 1.0, or 2.0 percentage points a year. Some argued that there were "speed limits" on the rapidity with which real income could rise and unemployment could fall: that rapid rises in production would generate short-term backlogs and bottlenecks that would make inflation worse. Others found such arguments unconvincing. As it turned out, the argument was not resolved because the economy approached U^* at a slow and steady enough rate that the speed limit was not an issue.

The noninflationary value of high unemployment. Perhaps the hardest question of all involves the value of recessions in limiting inflation. If the Phillips trade-off gets very flat to the right of U^* in figure 1, high unemployment has almost no value in fighting inflation; if it is steep, high unemployment has a great value. Depending on how one sees this question, then, one can either believe or not believe in recessions (temporary periods of high actual unemployment) as antidotes to bursts of inflation. Opinions vary widely on this issue, typically in a manner somewhat related to political points of view. Arthur Okun reviewed the evidence from six sophisticated statistical examinations of the matter and found that all suggest rather flat trade-offs in this range. An additional 1 percent of temporary unemployment reduces the inflation rate by about as much as the Department of Commerce will typically alter it with revised income and product data. If this is correct, even recessions may no longer stop inflation.

This discussion has proceeded as if the world were in a state where nobody expected inflation and where price and wage setting agents would sign contracts that had no built-in protection against it. Obviously, if inflation develops, these expectations are likely to change, and price and wage setting behavior will change along with it. In this section the simple model described in figure 1 is extended to encompass changes in expectations and, in so doing, it illustrates the second main cause of inflation.

There are two standard models of changing inflationary expectations. The first, adaptive expectations, which was developed by Milton Friedman and Edmund Phelps, has economic agents looking backwards at recent past rates of inflation.[1] If there was inflation in the past, price and wage setters expect it to proceed and they do not sign price or wage contracts without inflation protection. It matters little in this view whether the inflation protection is formal, as in explicit cost-of-living adjustments or indexing, or informal, where all wage bargains are simply escalated to make up for past inflation. The result is that the positioning of the Phillips relationship in figure 1 depends on recent past rates of inflation. In a typical Friedman story, illustrated in figure 2, the economy is initially positioned at U^* along Phillips relationship T_0 (T for trade-off and 0 for the fact that no inflation is anticipated). A new administration takes office and pledges to lower the unemployment rate to U_1. In the first year inflation proceeds at rate p_1, along the short-run trade-off curve. If inflationary expectations were stable, that would be the end of the story. But if they adapt, as Friedman and Phelps argue they would, future wage and price agreements would be

[1] Milton Friedman, "The Role of Monetary Policy," *American Economic Review* 58 (March 1968):1-17; and Edmund S. Phelps, "Phillips Curves, Expectations of Inflation and Optimal Unemployment over Time," *Economica* 34 (August 1967): 254-81.

FIGURE 2

The Phillips Trade-off with Adaptive Expectations of Inflation

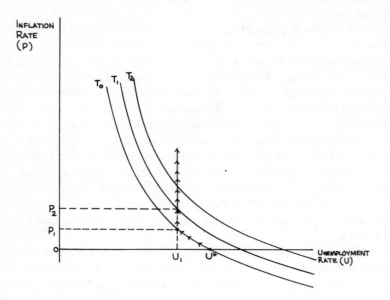

shifted up exactly by p_1, leading to a new trade-off T_1. If the unemployment rate were held at U_1, inflation would again get worse, the new rate would be p_2, the following year's trade-off is T_2, and the whole process repeats itself. Ultimately the economy would follow the path formed by the arrows, which in the limit implies no trade-off between unemployment and inflation. U^* becomes the only sustainable rate of unemployment for this economy, and while inflation and unemployment can be traded off against each other in the short run, they cannot be in the long run.

This fundamental amendment to the inflation story achieved almost immediate endorsement by most segments of the economics profession and within a few years was a standard feature of macroeconomics textbooks. On one hand, it accorded well with economic intuition, since it argued that sooner or later price and wage setters would figure out that inflation was prevalent and would adapt to it. On the other hand, it gave a perfect explanation for the inflationary epoch of 1965–73. Unemployment first fell because of excess demand fiscal policies during the Vietnam war and was then followed by the gradual adaptation of expectations, so that even after the excess demand was eliminated by the Nixon administration policies of the early 1970s, inflation was held up by the momentum of past history. It did not take long before the econometric estimates of price and wage equations demonstrated the mathematical properties of this adaptive expectations model.

While most of the profession still believes in something like this view of the inflation process, there are some dissonant notes. One is that in fact the theory may not have applied so well to the most recent recession. In 1975, for example, unemployment rose well above U* and stayed there for at least two years, almost as long as it stayed below U* in the late 1960s. Now the Friedman-Phelps theory should work in reverse: sustained high unemployment should reduce inflation below its expected value and eventually cause a steady deceleration of prices and wages. If this deceleration is now happening, it is well disguised indeed. There are several possible reasons why it is not happening: the Phillips trade-off becomes flat to the right of U*, thus preventing the deceleration from ever getting started; the 1975 period witnessed supply shock inflation, which also prevented the deceleration from starting; or the unemployment argument in the Phillips relationship is not the actual observed unemployment rate but rather the permanent unemployment rate that economic actors feel the government is committed to. In the 1960s actors might have felt that the government was committed to a permanent policy of lowering unemployment below U* (as official statements indicated), while in the 1970s the high unemployment was viewed as a temporary aberration due to the oil crisis or some other difficulty, which would be undone as soon as possible. With these modifications, the Friedman-Phelps theory can apply at the present time, but it should be recognized that the explanation is not quite so simple once such patently ad hoc modifications are attached.

The second major model of changing inflationary expectations is that of rational expectations. There are a number of variants of this model, developed by Robert E. Lucas and Thomas J. Sargent.[2] Their basic idea is that agents do not mechanically react to past rates of inflation, as in the adaptive model, but they understand the system and react to what will happen in a model of the economy that all agree on. They all know the effects of adaptive expectations and know that the only viable long-run rate of unemployment is U*. They also know that if supply shocks average out over the long run, the rate of inflation is ultimately a linear function of the rate of growth of the money supply. Hence, in the most prevalent rational expectations model of the economy, past rates of inflation and present unemployment conditions are in fact irrelevant—one has only to know the rate of growth of the money supply to "rationally anticipate" the rate of growth of prices.

Rational expectations models imply that monetary-fiscal policies can do little to control the real economy but a great deal to control the rate of inflation. Their spirit is that policies are important as instruments of control of the real economy because all actors in the real economy already know the equilibrium real position of the economy, and policies cannot disturb the economy from this equilibrium because the self-fulfilling prophecies of the private sector will

[2] Robert E. Lucas, "Expectations and the Neutrality of Money," *Journal of Economic Theory* 4 (April 1972): 103–24; and Thomas J. Sargent and Neil Wallace, " 'Rational' Expectations, the Optimal Monetary Instrument, and the Optimal Money Supply Rule," *Journal of Political Economy* 83 (April 1975):241–54.

always offset monetary-fiscal actions in real terms. But where the rate of inflation is concerned, monetary policy is invested with unusual power. Since economic agents look only to the Federal Reserve Board to determine the rate of inflation, it can control inflation. Any past inflationary sins, which perpetuate inflation in the adaptive model, are irrelevant in the rational model. All that is needed is to control future money growth.

While the simple beauty of the rational expectations cure for inflation is inspiring, the model may not be appropriate. Everything hinges on the fact that economic actors understand the economic system. If they are bewildered by it, as most professional economists certainly feel at times, the ability to see through policies lapses, and they may be forced to rely on adaptive ways of forming expectations. Indeed, if they feel others do not behave rationally even if they do, they may still find it worthwhile to behave adaptively. Most empirical tests of the rational model do not confirm its basic postulates, at least where price and wage movements are concerned, and it will probably be a while yet before the message sinks in sufficiently for the rational model to take hold.

The most recent important cause of inflation, originating in the peculiar inflation afflicting the United States economy since 1973, is from the supply side. Just as a rapid growth of demand can cause rising prices, so can a rapid contraction of supply. This happened in 1973, when the agricultural shortages forced up farm prices, and again when the Arab boycott and subsequent cartelization of the Organization of Petroleum Exporting Countries (OPEC) resulted in increased energy prices. Then, as a related development, the decline of the dollar in a world of fluctuating exchange rates forced up the United States prices of most internationally traded goods, raising United States price levels once again. Most analyses of the current inflationary problems in the United States give extraordinarily heavy weight to these supply shocks, or price increases essentially unrelated either to excess demand or to expectations.

Supply shock inflation is disturbing enough when the cause is external, as with food, oil, and the declining dollar. But it becomes particularly damaging when the source is internal, from specific artificial shortages or price increases legislated by Congress. In the past two years examples of such actions have been the increase in employer payroll tax rates as part of the social security system rescue package, the increase in minimum wages, legislated increases in farm price supports, environmental standards, and certain requirements of the Occupational Safety and Health Administration. All of these policies were enacted for perhaps perfectly good reasons, but they do raise price levels and compound the difficulties of controlling inflation. A way to deal with this problem in political economy will be suggested below.

At various times in the past it has been possible to associate inflationary periods mainly with one or another cause, but that does not appear to be the case today. In the late 1960s virtually all observers considered the inflation an excess demand strain caused by overexpansionary fiscal policy during the Vietnam war; in the early 1970s, the cause of the inflation that persisted long after excess demand had worn off was attributable to the momentum of expectations;

and in the mid-1970s, inflation resulting from supply shocks became prevalent. In 1977 and 1978, however, one can find traces of all strains. With the recent drop in the unemployment rate, it is likely that U is at least near U*. Further stimulation of the economy would therefore be unwise and could generate excess demand inflation. The outside supply shocks of the 1973–75 period have not continued, but there is at least some continuing slide of the dollar and the congressional actions that have raised certain prices legislatively. Through it all, expectations are still adapting to ten years of inflation, particularly to the 1973–75 supply shocks. Many of those supply shocks ultimately implied losses of real income to the United States's international trading partners, but as wage and price setting groups attempt to index their own bargains by full cost-of-living protection, a mathematical impossibility in an era when the overall pie has shrunk, expectations inflation will persist. It would be pleasant to rule out certain causes of inflation and focus intensively on just one, but that is impossible. All strains are now present, and all must be treated.

Through the persistent efforts of the *Wall Street Journal*, *Business Week*, and other such journals, the impression seems to be gaining ground that there is just one cause of inflation—deficits in the federal budget. It certainly may be true that the attitude that leads to government deficits is the same as, or related to, the attitude that engenders inflation, but more precision is needed about the economic reasoning. Just as there are three species of inflation, there are two species of deficits in the federal budget.

"Excess demand deficits" are the ones usually associated with inflation, and there is no question that they do cause excess demand inflation. The most prominent illustration is again the period of the Vietnam war when budget deficits ran on the order of $30 billion measured at the full employment level of income. Simultaneously, unemployment rates were about 3.5 percent, well below U*. The economy was clearly in an excess demand region, and overstimulative fiscal policy was clearly aggravating the problem day by day. This is a perfect illustration of how deficits could cause inflation, and it is perhaps not surprising that everybody learned that they could.

The other source of deficits in modern economies is not excess demand or rapid spending growth but what may be called "automatic stabilizer deficits." As the economy enters a recession with U rising above U* (in a range where excess demand inflation is present), a government deficit will develop automatically. Declines in personal income will automatically lower personal tax revenues, and rising unemployment will automatically raise unemployment insurance benefits. These movements are known as automatic stabilizers precisely because they insulate the incomes of the private sector against changes in the economy, prevent private spending from dropping any more than it already is, and stabilize the economy. They are perhaps the single most important reason that it is almost impossible for another Great Depression to occur in the United States. Moreover, since they are operative in a range where U is in excess of U*, they should not cause excess demand inflation.

This statement has to be qualified. For one thing, shrewd observers of figure 1 will point out that any force that lowers unemployment below what it would otherwise be will generate at least some inflation when the Phillips trade-off is not flat over the relevant range. This is true, but the automatic stabilizer deficits can still be absolved of responsibility for perpetuating inflation in two senses: the Phillips trade-off is certainly rather flat over ranges where U is fairly high, in excess of, say, 7 percent; and the whole range to the right of U* is a nonacceleration range. If the unemployment rate would only stay there, sooner or later inflation would go down, and automatic stabilizer deficits would do nothing more than keep it there. The difference between the inflationary potential of the two types of deficits is then ultimately the unemployment rate that prevails when the deficits are run.

A second qualification regards monetary policy. It may be that even though government deficits do not by themselves generate inflation, their existence on a large scale may force the Federal Reserve to monetize them or to buy up a large volume of interest-bearing securities by the simple expedient of printing money. Of course, ever since the Treasury-Federal Reserve Accord of 1951 this has not been formally true: the Federal Reserve is an independent entity and free to set the monetary policy it wants. At the same time, it will not remain independent for long if it wantonly violates the wishes of elected representatives, so it clearly does not have as much power as one would believe by examining the statutes.

Whether in fact the Federal Reserve does feel pressure to monetize deficits is essentially an empirical question, and in answering it one should again distinguish between excess demand and automatic stabilizer deficits. Excess demand deficits occur at a time when the economy is booming and the search for liquidity is driving up interest rates. Automatic stabilizer deficits occur when real income and interesting rates are falling. Virtually every observer feels that the Federal Reserve, at least in the short run, follows something of an interest rate target—when rates are rising it conducts open market purchases, and when rates are falling it conducts open market sales. If this is so, the Federal Reserve will feel much pressure to monetize excess demand deficits, thus making their inflationary potential worse, but it will not feel pressure to monetize automatic stabilizer deficits, thus preserving the feeling that these deficits do not generate at least excess demand inflation.

It might be helpful to conclude this section by returning to the present situation, in which every observer knows that large deficits and rapid inflation coexist. Are they related, and if not, why not? The answer appears to be yes and no. There is no doubt that fiscal policy is very expansionary these days, with a deficit that would be on the order of $30 billion if the economy were at full employment. There is also no question that the unemployment rate is reaching the edge of the accelerating danger zone. Hence there is a risk that soon there will be excess demand deficits and excess demand inflation and a serious risk that United States politicians will overdo it and take the economy into this range. Yet the continuing inflation of the past two years cannot be blamed on budget deficits. Over this time, unemployment was high enough not to be in the acceleration range, yet inflation continued. The obvious reason was that the other two causes of inflation—shocks and the momentum of expectations—were at work. It should be pointed out that the deficits during this time were at least in part automatic stabilizer deficits and they apparently did not put undue pressure on the Federal Reserve: monetary growth has been at the fairly responsible rate of 7 percent for the past two years.

The Cures for Inflation

Over the years, various observers have presented a large number of possible cures for inflation. The list is long partly because most cures have at one time or another been found wanting and have stimulated concerned observers to offer new suggestions.

The classical antidote for inflation, specifically excess demand inflation, is recession. If demand is excessive, tighter monetary-fiscal policies should be able to deflate the economy until the excesses are removed. Such a prescription would be the logical result either of a Draconian monetary policy to reduce the rate of money growth drastically, or of a rigorous fiscal policy aimed at eliminating deficits in short order. The main problem with these remedies is simply that their cost is enormous. Calculations from empirical estimates of the slope of the Phillips trade-off indicate that an additional percentage point of unemployment (raising the rate from, say, 6 to 7 percent) would lower the inflation rate by only about 0.5 percentage point (from 7.0 to 6.5 percent). To reduce appreciably the present inflation rate of about 8 percent would thus take either an enormous recession or an extraordinarily long one. Not only would such a recession impose staggering human costs and the usual losses of income, but it would probably be precluded politically. Perhaps a less entrenched commitment to high employment will make the anti-inflationary potential of recessions more believable, but again it is unlikely that Congress will agree to such a weakened commitment any time soon. By now most observers are persuaded that it is unwise to overstimulate the economy and reduce unemployment much, but that unfortunately does not mean that inflation will be cured by engineering great increases in unemployment.

Controls are another alternative. Scholars will long argue whether the price-wage control scheme first imposed by President Nixon in 1971 was successful in lowering inflation. Yet, even if it was successful then, there are good reasons for doubting that it could be again. For one thing, in 1971 the president already had statutory authority to impose controls, and he was able to take the economy by surprise. Now the president would have to seek authorization, and there would likely be a short burst of inflation as firms and workers tried to increase their prices and wages.

There is a much more serious long-run problem with price-wage controls. Since firms can produce numerous product variations, it is virtually impossible to police controls on the price side. Any scheme is then forced to identify violations of the guidelines by instances of rapidly rising profits. It is anomalous to legislate against high profits in a free enterprise system that works according to the profit motive. Of course, in an ideal scheme it would be possible not even to try to police product prices but just control wage increases, relying on product market competition to bring prices into line. This strategy may turn out to be more effective than might be supposed, given the long-run virtual constancy of income shares. But again it is a rather academic point, for the chances that labor representatives will agree to a scheme featuring controls only on wages are remote indeed. Presently, labor representatives will not even agree to a scheme that does have a provision for attempts to control product prices.

Simply saying that controls are not perfect is not a sufficient reason to dismiss them, because if other measures do not work, new controls may be necessary regardless of their costs. Hence one measure that would be helpful in fighting inflation is a procedure by which the machinery for controls could be constructed without actually using it and without generating a lot of anticipatory price-wage increases in the meantime. Congress would not pass controls legislation as it did in 1970, when it was opposed by the administration that ultimately benefitted from it. But another technique might be useful. All firms could be required to record with the government their basic price and wage levels of the preceding month. Those prices and wages would then be the ones used for controls or for any measures to tax firms on the basis of price or wage increases. They would be on record and available for audit by government agencies, with perhaps the same types of penalty mechanisms now used by the Internal Revenue Service. Most important, they would be fixed. Meantime, any price or wage increase in anticipation of controls would increase the firm's susceptibility to controls if they come about. The base level for the firm could be updated at the general rate of inflation, and the administration should also be given the power to exempt industries like petroleum, as the circumstances warrant.

Because of the difficulty in designing a workable controls scheme, Sidney Weintraub, Henry Wallich, and Arthur Okun have designed variations of tax-based incomes policies (TIP). The basic idea is to permit firms or workers to raise prices and wages if they want to but to make it unprofitable for them to do so. This could be done either by penalizing firms granting large wage increases, as in the Weintraub-Wallich scheme, or rewarding workers taking small increases, as in the Okun scheme. Only some of the obvious characteristics of TIP will be noted here. A general scheme, as a reward scheme would have to be, forces administrators to grapple with all the complexities of the income tax system along with all the complexities of price-wage controls. The penalty scheme could be much simpler and focus on the large bargaining units of the economy, but even then the idea of guiding such a measure through Congress would discomfit even the most capable lobbyist. Finally, in regard to the earlier discussion of deficits and inflation, the TIP strategy can be thought of as a way to use budget revenues to induce firms and workers to behave responsibly or to tax them if they are irresponsible. Either way the greater the inflation, the smaller the deficit.

For obvious political and economic reasons, administrations and legislators usually reject extreme measures, and the typical compromise features informal guidelines, enforced with varying degrees of intensity. The major advantage of voluntarism is that it is less radical. It can be imposed or discarded without congressional approval and without much publicity, and it can be used selectively. Often it is difficult to draw up precise standards of inflationary behavior that would apply in every case, as is necessary for either controls or TIP, but it is not difficult to know that a particular action of a firm or union was inflationary. Various measures can then be used to threaten or make an example of such a firm, often resulting in a highly publicized partial backdown. The importance may be minor, but at least excessive inflationary behavior may then be cured.

The disadvantages of informalism are just as obvious. One is that there is no formal enforcement scheme, and the government's effort may seem more rhetorical than effective. Unless real punishments are to be found, the government risks generating real animosity and being ignored, as any recent speech by George Meany amply indicates. Finally, there is an element of perversity in any informal scheme: those who do not engage in inflationary behavior transfer real income to those who do. Over time, these transfers will seriously undermine the whole effort.

In the preceding discussion both the state of aggregate demand in the economy and the implicit social indicator of the responsiveness of labor markets to the employment needs of workers was the unemployment rate. The fundamental policy conflict is that it is impossible to raise employment demands and allow people to work all they want without overstimulating the economy and causing excess demand inflation. But what if the link were broken? What if it were possible, say, to raise the demand for low-wage workers, giving them better opportunities for advancement, without raising the demand for high-wage workers? It is possible that this change in the composition of employment demand would represent a social policy improvement and be noninflationary. A decade ago Charles Holt suggested a series of such policies aimed at filling inflation-creating job vacancies with low-wage and otherwise unemployed workers—improving job training opportunities, better placement services, and so forth. Not much ever came of those suggestions, but a similar idea has been suggested lately by Martin Neil Baily and James Tobin in connection with the Comprehensive Employment and Training Act (CETA).[3] Two of the titles of this act provide for a form of public sevice employment working through local governments. If the CETA wage is kept low, say at the minimum wage,

---

[3] Martin Neil Baily and James Tobin, "Macroeconomic Effects of Selective Public Employment and Wage Subsidies," *Brookings Papers on Economic Activity*, no. 2 (1977):511-44.

local governments will be hiring otherwise low-wage and unemployed workers, who presumably do not have much wage bargaining power, hence making for what should be a noninflationary expansion of overall employment demand. Indeed, CETA might even be thought of as a gentle but effective way to keep state and local wages under control, because the availability of public employment grants will give state and local governments a ready reserve army of the publicly employed to temper the wage demands of regular public sector employees. Empirical evidence on this point is scanty, but it is true that the recent large-scale expansion of CETA has been coupled with surprisingly moderate increases in state and local wages. Once again, if CETA does provide a way to expand employment demand in a somewhat noninflationary manner, it will again be true that extra federal deficit spending can be used to reduce inflation.

While United States policymakers have not been able to deal with inflation and unemployment very well, they have been successful in protecting various groups against the consequences through transfer restructuring. All government transfer programs are indexed against inflation now, at least ensuring that for this portion of their income the aged, unemployed, veterans, disabled, and welfare recipients do not bear any costs. Moreover, the gradual liberalization of provisions of unemployment insurance has made unemployment far less damaging to those becoming unemployed than it was in the 1930s.

Since inflation is likely to linger, it would take an extremely dispassionate observer to propose eliminating the indexation of transfer payments, so that the aged and helpless would bear the brunt of inflation. It is not even obvious that it would do any good, given the remote connection between the spending habits of these groups and price and wage bargains in the economy. (Reductions in social security payments will, of course, cause some reduction in aggregate demand, but these changes can easily be neutralized by tax changes.) But it may be fruitful to reexamine the unemployment insurance system. Martin Feldstein has proposed that unemployment benefits be made taxable, hence encouraging workers to search harder for new jobs in a spell of unemployment and lowering the nonaccelerating inflation rate of unemployment. Since firms are not fully taxed according to their previous levels of unemployment, there is at least some slight subsidy of those firms and industries that generate many temporary layoffs. If all firms were fully "experience-rated," at least some reduction in the nonaccelerating rate of unemployment could again be expected. Feldstein himself agrees that these two measures would be of rather modest empirical importance. However, by shifting down the rate of unemployment at any level of inflation, both would shift the Phillips trade-off inwards and allow for at least some noninflationary expansion of employment demand.

A final measure is assuming increased importance with the realization that government itself does a great deal to generate inflation through legislation that might be thought of as creating artificial supply price increases. A few specific measures were listed above, and they can at times be responsible for significant increases in price levels. In 1977 alone, the net result of all government actions to raise social security taxes, minimum wages, farm price supports, and so forth was estimated to raise price levels by an excess of 1 percentage point—twice as much as an extra percentage point of higher unemployment rates. Those who seriously propose recessions as an antidote to inflation should propose moratoriums on such measures all the more seriously. Now that the short-term financing needs of social security are met and the double indexation problem solved, new employer tax increases should be unnecessary for the next ten or twenty years. For farm supports and minimum wages, there are alternative ways to aid farmers and low-wage workers that do not directly generate higher prices and wages. The matter of environmental and health standards is harder—nobody wants a stable dollar at the cost of polluted air or an unsafe workplace, but it is not radical to propose structural changes in the way standards are set that at least ensure that the price-raising impacts of new standards are considered in forming decisions and that cheaper and slightly less general measures are considered as options. One such structural change would be to give these agencies an inflation budget—they would be allowed to raise price levels only by a fixed percent in a given year—and let them set their own priorities and ask for "budget" requests exactly in the manner that other agencies ask for new spending authority. On the other side, the renaissance in the Civil Aeronautics Board provides a lesson that it is possible for the government to take measures that encourage price cutting as well.

One caveat here is that, just as deficits do not always cause inflation, lower prices are not always accompanied by improved economic welfare. In the area of energy, for example, supplies simply are scarce, and the longer prices are held down artificially, the scarcer they will become. At least in this instance prices must increase, even if some inflation results. Another is perhaps the international value of the dollar. Eventually the United States balance of payments deficit must be eliminated, even if that takes a further decline in the dollar.

Conclusion

This review of some of the commonly discussed ways to stop or reduce inflation has found no panaceas. There appears to be no policy or policy mix that can bring about either a dramatic or a rapid reduction in inflation without causing some other serious problem. However, the measures discussed are not mutually exclusive, and there is no reason why a package could not be put together to bring about a slow and steady reduction in inflation rates. The questions of controls and TIP aside, a sensible package could include elements of all measures—a macro policy that avoids bursts of excess demand inflation, a law requiring that base prices be recorded, attempts to improve the state of the low-wage market by vacancy-filling or demand-switching policies, structural changes in unemployment insurance, and a concerted governmental effort to lower important product prices and wages. Compared with present policies, this strategy would be geared to having the government

146 EDWARD M. GRAMLICH

show it means to stop inflation: it must stop passing direct price-increasing legislation in response to pressures from important interest groups, it must not endorse legislation such as the original Humphrey-Hawkins bill that specifically violates the structures on macro policy, and it could clearly signal its intentions with the price-wage disclosure law. This firm adherence strategy should be given time to yield some reductions in inflation rates. But if the strategy proves to be inadequate, either because the government cannot stick to the regimen or because the private sector does not respond, then it will undoubtedly be necessary to go to something more drastic, such as controls or a TIP plan.

The Anti-inflation Leverage
of Investment

ROGER E. BRINNER

The issue of productivity and inflation is more complex than popular discussion has indicated. Too many discussions operate on the following two premises. First, prices reflect relatively stable markups on labor costs. Labor costs are defined as compensation (wages plus fringes and payroll taxes) per unit of output or, equivalently, compensation per hour divided by output per labor hour. Second, labor compensation increases are independent of movements in output per hour. Wage negotiations are assumed to focus on retrospective and prospective living costs and, to a limited extent, on the scarcity of labor. Productivity enters as a peripheral determinant, if at all. From these premises, it is concluded that any increase in labor productivity will automatically translate into a reduction in price inflation and, as a corollary, that increased capital formation will boost output per worker and thus cut inflation.

There is a lot of truth in this "logical" framework but also much that is questionable. If the two premises were true, the conclusion would have to be accepted, and one could proceed to catalogue and rank alternative policy measures to stimulate capital formation. Unfortunately, these widely accepted premises hide significant errors. It is worth clarifying these points before assessing the still substantial, inflation-control benefits of capital formation.

There are definite conceptual limits to the price side gains to be obtained from additional investment, because the capital costs must eventually be covered by higher profits. Up to a point, these higher profits can be generated by the lower labor or energy unit costs associated with an investment. Beyond this point, extra investment becomes inflationary because it represents a higher total cost method of producing output. Tax incentives for investment can be devised to induce businesses to go too far and make decisions that are not optimal at a national level, though correct at the firm level; but these subsidies will have to be paid for by higher taxes elsewhere or by lower government services.

Thus the shortcoming of the first premise is that prices reflect full costs in a competitive economy, not just labor costs. Productivity enhancement must be thought of in the more general sense of total factor productivity. In this vein, a subsequent section of this essay will report on the extensive benefits to be obtained through additional spending on research and development, a sphere of activity with a very high rate of return.

The second premise is also weak, especially in any long-run context, since changes in the real product per labor hour will be reflected in negotiated wages. In the extreme case in which dollar wages fully and promptly rose to match an increase in real productivity, unit labor costs would be independent of productivity. Then, even if the first premise were true, price inflation would be independent of productivity.

However, it is clear from statistical research that the wage-labor-productivity response is neither full nor prompt. In the short run, wage negotiations do appear to be dominated by factors such as past or expected inflation and unemployment, rather than by real product growth. In the first place, productivity growth is extremely diverse across firms or industries, yet these firms compete for a common pool of labor resources. Wage offers therefore tend to fall in a relatively compact pattern dominated by inflation and labor market tightness. Higher productivity growth can therefore succeed in reducing labor cost pressures.

Finally, it should be noted that some economists would argue that inflation is a purely monetary phenomenon, that the Federal Reserve Board can choose any desired rate of price increase by setting the appropriate rate of money creation. In one sense, this argument is correct; the available liquidity must support the dollar volume of transactions in a market economy (that is, demand must equal supply). The dollar volume growth is the sum of the physical volume growth and price inflation. Given the physical volume growth, the Federal Reserve can set the inflation rate by adjusting the liquidity growth. But there are two problems with this chain of logic. The Federal Reserve's actions can influence the physical volume growth by sending the economy into a recession, obviously affecting current output but also cutting the long-term potential by curtailing capital spending. Equally significant, the Federal Reserve is not free politically to choose any rate of liquidity growth it desires. Because of the short- and long-run implications of monetary policy, the growth of the money supply is nearly as endogenous to the economic system as wage or price changes themselves. In short, money growth is as much a result as a cause of inflation.

Even with these qualifications, the initial premises and conclusion have significant validity, particularly in the short run. Wage increases are dominated by the influences of past price behavior, while pricing patterns correspond to unit labor cost movements. Accelerated growth in labor productivity can therefore drive a larger wedge between wages and prices, providing room for price deceleration. The wedge is expanded if the added labor productivity is not at the expense of too much capital productivity. The most potent device to achieve such progress is research and development.

The Necessity of Research and Development

Research and development (R&D) is the only possible way to generate the knowledge and flexibility required for a business, or indeed a national economy, to progress and stay competitive. This postulate has been only superficially recognized in the past by business and government, but the failure of American enterprises to cope fully with the shocks of the 1970s has led to analyses that should awaken the necessary awareness of the role of R&D.

There are three major reasons why R&D has been overlooked. First, it is particularly difficult to measure any aspect of R&D activities beyond the current year expenditure. In contrast, one can add up current investment in fixed capital, obtain reasonable estimates of its depreciation, and then approximate the value of the accumulated capital stock. The result can be approximately checked with engineering and physical retirement data. Yet how can one locate the stock of knowledge, measure how much is forgotten or is transplanted to other industries, or reliably determine the profitable lifetime of even the successful research efforts of a given firm? How is a largely external observer, an economist, to be expected to form reliable opinions?

Not only do economists have a hard time measuring R&D, but they also fail to appreciate its broad significance for economic performance. Finally, even if they do suspect its impact, they are too willing to assume that the market will ensure that the proper volume of research efforts is forthcoming from the private sector.

What aspects of the economic model lead to this myopia? Several assumptions appear all too often in various strengths in economics, and each could lead an economist or a policymaker to underestimate the dynamism of an economy and hence the critical role played by R&D. It is assumed, for instance, in classical economics that full employment is guaranteed by flexible wages and prices. Given this absence of any institutional rigidity, inflation is purely a monetary phenomenon, even in the short run. Thus, even if unemployment problems arose, policy would quickly be adjusted toward stimulus without fear of igniting inflation. No extra policy levers are needed. World trade is balanced with each country producing according to its comparative advantage. Trade deficits are not a policy constraint. Moreover, within each country and perhaps across countries as well, knowledge is readily available and, if not static, at least predictably expanding. This is true for the full spectrum of opportunities, products, processes, and occupations—not a particularly challenging world for capital, labor, or government. As a result, there are no genuine surprises. To the extent that uncertainty is present, it is in the form of a confidently held probability distribution across known alternatives. The required degree of flexibility of response is thus sharply limited compared to the real world.

Finally, the market works. Private decisions reflect full social costs and benefits: no regulations, taxes, and tariffs; no spillover benefits or costs; and no difficulties of unequal income or wealth distribution that might complicate policy formulation and redirect it from narrow questions of efficiency to broader questions of equity. As a result of each of these assumptions, an economic problem will be misunderstood, a policy will fail because it does not recognize this flaw, and a role for R&D will be ignored. A convincing case can easily be made that greater attention to expenditures on R&D will make a fundamental contribution to controlling inflation, expanding employment, and raising productivity and hence living standards.

An analysis of output, employment, and price behavior in manufacturing industries over the past three decades indicates that high-technology industries have surpassed low-technology industries according to all meaningful aggregate economic indicators. High-technology industries expanded at a 6.7 percent compound rate from 1950 to 1974, compared to 2.3 percent for low-technology industries. Output per employee increased 4.0 percent in advanced industries and only 2.0 percent or less in traditional activities. The favorable labor productivity record is mirrored in the price records of 0.5 percent annual inflation in high-technology compared to 3.0 percent in low-technology firms. The gains in output per worker were not at the expense of employment. The job gains of rapidly modernizing industries surpassed their conservative counterparts by a substantial margin of 2.6 percent to 0.3 percent. The enhanced domestic and international competitive posture generated more than enough demand to expand employment at a rapid pace.

To classify industries into technological strata, an index of research effort (IRE) was created, equal to the average ratio of research and development expenditures to gross product originating. A natural grouping suggested itself and designated that industries with an IRE of 0.07 or better were termed "high technology" and those with an IRE below 0.02 as "low technology."

National Science Foundation (NSF) data are available at a reasonable level of disaggregation for total research and development spending by industry, and the Bureau of Economic Analysis provides corresponding data on real and nominal product, prices, and employment. Examination of these ratios suggested a breakdown into high, low, and mixed technology. The line between high and mixed technology was defined as 0.07, the average ratio of research and development expenditures to output for all of manufacturing. Similarly, the division between mixed and low technology was defined as 0.02, the average ratio of total expenditures for research and development to the gross national product.

In theory, monetary and fiscal policy should be able to keep the economy on a relatively full-employment path, buffering outside shocks to keep long-run employment growth approximately equal to expansion in the labor force. If such a theory were accurate, the creation and adoption of high technology would have no impact on aggregate job creation, and the exclusive role of new technology would be the enhancement of per capita living standards. On the other hand, even a casual observation of economic history suggests additional employment benefits of new products and processes.

Advanced industries generate innovative products for which there are high-growth markets at home and abroad. This product demand leads these firms to attract workers from other sectors of the economy, employing them in more productive occupations. If the economy is near full employment, high-technology industries primarily perform the function of reallocating labor to more effective uses, rather than expanding national employment; if slack does exist in the job market, the growth industries can be expected to increase domestic employment.

It can also be argued that high-technology industries have a significant, additional impact on employment as a result of their contribution to price stability. It is unquestionably easier for macro policymakers to counter recessionary shocks if they are not simultaneously challenged to curb inflation. As noted earlier, the price record of industries with a strong research and development effort is clearly superior to those with weak research efforts. Thus, indirect cyclical benefits enhance the more obvious long-run gains. As for employment growth rates, high-technology industries have a clear margin of superiority over the low-technology industries, as figure 1 indicates. The contrasts are equally sharp when labor productivity increases are examined as in figure 2. The trend rate of increase in real output per employee of 2.3

FIGURE 1

Compound Annual Growth Rate of Employment

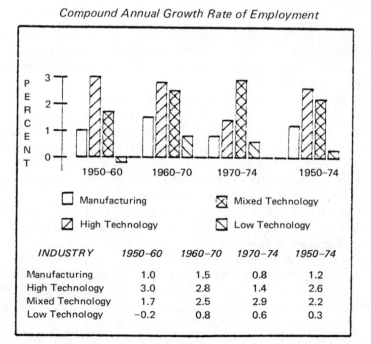

INDUSTRY	1950-60	1960-70	1970-74	1950-74
Manufacturing	1.0	1.5	0.8	1.2
High Technology	3.0	2.8	1.4	2.6
Mixed Technology	1.7	2.5	2.9	2.2
Low Technology	-0.2	0.8	0.6	0.3

FIGURE 2

Compound Annual Growth Rate of Output Per Employee in Real Terms

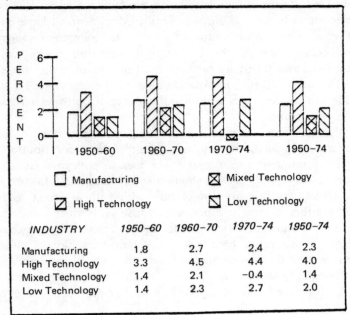

INDUSTRY	1950–60	1960–70	1970–74	1950–74
Manufacturing	1.8	2.7	2.4	2.3
High Technology	3.3	4.5	4.4	4.0
Mixed Technology	1.4	2.1	−0.4	1.4
Low Technology	1.4	2.3	2.7	2.0

percent a year for all manufacturing was led by 4.0 percent a year in high-technology industries. The manufacturing average was substantially depressed by the 1.4 and 2.0 percent improvement in labor productivity in industries with mixed or low research efforts.

Figure 3 demonstrates that the aggregate effect of increases in employment and productivity is, by definition, reflected in the increase in the rate of real growth of high-technology industries. The new products of advanced research have generated a ready market at home and abroad. Capital equipment embodying advanced technology is a leading United States export sector, permitting the United States to import necessary raw materials to enhance the living standards of its trading partners and its own.

Finally, as figure 4 indicates, high-technology industries have shown increases in employment while curbing inflation. During the 1950s, the output prices of advanced industries rose at only 1.6 percent a year, compared to a 3.0 percent average for low- and mixed-technology industries. The 1960s presented an even sharper differential: −0.8 percent (high) compared to 1.4 percent (mixed) and 2.0 percent (low). The margin of superiority rose again during the early 1970s. High-technology industries generated inflation averaging only 1.3 percent a year, while prices in the mixed sector accelerated to a 7.5 percent pace and those in the low sector increased to a 5.3 percent pace. The

FIGURE 3

Compound Annual Rate of Growth of Output in Real Terms

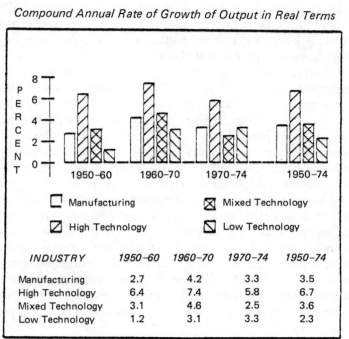

INDUSTRY	1950–60	1960–70	1970–74	1950–74
Manufacturing	2.7	4.2	3.3	3.5
High Technology	6.4	7.4	5.8	6.7
Mixed Technology	3.1	4.6	2.5	3.6
Low Technology	1.2	3.1	3.3	2.3

FIGURE 4

Compound Annual Rate of Growth of Prices

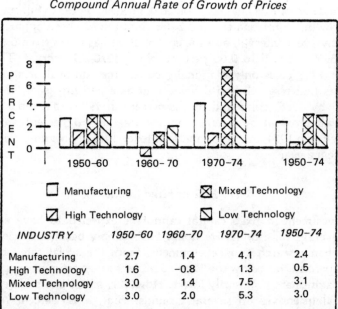

INDUSTRY	1950–60	1960–70	1970–74	1950–74
Manufacturing	2.7	1.4	4.1	2.4
High Technology	1.6	–0.8	1.3	0.5
Mixed Technology	3.0	1.4	7.5	3.1
Low Technology	3.0	2.0	5.3	3.0

favorable price behavior of high-technology industries is not an inevitable result of rapid increases in labor productivity; costs for fixed capital and R&D expenses must also be met. However, the rate of return has clearly been sufficiently large to keep total cost increases at a minimum and thus to hold price increases at very low annual rates.

Many economists have sought to quantify the rate of return to research and development expenditures. A small data base and the absence of an observable capital stock of accumulated knowledge have precluded precise estimation, but a consensus appears to exist on a number of points: the private rate of profit derived from R&D expenditures is substantially above the return on traditional investments; conceptual and data limitations make any precise estimate hazardous, but an approximate figure of 15 to 20 percent emerges from several studies, compared to the usual 10 to 15 percent return on fixed capital investments; and the private return to the firm initially sponsoring the research is only a fraction—perhaps one-third to two-thirds—of the total return received by the economy. Through further analysis at the macroeconomic level, the social and private rate of return has been estimated to be at least 17 percent and perhaps as high as 35 percent. The margin between the total and private returns reflects the spillover benefits not appropriable by the sponsoring firm. Patents and licensing agreements are imperfect; some research needs further development that the initial firm does not choose to pursue, but it is followed up by other firms.

The relatively high return implies that the sharply declining share of GNP devoted to R&D since the mid-1960s has had and will continue to have a serious negative impact on aggregate productivity growth and inflation. During the past two decades, R&D has contributed 0.3 percent a year to full-employment, capacity growth. Unfortunately, a 0.2 deterioration has been apparent in each successive five-year interval, and the contribution has fallen from 0.63 percent in the 1955–60 interval to 0.05 percent in the 1970–75 interval. The official outlook for 1975–85 is only marginally better: the National Science Foundation projects that research and development as a percentage of GNP will be 2.0 percent by 1985, compared to 2.2 percent in 1976, that industrial R&D spending will grow at an average annual rate of 3.5 percent adjusted for inflation between 1974 and 1985, and that federal R&D programs will increase by 2.6 percent a year.

The Role of Fixed Capital

Greater investment in fixed capital cannot be expected to have equal anti-inflation leverage on a dollar-for-dollar basis simply because it has been less neglected than research and development. Since the social rate of return is close to 12 percent, far below the 17 to 35 percent range estimated for R&D, the total cost savings are necessarily lower. However, a case can still be made for fixed capital incentives on several grounds. First, a 12 percent real return is probably more than the appropriate public discount rate; almost anyone would choose $1.12 next year at the expense of $1.00 this year, particularly when the $1.12 is indexed to the intervening inflation. Second, it has been well documented that capital taxation is perversely, accidentally severe when prices are increasing rapidly. Finally, the greater the level of fixed capital investment, the more rapidly new technology from R&D can be embodied in production processes.

Two or three years ago, the avoidance of premature bottlenecks would have been a fourth argument for fixed capital incentives. Many writers worried that industrial capacity would be fully utilized in this recovery long before labor markets indicated full employment. In fact, the post-1975 growth has seen relatively balanced absorption of fixed capital and labor.

Unfortunately, this balanced absorption reflects unusually strong employment gains necessitated by weak growth in labor productivity. Elsewhere, the author has analyzed the source of this phenomenon and found the answer in exceedingly weak fixed and R&D capital spending over the last decade. Only a partial reversal is to be expected in the 1980s. While fixed capital expansion may have a comparatively limited leverage on inflation in contrast to R&D, its magnitude establishes it as the fundamental determinant of labor productivity and hence per capita living standards.

Capital spending fell sharply during the last recession, and the fixed investment share of total demand made a delayed recovery. Low profits, high energy costs, high-risk premiums, and the recent fiscal-monetary policy mix were all contributing factors. In most cases, a low-profit share of national income could not be explained by low capacity utilization rates; a downtrend had been visible since the late 1960s. The most fundamental explanation was that productivity growth had decelerated universally but real wage growth had now slowed by an equal magnitude. The investment impact of the resultant cash flow squeeze was augmented by a reversal in the historic pattern of capital goods inflation falling below consumer price inflation.

The anticipated rate of return on labor-saving investment would be quite high were it not for energy, risks, and policy. First, recent research supports the hypothesis that capital and energy are complements, not substitutes, and that the actions of the Organization of Petroleum Exporting Countries have sharply cut the optimal capital intensity of industrial economies. In other words, the incentive to invest in energy conservation or discovery projects (such as insulation, computer-controlled climates, and costly offshore drilling rigs) may be more than offset by the disincentive to purchase energy-using machinery elsewhere in the economy. Second, the turbulence of the 1970s, with food and energy price explosions, volatile exchange rates, and vulnerable final demand, has inevitably made business more cautious about capacity expansion at any particular expected rate of return. Finally, inflation has led governments to stimulate with fiscal policy—particularly spending—and to restrain with monetary policy. High interest costs resulting from this mix undeniably curb investment appetites.

Most respected forecasts envision some resolution of these problems and a gradual recovery of fixed investment. Growth is proceeding, though at a mildly erratic pace, and final demand expectations will be raised. The real price of energy is predicted to be essentially flat at its current level, and policy is being tilted toward wage restraint and tax cuts rather than toward government spending to attempt a traditional and quick but temporary fix of employment problems. Monetary policies are as expansive as inflation fears will permit.

Policy Prescriptions

The most efficient inflation control program in terms of tax dollars foregone through fiscal stimulus can be obtained from strong tax incentives for research and development. If the total return is in fact twice the private return to the initial investor, a 25 percent tax credit for R&D wages, supplies, and fixed capital spending can be justified. If the investing firm immediately writes off the expenses of the project, this would approximately double the anticipated private return, thereby equating it to the full national return, as shown in table 1. Revising the illustration to include alternative tax rates, or to allow only

TABLE 1

The Impact of a 25 percent R&D Tax Credit on the Private Rate of Return

Cash Flow	Cash Flow Pattern					Private Rate of Return
	Year: 1	2	3	4	Etc.	
Gross flows	−100	20	20	20		20%
− Associated taxes	−50	10	10	10		
= Net without credit	−50	10	10	10		20%
+ 25% R&D tax credit	25	0	0	0		
= Net with credit	−25	10	10	10		40%

Note: For simplicity, assume that annual gross project cost is $100 in year 1 and nothing thereafter, annual gross project return is $20 in year 2 and beyond; and the incremental profit tax rate is 50 percent.

depreciation rather than expensing of the fixed capital component of an R&D project, would naturally modify the estimated private returns, but the same qualitative conclusion would remain. A tax credit of a substantial magnitude is called for to lead the private entrepreneur to make the socially optimal decision.

This argument can be amplified by recognizing that society can effectively pool the risks of diverse R&D activities to reduce average risk exposure. The individual firm or inventor can only do this to a limited extent and will therefore require a notably higher anticipated return on R&D projects than on typical fixed capital projects. Because the risk is reduced for the nation as a whole, a subsidy is again indicated to provide the proper private incentive.

Although defensible on efficiency grounds, as dramatic a tax credit rate as 25 percent is likely to draw substantial opposition since both technical and equity issues suggest a more moderate step, such as expanding coverage of the current 10 percent investment tax credit (ITC) to all R&D expenses. First, it would be difficult to draw a legal line of demarcation between R&D-related fixed capital spending and other spending that already qualifies for the standard 10 percent ITC. Second, sharply accelerating the transition of the industrial base to a high-technology mode could create short-run employment problems—shortages of scientific personnel and surpluses of workers in firms unwilling or unable to take advantage of the incentive. A related problem is that of the stockholders in low-technology industries who will see their wealth diminished. If a higher credit is desired, comprehensive assistance modeled after current foreign trade adjustment policies would be appropriate.

The investment tax credit is probably the preferred incentive. In terms of extra investment per dollar of tax revenue loss, the consensus of the economics profession is the following ranking of investment incentives:

Best: Investment tax credit
Middle: Accelerated depreciation
Worst: Corporate rate cut

Moreover, the ITC could be defined on an incremental basis to maximize its effect. In this instance, the credit would be granted at a higher rate on R&D beyond a firm's average (relative to sales) for some reference period. Accelerated depreciation is already permitted for some R&D activities, with expensing of some components and standard accelerated depreciation of fixed capital components. The principal alternative to the tax approach would be direct grants to research institutes, universities, and firms. The associated bureaucratic oversight is a sufficient liability to imply preference for tax incentives.

Beyond this specific suggestion, a more general prescription is to change substantially the national monetary-fiscal policy mix. Simulations with the Data Resources, Inc., model of the United States economy indicate that expenditures restraint offset by monetary ease would produce a final demand mix significantly slanted toward investment. In this case, the extra liquidity provided by the Federal Reserve would support a higher volume of real output rather than a higher price level.

These proposals to stimulate investment are the most effective route to expanding productivity and living standards. They would achieve the long-term goal of controlling inflation without subjecting the economy to recurrent recessions. Stringent monetary policy, one alternative currently popular in the financial press, might have a slight effect on the current inflation but would extract a heavy toll in foregone investment as businesses cut back in response to vanishing final demand and high financing costs. An equally misguided approach would be to attempt a sudden balancing of the federal budget by, for example, raising payroll taxes to put social security on a so-called insurance basis. On one hand, the associated skyrocketing labor costs would provoke further inflation. On the other hand, final demand would be so depressed that capital spending would again sharply decline, rather than rising to absorb the presumed increment to national savings. The best mixture combines selected investment tax incentives, tight federal spending constraints, and more liberal monetary policy.

The last five years attest that the United States is an open economy competing intensively with other advanced industrialized nations and with emerging industrial countries such as Korea. World comparative advantage is in constant flux, and unless the United States continues to enhance its technology it will be faced with low domestic productivity growth and a declining dollar. The latter would be a straightforward reflection of a diminishing quality advantage by the United States that would need to be offset by lower foreign prices for its products. Such a development directly implies a lower standard of living relative to those parts of the industrial world success-fully embracing modern technology. Attention to high technology growth is by no means a secondary matter for the United States.

Another version of this essay with quantitative details is available from the author.

Tax Incentive Proposals

HENRY C. WALLICH

During the twelve years that disruptive inflation has plagued the United States, its virulence has varied from as high as 12.0 percent in the fourth quarter of 1974 to as low as 1.5 percent in the second quarter of 1967. But the experience has made clear that no one has learned to live with inflation. Increasingly, inflation is seen for what it is—a serious addiction that gradually undermines the vitality and even the viability of the addict.

While inflation is being forecast for the indefinite future at a rate close to its present level, there is no reason to believe that it will stabilize if it is left alone. Inflation has shown itself in recent years to be highly inflexible downwards. It has shown no similar inflexibility upwards. Any one of a number of factors could send inflation spiraling again. Pressure of demand on limited manufacturing capacity, a major wage breakthrough resulting from special circumstances that nevertheless could set a pattern, food prices, or oil prices could trigger off higher inflation that would then work its way into wages and become resistant to any decline. Such a ratchet mechanism is a real threat. Further acceleration of inflation almost certainly would, after a short interval, lead to renewed increases in unemployment. Thus there is no other choice but to try to reduce unemployment and inflation simultaneously.

Largely because of concerns like these, a consensus has developed that the economy must be allowed to grow at only a moderate rate. Idle resources, human and material, can be absorbed only gradually. Moreover, the noninflationary limits to that absorption leave a distressingly high margin of unused resources even in the long run.

Incomes policies have been suggested as a means of curtailing inflation more rapidly. Generally, however, incomes policies are associated with wage and price controls, or at least are seen as a step in that direction. This concern has helped create an interest in a tax-based incomes policy (TIP) that cannot be charged with that defect because it is specifically designed to give full effect to market forces. While numerous versions of TIP exist, their common characteristic is a reliance on the tax system as a means of inducing more moderate behavior of wages and prices. The Carter administration's proposal for real wage insurance is an example of one possible version of the scheme. It would be worthwhile to discuss a variant that was developed by Sidney Weintraub of the University of Pennsylvania and the author.

The essence of this plan consists of a tax penalty on firms granting wage increases that exceed a guideline. The restraint is on wages rather than on prices. But the tax is paid by the firm; in this way, evenhandedness is maintained. The plan can be extended to include a restraint on profits if that is regarded as necessary. To begin with, however, the adequacy of a plan that focuses on wages combined with a corporate tax should be explained.

A considerable body of research indicates that in the long run prices are basically determined by wages. Nonwage factors such as those mentioned earlier—demand pressures and nonwage costs—may initiate price movements; since wages and other labor compensation amount to 75 percent of the GNP, however, wages are unavoidably the principal factor in prices. A deceleration of wage increases, therefore, will necessarily restrain price increases.

If prices follow wages, wage restraint will not lead to any reduction in real wage increases. Given productivity gains of, say, 3 percent, labor will obtain the same increase in real wages with a 5 percent wage increase and 2 percent inflation as it would with a 9 percent wage increase and 6 percent inflation. The gains from productivity are all that the economy can give to labor, unless they are to be taken away from someone else. These gains will go to labor at any level of inflation, so long as the gap between wages and prices—as it normally does—equals productivity gains. Wage restraint, therefore, imposes no sacrifice on labor in real terms. On the contrary, by reducing the threat of inflation, wage restraint would permit the economy to move more rapidly to lower levels of unemployment, thereby benefiting both labor and all others who share in the national income.

A tax to be imposed on firms granting excessive wage increases could take one of several forms. It could be imposed as an increase in the corporate income tax, as a payroll tax, through disallowance of wage increases as tax deductions, or in other forms. The plan could also be structured in the form of a tax reduction for firms avoiding excess wage increases.

Disallowance of excess wage increases as tax deductions has the advantage of having already been on the statute books after World War II and after the Korean war. An increase in the corporate income tax has the advantage that it could easily be scaled in proportion to the magnitude of the excess. This would help to make the penalty or threat of a penalty effective while largely eliminating controversies over marginal excesses. A rise in the corporate income tax, moreover, could be shifted less easily than a payroll tax or denial of deductibility. On the other hand, it might adversely affect the ability of the firm to invest.

The setting of the wage guideline requires a governmental decision. A maximum wage increase equal to long-run productivity gains plus half the current rate of inflation might be appropriate. The guideline would in no way interfere with the functioning of the market, since firms and unions would be entirely free to make settlements above or below it. Thus the concern that the guideline would become a first step on the way to a system of controls would be unwarranted. Likewise there seems to be no reason for expecting the "maximum to become the minimum," since the guideline would not represent a maximum. The guideline would be lowered periodically as inflation was reduced.

A good case can be made for subjecting only a limited number of large corporations to the guideline and tax. In a period of inflation like the present, which is maintained because one high wage settlement leads to another and because there is no excess demand for labor, moderation in the settlements of large firms and some consequent slowing of the price trend would probably lead to moderation for most employers. Limiting the plan to large firms would greatly ease administrative complexities. However, an alternative and opposite procedure could also be envisaged—to cover unincorporated as well as incorporated businesses.

The fact that laws disallowing excess wage increases under the wage and price control legislations following World War II and the Korean war have been on the books suggests that the technical problems of measuring excess wage increases have been considered by the legislature and not found intractable. There are, of course, a wide range of technical problems to be resolved. In an economy characterized by multicorporate enterprises, how is the tax-paying unit to be defined—as a plant, a corporate entity, or an entire conglomerate? Are the excesses to be measured by total payroll and total employment or by individual categories of workers, allowing for overtime and fringe benefits that include deferred compensation, cost-of-living adjustments, and health insurance? How are new firms or firms with losses, multiyear labor contracts, or numerous subsidiaries to be dealt with? Should the TIP penalty be applied for one year only, for a fixed multiyear period, or for a lengthy or indefinite period?

A large number of decisions will have to be made in writing the tax regulations. This is the same analysis, however, that firms and unions engage in during wage bargaining sessions and that the Council on Wage and Price Stability must also undertake. Furthermore, the initial evaluation of a wage package, which would form the basis for a pay-as-you-go approach to the tax, can be revised on eventual audit by the Internal Revenue Service. Since the tax penalty would be proportionate to the degree of infringement of the guideline, minor differences between the taxpayer and the tax authorities would not involve large amounts of tax and could be compromised, as are many differences arising in tax audits.

It was noted earlier that the wage guideline proposal does not contain a corresponding restraint on prices because prices can be expected to follow wages. However, if the evidence supporting this view is not generally accepted, a supplementary device could be introduced that would serve to restrain profits and not prices. A failure of prices to follow wages would tend to show itself in a corresponding change in profits. Labor would have a legitimate right to expect that no special benefits for profits should emerge if it accepts a wage guideline. To ensure that this expectation is realized, the corporate income tax could be raised to prevent the rise in total after-tax profits from exceeding some historical relationship to the gross national product (GNP). This increase would be proportionate to the "excess profits" of the corporate sector as a whole but not related to the profits of any particular corporation.

As a practical matter, such a tax increase would probably never be triggered. But if it were, the increase in the corporate tax could hardly amount to more than a few percentage points. Such a tax would be an "incomes policy" in the proper sense of the term, since it would be specifically designed to deal with income shares. The setting of a profit share, presumably in the light of historical experience and the need for business capital expenditures, would be one of the difficult decisions to be made under this approach.

To the extent that the tax measures proposed here are cast in the form of tax increases for exceeding a guideline rather than tax reductions withheld, some incremental revenues would be collected. Their magnitude would depend on the nature of the guidelines set and on the magnitude of penalties in relation to violations. These additional revenues could be utilized to reduce the income tax burden. Given the uncertainty of these additional revenues, however, a precise link could probably not be established.

So long as these arrangements do not involve carryovers from the operative period of the plan, they should be terminated when inflation ends. It might be better to reintroduce the scheme if inflation should revive thereafter rather than to perpetuate it at a time when it is not needed. Even after termination of the plan, a better understanding of the role of wage increases in price determination should prevail and should make it easier to avoid renewed bursts of inflation.

Alternatively, the arrangements could be kept alive even during a period of stable prices as a means of permanently facilitating lower rates of unemployment. It is the pressure of strong demand for labor that, at low levels of unemployment, tends to induce excessive wage increases. The threat of such increases, implying demand-pull inflation, in turn prevents the adoption of fiscal and monetary policies that would lead to such lower levels of unemployment. If the wage-increasing effect is restrained by a tax-based incomes policy, the achievement of permanently lower levels of unemployment should be within reach.

It should be clear, however, that TIP cannot serve as a counterpoise to, or justification for, overly stimulative fiscal and monetary policies. The rate of growth of the money supply would have to be reduced in line with diminishing inflation and eventually would have to be stabilized at a level consonant with the rate of real growth and the trend in velocity. Fiscal policy would have to limit the government's demands on the credit markets to whatever could be financed with that rate of money growth at stable prices and interest rates consistent with full employment.

Incomes Policies

JOEL POPKIN

The search for a set of incomes policies to reconcile the objectives of full employment and price stability has intensified recently in the United States. The reason is that over the past year inflation in the United States has risen to a higher rate and shows no signs of falling in any fundamental way. This acceleration has occurred in a world environment in which inflation rates in most other industrialized countries have remained constant or have decelerated. This recent behavior of inflation in the United States has resulted in a substantial decline in the exchange value of the dollar, particularly with respect to the German mark, the Swiss franc, and the Japanese yen.

Periodic efforts to come to grips with inflation frequently result in the reinvention of the wheel as old policies are tried again. However, the recent search has brought to the fore a new approach to controlling inflation. It is based on the use of the tax system; major proposals regarding this approach have been advanced by Henry Wallich, Sidney Weintraub, and Arthur Okun. Given the conjunction of a renewed search for tools to combat inflation and the innovation of a new set of potential tools, this essay will set forth a view of the structural problems in the United States that by limiting the effectiveness of traditional anti-inflation tools motivate the search for new ones; assess the effectiveness both of previously articulated (and implemented) incomes policies and also of the newly conceptualized ones; and present recommendations based on the structural problems described and the analysis of proposals to combat them.

That there is a need to introduce incomes policies at all is frequently interpreted as evidence of the failure of the science of economics, if not of economists as well. This view is unfortunate, because the problem lies not so much with the body of economic theory as with the way in which it is articulated. Supporters of the two leading theories—monetarist and Keynesian—purporting to explain how changes in the aggregate price level are determined have spent too much time trying, inconclusively at that, to demonstrate the absolute validity of their views. What is not studied adequately, and therefore remains largely unarticulated, is the length and other characteristics of the time path by which these policies can produce the results ascribed to them by their champions.

The ways in which these policies work depend on the structure of the economies on which they are imposed. The fact that for the United States most monetarist models indicate that it takes about twenty-four months for a change in the money supply to affect prices, and that in the interim it will affect output and employment, says something about the structure of the United States economy. Similarly, as Lawrence Klein said in his 1978 presidential address to the American Economic Association, the failure of Keynesian models to predict the acceleration of inflation suggests that such models do not adequately take into account the detailed structure of the economy. In particular, they have failed to specify what determines supply and demand and their rates of change in specific markets, especially intermediate markets through which goods pass on their way to being counted as part of final demand of the gross national product (GNP).

The need for a separate policy to control inflation should not serve to indicate that either Keynesian or monetarist policy is wrong in its predictions about the long-run results of fiscal and monetary policy; the evidence is not all in and may never be. Their results take time to appear, and the intervening costs may be greater than the body politic is willing to tolerate.

Structure of the United States Economy

What are these structural characteristics of the United States economy that insulate it for an intolerably long time against the anti-inflationary stance of monetary and fiscal policy? There are two of primary importance. One has to do with product markets, and therefore prices, and the other with labor markets and wages.

Gardner Ackley was probably the first to articulate the consequences for the overall inflation rate of an economy in which prices in some sectors responded in the short run to changes in demand, while prices in others seemed to be characterized by "cost-pass-through" behavior. That is, in some sectors, margins or markups over unit costs increase and decrease with demand, while in others they are fairly constant. Ackley and Charles Schultze, whose work appeared at almost the same time, argued that a policy of expansion would first raise prices in demand-sensitive sectors. This, in turn, raised costs in industries purchasing materials from demand sensitive sectors, which were then passed through with constant markup. Agriculture and some of the other primary producing industries were identified as "demand-sensitive" industries.

In recent research the author has identified more exactly the sectors characterized by demand-sensitive margins and those characterized by cost-pass-through behavior. The results are not startlingly different from early characterizations. It turns out that the price behavior of industries extracting raw commodities and those producing primary manufactures—those manufactures that are the first stage in the transformation of raw commodities to finished products, in the main—can be characterized as demand sensitive. The price behavior of the bulk of the remainder of the economy—processor of semimanufactures and producers and distributors of finished goods and services—is characterized largely by the pass-through into prices of cost increases, subject to a fairly constant markup. In other words, the closer an industry is to final demand, the less likely is its margin to be responsive to changes in demand.

Since the first impact of restrictive monetary or fiscal policy designed to slow inflation is on industries at or near final demand, the first impact of a reduction in money demand is on a set of industries whose prices in the short run are insensitive to such reduction. These industries tend to keep prices where they are and bear the brunt of such restrictive policies through a reduction in sales or production volume. It is only when such declines in sales and production are passed back, through the stages of processing, to those industries in which margins are demand sensitive that price relief begins to occur. This process can take some time; its interim product is a reduction in real output and in employment. The public will not long endure these consequences, and policymakers are pressured to reverse the policies that brought them about before they begin to have any pronounced effect on margins. If it were true that margins became more responsive to demand the closer an industry was to final demand, the overall responsiveness of prices to changes in monetary and fiscal policy would be much greater, and smaller reductions in output to bring about a slowdown in prices would be required.

The second aspect of the United States economy bearing on the intractability of inflation has to do with the behavior of wages. Table 1 contains annual rates of change in average hourly earnings in manufacturing for nine industrialized countries for which such data were available from 1960 to 1977. For this analysis, it would have been preferable to use a wage measure that reflected straight-time wages better than average hourly earnings that reflect cyclical swings in premium pay for overtime and in the mix of employment between high- and low-wage industries. But such data are not available on an international basis, so a measure of average earnings is used to approximate wages. For each country, several summary statistics are calculated and appear at the bottom of the table. One is the mean, or average, rate of change during the eighteen-year period. Another is the average absolute year-to-year change in the rate of change of wages. This measure shows the extent to which wage changes have fluctuated from year to year. A third statistic is the ratio of the latter mean to the former mean. It measures wage rate change flexibility, the observed degree to which wage rate increases can be expected to accelerate or decelerate in the typical year relative to the typical speed at which they are rising generally. This ratio is termed wage flexibility. Wage flexibility in the United States is the lowest relative to that of the other countries in the table. It is about half that

TABLE 1

Percentage Change in Average Earnings in Manufacturing,
Selected Industrial Countries, 1960-77

Year Ending Fourth Quarter	Australia	Canada	France	Germany	Italy	Japan	Norway	United Kingdom	United States
1960	4.1	3.4	8.0	9.3	5.0	7.1	2.2	6.6	3.0
1961	3.4	3.3	7.7	7.5	4.8	13.8	10.6	4.6	2.9
1962	0.1	1.6	8.9	8.7	13.7	6.6	5.8	4.3	2.9
1963	2.1	4.8	8.2	6.6	13.3	12.7	5.5	2.8	2.8
1964	5.3	3.0	6.6	8.6	15.4	10.6	6.9	5.1	2.7
1965	2.5	5.9	5.7	6.6	5.5	6.9	8.1	7.1	3.9
1966	5.4	5.6	6.0	6.2	3.9	13.6	7.5	5.0	3.8
1967	4.5	7.9	5.9	4.1	4.6	13.2	8.3	5.4	4.9
1968	9.2	7.3	16.5	5.6	3.3	15.6	10.3	7.4	7.0
1969	3.1	8.0	8.1	9.8	10.1	16.5	7.0	5.9	5.4
1970	5.3	8.4	10.9	15.2	22.6	18.3	15.2	12.9	4.1
1971	14.1	8.7	11.3	7.5	11.8	11.9	9.4	11.2	6.9
1972	9.0	8.0	11.5	8.2	13.0	17.6	9.5	16.8	7.4
1973	14.3	9.9	15.5	10.2	28.7	26.0	11.0	12.2	7.8
1974	35.6	16.5	20.6	12.3	20.6	23.7	21.0	21.9	9.6
1975	11.4	12.9	15.9	7.7	23.0	9.6	17.6	29.3	7.3
1976	14.1	12.6	14.9	5.8	28.3	13.0	16.5	12.1	8.2
1977	14.8[a]	11.2	12.0	7.4	23.6	8.1	8.7[a]	3.7	8.8
(1) Average year to year change	8.8	7.7	10.8	8.2	14.0	13.6	10.1	9.7	5.5
(2) Average change of year to year changes without regard to direction	5.7	1.7	2.7	2.5	5.4	5.3	3.6	4.5	1.0
(3) Earnings flexibility (2) ÷ (1)	0.65	0.22	0.25	0.31	0.39	0.39	0.36	0.46	0.18

[a]Preliminary, first three quarters at annual rates.

of the average for the eight other countries. The same calculations, for the same countries and years, were made for prices and appear in table 2. Price flexibility in the United States is not lower than that of these countries; in fact, it is somewhat greater than their average. Given its very low wage flexibility and average price flexibility, the flexibility of prices with respect to that of wages in the United States is the highest of any of these countries. (The ratio of price flexibility to wage flexibility is found in the last row of table 2.)

Why, then, are wages in the United States less flexible than in most other major industrial countries? The answer lies in the fact that wage bargaining is more decentralized than in the other countries and is staggered over time, reflecting the fact that many important labor contracts run for overlapping three-year periods. Countries displaying the highest degree of wage flexibility are those in which a few labor leaders bargain for a large part of the labor force, and bargaining takes place annually for the most part. In such countries, particularly those in which labor is part of the government, it is possible to reach agreements that provide for rather marked deceleration or acceleration in rates of wage increases from year to year. This is not the case in the United States. In the United States wage flexibility is highest in transportation and public utilities, mining, and contract construction where either one or just a few unions represent a sizable proportion of workers and contracts are multiyear, or bargaining is less concentrated but largely annual, as in construction. In the re-

TABLE 2

Percentage Change in Consumer Prices, Selected Industrial Countries, 1960-77

Year Ending Fourth Quarter	Australia	Canada	France	Germany	Italy	Japan	Norway	United Kingdom	United States
1960	4.6	0.7	3.5	0.8	1.5	3.2	1.6	1.8	1.3
1961	0.8	0.4	3.7	2.7	2.6	8.2	3.1	4.3	0.8
1962	0.1	1.7	4.2	2.7	5.7	4.5	4.5	2.5	1.3
1963	0.5	1.7	5.3	3.1	7.6	8.2	1.4	2.2	1.4
1964	4.0	1.8	2.4	2.5	5.9	5.1	8.5	4.4	1.1
1965	4.0	2.8	2.5	4.0	3.4	6.1	2.6	4.5	1.9
1966	2.4	3.9	2.8	2.8	2.1	4.1	3.8	3.8	3.5
1967	3.2	3.8	3.3	0.7	3.7	5.7	4.9	2.1	2.8
1968	2.6	4.2	5.3	3.3	0.8	4.5	3.5	5.6	4.7
1969	2.9	4.6	5.8	1.9	4.0	5.9	3.4	5.2	5.8
1970	4.9	2.1	5.2	4.0	5.3	7.8	12.0	7.7	5.6
1971	7.1	4.1	5.8	5.7	4.7	5.4	4.9	9.3	3.5
1972	4.5	5.2	6.9	6.2	7.2	4.5	8.3	7.7	3.4
1973	13.3	9.1	8.3	7.3	11.6	16.4	7.7	10.3	8.4
1974	16.2	11.9	15.0	6.4	24.7	24.6	9.5	18.2	12.1
1975	14.0	10.2	9.9	5.6	11.6	8.5	11.6	25.3	7.3
1976	14.4	5.9	9.9	3.8	21.1	9.4	8.4	15.0	5.0
1977	9.3	9.1	9.2	3.7	15.5	6.2	9.0	13.1	6.7
(1) Average year to year change	6.0	4.6	6.1	3.7	7.7	7.7	6.0	7.9	4.3
(2) Average change of year to year changes without regard to direction	2.2	1.5	1.4	1.2	4.1	4.0	3.0	2.9	1.6
(3) Price flexibility (2) ÷ (1)	0.37	0.33	0.23	0.32	0.53	0.52	0.50	0.37	0.37
(4) Ratio, price flexibility to earnings flexibility	0.57	1.50	0.92	1.03	1.36	1.33	1.39	0.80	2.06

maining industries, which are characterized by decentralized bargaining, wage flexibility is only 60 percent of that of the other three, either because there are many unions such as in manufacturing or widespread decentralization as in the service sectors.

It is also interesting to note that the overall decentralization and staggering overtime of wage bargaining results in a lower wage flexibility measure for non-farm wages in the total private economy than for the average of its seven major industrial sectors. This finding is consistent with the view that today's wage bargains are influenced by the settlements achieved by other groups of workers in the recent past. In other words, there is a wage structure that from time to time gets out of line and causes pressures, sometimes called coercive comparisons, which result in a particular group getting a large, catch-up wage increase even though economic conditions may not seem to support it at the time. Such leap-frogging in specific industries in particular years leads to the phenomenon that wage flexibility for the total private nonfarm economy is less than the sum of its parts.

These results show that sizable year-to-year changes in wage rate increases are achievable for the most part only when a few actors represent a large number of workers or bargaining takes place annually. As a result of relatively decentralized bargaining and the prevalence of contracts of more than one year's duration with staggered expiration dates, aggregate wages tend to behave like a twenty-six-month average, accelerating and decelerating only slowly. This inertia has been the key element of the structure of the United States economy that has thwarted attempts to control inflation by monetary and fiscal policy. It limits the ability of policymakers to reduce dramatically the rate of inflation in order to create and reinforce expectations that inflation can slow as well as accelerate.

Given these key elements in the structure of the United States economy that impinge on the ability of monetary and fiscal policy to control inflation, it can be argued that there is a need for another set of policies—incomes policies—designed specifically to combat inflation, working within the framework of traditional macro tools.

An Assessment of Various Proposals

In turning to an examination of incomes policies, both ones that have been tried before and those conceived recently, it is useful to set forth standards for an effective policy against which various proposals can be evaluated. The first criterion and substantive feature required of an incomes policy is that it bring down the rate of inflation, while leaving relative prices, and therefore resource allocation, unchanged. The second criterion, political in nature, is that it be capable of enactment, which is largely dependent on whether the policy exacerbates industrial and political conflict. Frequently, these two requirements are interactive.

A third criterion, perhaps more subjective than the first two, is also important: an effective incomes policy must show clearly discernible results in a relatively short period of time. It is difficult to maintain the active support of the affected parties without demonstrating that their efforts are worthwhile. The most difficult obstacle to achieving this is wage inertia.

It is appropriate to evaluate various incomes policies in the light of these criteria. While there are a number of variants, incomes policies can be analyzed in four groups as they apply to the United States since the end of World War II.

"Voluntary micro policies," the selective use of persuasion by the government, are usually focused at sectors where wage and price behavior is thought to exert a strong influence throughout the economy. It is sometimes done openly, usually in an attempt to solidify public support, but it has been done privately as well. Some argue, however, that behind-the-scenes persuasion is likely to be more effective. Micro jawboning is usually accompanied by government actions in the sphere in which it has direct control; in most countries, controlling public sector wages accompanies micro jawboning—in fact, all forms of controls.

"Voluntary macro policies" establish voluntary economywide guidelines for wage and price behavior, implemented through government persuasion, usually on a selective basis. The guidelines, employing either an explicit numerical target for wage and price increases or a target expressed in terms of a percentage reduction per year in the rate of increase in wages and prices, are usually the same for all to whom they apply.

"Mandatory wage-price controls," legally enforceable guidelines for wage and price behavior, are broad in scope but with selected exclusions. Frequently prenotification of wage and price increases is required, as well as ex post facto audits.

"Tax-based incomes policies" use a system of subsidies and/or penalties to enforce the achievement of guideline objectives. The subsidies and penalties are calculated as increases or decreases in the tax liabilities of those filing income tax returns. This system is the only one of the four that has not been tried in the United States.

Each of these wage-price policies will be assessed to see how well it meets the criterion of reducing overall wage and price increases without altering the relative structure of both wages and prices. Their relationship to each other—that is, the relative shares of wages and profits in national income—will also be examined. The first and general point in this assessment is that within specific markets, whatever their characteristics with respect to such factors as degree of competition and bargaining power, wages and prices are ultimately determined by both supply and demand. Therefore, the appropriate price for a factor of production is related not only to its productivity but also to its demand. The demand side of price determination is frequently set aside in considering incomes policies; yet no one would be willing to settle for wage increases proportional only to his productivity (and changes in the cost of living), foregoing the opportunity to benefit as a result of possessing something for which the demand has risen relatively. If this point is made in somewhat personalized terms, it is only to sharpen the argument that not interfering with relative price change is not just an abstract term economists use when discussing the efficient allocation of resources; it may well be a deeply ingrained part of the fabric of American life, the source of the kinds of incentives that lead to growth.

How, then, do the various types of incomes policies attempt to meet these criteria of leaving relative prices unchanged? Voluntary micro policies reflect the notion that if one holds down selected prices and wages, disturbing the equilibrium of relative prices, other wages and prices will fall into line, and a new equilibrium position will be reached at which the inflation rate will be lower, but relative prices and wages will be restored to the same position they occupied before the initial policy action. This approach, in principle, leaves relative prices undisturbed in the long run.

Obviously, this approach can take a long time, from the initial shock to the attainment of a new equilibrium in relative prices around a lower overall inflation rate. For one thing, the initial shock may be difficult to achieve. The government must first identify a firm, an industry, or a labor union that has disturbed the relative price structure in an inflationary direction. Then it must convince the alleged promulgator that it has done so and get it to create another, disinflating shock. But that is just the first step. The government must then convince the other actors in the economy, when they are ready to initiate price and wage actions, to follow the leader in the direction of a new equilibrium. The staggered nature over time of collective bargaining is an important element in the time lags from start to finish under this approach, and most other ones for that matter; it takes about three years to reach wage behavior in the entire work force. In the interim, if the approach is working, continual small reductions, perhaps imperceptible over short periods of time, should occur. It is hard to measure and report the kind of progress that could accelerate the process by favorably altering expectations. Moreover, if farm prices escalate because of shortages or if war breaks out and the energy shortage worsens, it is unlikely that the process will continue.

In contrast to the micro approach, voluntary aggregate guidelines set forth an immediate target of persuasion. Influence is used to achieve a reduction to a specific figure in rates of increase in wages and prices, as wage and price decisions are made. It seeks, therefore, to achieve a fairly simultaneous reduction in both wages and prices, leaving the relative price structure undisturbed. Here also the degree of simultaneous response that can be achieved on both the wage and price side is limited by the staggered nature of labor contract expirations. Again, it can take several years to achieve targets, and the course is precarious with respect to shocks like those from farm and energy prices mentioned earlier.

Then, too, aggregate guidelines focus on the structure of relative wages and prices from the supply side only. A wage guideline is usually based on productivity and the degree to which inflation currently exceeds it. Firms are then persuaded to price according to the behavior of wages and trend productivity. In industries where productivity exceeds the national average, the object of persuasion is to reduce prices relative to the average and increase them in industries with productivity trends lower than the national average.

Aggregate guidelines are thus a cost-pass-through phenomenon, defended by their proponents on the basis described earlier that cost-pass-through is the pervasive form of price behavior. Thus the approach tends to ignore the fact that industries experiencing rapid demand growth frequently display productivity growth that exceeds the national average. In such industries, the savings through productivity must be passed through to prices. It cannot be reflected in widening margins as allocative efficiency would suggest it should. Of course, the government could overlook using its powers of persuasion in such a situation. But if there were too many of them or they were highly visible, the whole concept of voluntary cooperation could be undermined, as indeed it has in the past. Finally, with respect to any voluntary program, there are the basic problems that income may be redistributed from compliers to noncompliers. Always in the micro approach and frequently in the macro one, certain businesses and labor unions are targeted to receive the brunt of attention, usually because they are highly visible.

Mandatory wage and price control programs are similar in operation to voluntary macro guidelines, except that they are enforceable. With authority to grant exceptions, the government can try to guess at the relative wage and price structure that would otherwise obtain. But most observers consider the administrative cost of such a program quite high. Furthermore, many think the indirect costs of the disincentives are high, particularly with respect to investment, arising from government intrusion into markets on such a broad scale. This latter objection is easy to demonstrate for industries experiencing excess demand as in many primary producing industries during controls in 1973–74. It is harder to demonstrate in cost-push situations. Perhaps the most fundamental objection to mandatory controls is that they put government into the marketplace further than most Americans are willing to tolerate.

Partly because it takes government out of the direct process of price and wage setting and partly because it helps relative prices and wages to respond to market forces, the tax-based incomes policy (TIP) has recently become a leading contender among policies to combat inflation. In providing tax subsidies that more than reward anti-inflationary behavior and less than fully punish inflationary behavior, some scope is left open for adjusting individual prices and wages to the supply and demand conditions of specific sectors.

There are two main types of TIP plans—those that provide for penalties only and those that also provide for rewards. Within each type, two variants relate to whether both employers and employees are directly involved in tax payments and rebates to the government. The earliest TIP proposal and one that has gained support because of its ease of administration was developed by Henry Wallich and Sidney Weintraub. Their plan involves penalties only and directly affects only about one thousand large employers. The plan calls for a tax penalty to be paid by employers who grant, in the aggregate, an increase in total compensation per full-time worker in excess of some guideline figure. No provision applies to prices; the assumption is that, in the aggregate, prices are determined by a constant, even falling markup over labor compensation less labor productivity. Thus relative markups and wages could change. Firms could further affect relative wages by granting aggregate wage increases in excess of guidelines if they were willing to pay the tax penalty.

Of course, the fact that there is no limit on price increases raises a potential problem, as well as an actual one, in gaining labor support for such a proposal. However, the plan does seize on a major problem area of structural inflexibility discussed earlier—the relative insensitivity of many margins to changes in demand—and turns it into an important simplifying force.

The relative operational simplicity of the Wallich-Weintraub plan is offset to some extent because it is somewhat less effective than the more complex programs in providing the maximum possible incentive for anti-inflationary market outcomes. More such incentive is provided by the approach of Arthur Okun, one variant of which includes not only penalties for firms exceeding the guidelines but also subsidies for employees of firms adhering to such guidelines.

The third criterion is that an incomes policy produce readily discernible results promptly. The speed with which this can be accomplished is limited by the structural problems that arise because of the pervasive nature of fixed markups and of wage inertia. Of the two, wage inertia is more important because the wage share of income greatly exceeds the profit share.

It is usually impossible to select an achievable wage guideline perceptibly below the actual rise in wages. Existing labor contracts providing for deferred increases and cost-of-living adjustments place a floor below which the guideline cannot be set. Given the feasible range within which a wage guideline can be selected, under any form of incomes policy, such action is not likely to produce the framework for a swift and marked reduction in the inflation rate. In fact, there was no marked reduction in wage-rate increases during the successfully regarded Phase II of the Nixon control program of 1971. Wage rate change in the year preceding the August move to controls was 7.2 percent. During the year and a half of Phases I and II of the program that rate decelerated by 1 percentage point. This pace of reduction on an annual basis is about consistent with what could now be expected from a mandatory guidelines policy of the types of that have been discussed.

Recommendations

The thrust of this analysis has been to illuminate the basic structural inflexibilities in the economy, with respect both to wage behavior and unit margin behavior, and to indicate that under the best of circumstances an incomes policy, even a mandatory one, can be expected to yield only moderate reductions in the inflation rate. More dramatic results—greater disinflation and quicker response—would seem desirable. Two approaches may be taken to accomplish this.

A radical approach would outlaw multiyear labor contracts. Their advent just after World War II was viewed favorably by both labor and management because they reduce the costs of annual bargaining, including strike possibilities, and provide certaintly into the future with respect to income and major cost element. Further, many economists and policymakers view multiyear contracts as a restraining influence on the ability of inflation to escalate rapidly. Although they do exert such an influence, they preclude a rapid deceleration in the inflation rate as well. While dampening the potential for both sharp acceleration and deceleration, however, they may also impart an asymmetry in practice by encouraging policymakers to err on the side of adopting policies that add directly to costs or overstimulate the economy, since they tend to defer the increase in inflation that such policies ultimately produce.

If bargaining were annual, the potential for a rapid rise in inflation would be quite high, but the prospect that it would occur quickly might strongly deter actions in economic policy by elected officials because they would fear the speed with which the consequences would become apparent. On the other hand, policymakers might be induced to pursue more restrictive policies because of the potential for rapid deceleration of inflation and because they could accomplish more in a shorter period of time, obviating the necessity of putting the economy into a lengthy period of recession or slow growth. Thus multiyear bargaining, while reducing the potential amplitude of swings in the inflation rate, may be responsible for imparting a rising secular trend to that rate. Annual bargaining, in contrast, while increasing the potential amplitude of fluctuations in the rate, may impart a downward secular trend to inflation.

The likelihood that a shift to annual bargaining may increase the sensitivity of inflation to traditional macro tools and increase the United States's potential to reduce inflation is a necessary, but probably insufficient, condition to urge its adoption. It is also necessary to consider the potential cost of the increase in labor-management frictions that could result. While the actual costs of more frequent bargaining and the reduction in telescoping of the horizon within which future costs are known are not insignificant, the greatest threat posed by annual bargaining is its potential for increasing strike activity. Some increase in the number of strikes is a likely result, although it is not equally clear that days lost per year would rise as much. It may be easier to agree on terms of a settlement that will last only for twelve months. In short, the increased costs of annual bargaining is its potential for increasing strike activity. Some increase in outweighed by the benefits of providing a framework in which inflation can decelerate.

A less radical approach would involve the use of that part of the tax system that directly influences costs and prices in ways that would reduce the rate of inflation. Such policies include one-time or staged reductions in social security, state and local sales, and federal excise taxes. (Direct subsidies could be substituted for minimum wage increases.)

Two common arguments oppose this approach. The first holds that as a result general revenues, a sometimes seemingly bottomless source of funds, would be used to pay for programs that should stand on their own. This argument is advanced, in particular, with respect to the social security system. However, safeguards could be built in. For purposes of stimulating the economy or adjusting the progressivity of the income tax structure for the effects of inflation, periodic tax acts seem to be a permanent part of the economic scene. When these tax cuts are considered, there is no reason in principle why they could not be split between the income and other taxes that directly affect inflation and subjected to a ceiling on budget expenditures. The second argument against this approach is that the potential reduction in costs and prices such taxes represent might not, in fact, be passed through. This argument suggests that some kind of incomes policy might be a useful adjunct.

Conclusion

This essay has documented the two main structural obstacles in the United States to reducing inflation by the traditional macroeconomic tools of monetary and fiscal policy. These obstacles are the short-run insensitivity of wages and, to some extent, of markups over costs to both of these policies. It has shown that, among major industrial countries, year-to-year wage flexibility—the degree to which wage increases slow or accelerate—is lowest for the United States, while United States price flexibility is about average. Lack of wage flexibility in the United States is due to the prevalence of multiyear labor agreements whose expiration dates are staggered over time, coupled with a wage catch-up phenomenon, the tendency of some groups of workers to try and frequently succeed, even during recessions, in restoring or improving their ranking in the wage structure vis-á-vis workers who bargained in the recent past. Such behavior in labor markets produces wage inflexibility or inertia, that is, the tendency of wage rates to behave like a thirty-six month moving average, accelerating or decelerating only slowly.

The presence of wage inflexibility considerably limits the ability, not only of fiscal and monetary policy but also of various incomes policies, to reduce dramatically the rate of inflation in a short period of time. An important criterion of an effective incomes policy is its ability to produce a perceptible reduction in inflation promptly enough to maintain the cooperation of business and labor participants. In this respect, all incomes policies are lacking. With respect to two other criteria—the potential to reduce the rate of increase of aggregate wages and prices while leaving relative wages and prices responsive to supply and demand and the ability to attract broad public support—some incomes policies are shown to be better than others.

Since no one incomes policy is clearly superior in meeting the last two criteria and all fail in meeting the first, this essay has made two recommendations. The first is to prohibit multiyear labor contracts. Though radical, it is intended to cope directly with the structural problem of wage inertia. Despite the potential problems of such a prohibition, the net result would be beneficial with respect to combatting inflation and would outweigh the various potential increases in costs attendant to more frequent bargaining.

A second recommendation, less radical, is to reduce one or more taxes that directly affect costs and prices, such as social security or state and local sales taxes. Such action, if passed through by business and labor in their market decisions, could produce a quick and marked reduction in the inflation rate and, by reversing the inflationary spiral, provide a basis for continued deceleration in wages and prices. Since a necessary condition for the success of such a policy is that tax reductions be reflected in costs and prices, some kind of incomes policy may be a necessary adjunct to this recommendation.

Unemployment Policies

MICHAEL L. WACHTER

This essay analyzes three aspects of the unemployment problem. The first is the cyclical character of unemployment. Is cyclical unemployment an important part of today's problem? The second is the level of the sustainable unemployment rate. Why has that rate increased from about 4 percent in 1954 to over 5.5 percent today? The third has to do with policy options. What are the uses and misuses of monetary and fiscal policies in the current economic environment? What types of structural supply side policies would reduce the unemployment rate without creating upward pressure on the inflation rate?

Both the current unemployment rate and the gross national product (GNP) indicate that the United States has fully recovered from the 1974–75 recession. The persistently high level of unemployment is approximately equal to the unemployment rate that can be maintained without accelerating inflation— hereafter referred to as the equilibrium unemployment rate or U*.

This equilibrium rate of unemployment, which the author estimates to be between 5.5 and 6.0 percent, is the lowest unemployment rate that monetary and fiscal policy can achieve without rekindling inflation. At that level, the pool of job seekers is heavily unbalanced toward unskilled workers. The unemployment rate of skilled workers (broadly defined) is commensurate with the notion of frictional unemployment. Therefore, any overall expansion of labor market demand is inflationary because it increases the demand for skilled workers and capital—inputs not available at current money wage and price levels.

In addition, recent research on low-wage labor markets has stressed that numerous unskilled jobs remain unfilled when the national unemployment rate is close to the equilibrium rate of unemployment. That is, unemployed lower skilled workers and unfilled jobs coexist in the same geographical and occupational labor markets. The reason most often used to explain this phenomenon is that the unfilled jobs are unattractive because of their low wage rates and promotion opportunities. Given the existence of welfare payments that are competitive with the low market wage offered by these unfilled jobs, the unemployed have little incentive to accept the available jobs on a permanent basis. This feature of low-wage labor markets will be discussed in detail below in the section on structural unemployment. The main implication for macro policymakers is that even the unskilled labor market may be relatively tight at U*.

Cyclical Unemployment

One of the major problems in the anti-inflation battle is that the appropriate unemployment rate target for stabilization policy is unknown. How far can the monetary and fiscal authorities push down the unemployment rate without causing accelerating inflation? In the 1960s it was argued that uncertainty about the length of the lagged response of economic activity to aggregate demand policies was the key problem in fine tuning the economy. Although that problem still exists, it is small compared with the issues raised by the uncertainty over the level of the sustainable unemployment rate. The equilibrium unemployment rate of 5.5 percent is a point estimate with a large standard deviation. The unemployment constraint could easily be over 6 percent. The coming of labor force age of the baby boom cohort, the associated increases in female participation rates, and the changing level of government transfer programs have contributed to increasing that rate from 4.0 percent in the mid-1950s to 5.5 percent today. In addition to the changing labor market factors, numerous other variables—including such diverse elements as the slowdown in the trend rate of growth of productivity and changes in the terms of trade—could also affect the equilibrium unemployment rate. An alternative method of calculating this rate is simply to analyze the inflation data over the postwar business cycles, to find the periods with stable inflation rates and their corresponding unemployment rates. Calculated this way, the equilibrium unemployment rate is higher than when estimated demographically throughout the past two decades. It should be recognized that this approach to estimating U* generally yields a figure for the current period that is well above the 5.5 percent.

Another indication that U* may be above 5.5 percent is the shifting relationship between capacity utilization and the unemployment rate. For any given unemployment rate today, capacity utilization is apparently much higher than it was in the 1960s. The availability of labor was the constraining factor in the 1960s, but now the availability of capital is the constraining factor. Inflation in the Wharton model tends to accelerate when capacity utilization is around 93 percent. In the current Wharton forecast, capacity utilization in 1979 will be just above 93 percent and unemployment will be approximately 6.2 percent. That is, the inflation point on the capacity utilization rate will be reached when the unemployment rate is still 6.2 percent. That is not to say that 6.2 percent is the new equilibrium rate of unemployment. But the capacity numbers are a source of concern, and the 5.5 percent figure that results from the demographic adjustment may be too optimistic.

The Carter administration and Congress continue to adhere to an unemployment rate target between 4.5 and 5.0 percent. For example, the Congressional Budget Office uses a 4.9 percent estimate of full employment. Furthermore, the shift from a 4.0 percent to a 4.9 percent unemployment rate target is only a recent development. Although policy should be aimed at achieving unemployment rates below 5.5 percent, the evidence suggests that this optimistic target can only be reached by adopting structural policies in place of expansionary monetary and fiscal policies. An outline of these structural policy options is discussed below. For policymakers, however, it appears that the low or optimistic unemployment target is to be achieved largely through the use of monetary and fiscal policy.

The evidence discussed above suggests that 5.5 percent may be a useful point estimate but that the equilibrium unemployment rate is more likely to be above rather than below 5.5 percent. An equilibrium rate as low as the government target is unlikely. The government's use of an overly optimistic unemployment rate target has a number of important implications. First, maintaining too low an unemployment rate target results in overexpansionary demand policies and thus accelerating inflation. In the late 1960s the government target was 4 percent and U* was approximately 4.9 percent. By the mid-1970s, when the government target was lifted to 4.9 percent, U* had increased to 5.5 percent. This can explain the increase in the inflation rate, from an average of 1.5 percent in the early 1960s to approximately 8 percent today.

Second, the "full-employment" budget surplus is seriously overstated by calculating that figure on the basis of a 4 or even 5 percent equilibrium unemployment rate. The result is a tendency to believe that fiscal policy is more restrictive than it actually is. Using a 4.9 percent full-employment rate, for example, the Congressional Budget Office calculates a full-employment surplus of −10.3 billion in 1977, −11.2 billion in 1978, and +1.5 billion in 1979. Replacing a 4.9 percent with a 5.5 percent target would change the projected full-employment surplus to a significant deficit for 1979 and would increase the size of the deficits for 1977–78. In other words, if the equilibrium unemployment is 5.5 percent, the economy has been running a large full-employment budget deficit over the last several quarters of accelerating inflation.

In addition, the higher estimate for U* explains why the famous fiscal dividends expected to result from ending the Vietnam war and the 1974 recession never appeared. Without accepting accelerating inflation, one cannot fund new programs or expand old programs from the tax revenues to be collected when the unemployment rate falls below 5 percent. Keynesian economics suggests that the budget should not be balanced over the cycle; rather, on average, it should be in deficit during recessions and in surplus during periods of tight product and labor markets. Using a U* of 5.5 to define the boundary between tight and loose product and labor markets indicates that the budget has been in a full-employment deficit continuously over the past decade of rising inflation rates.

Third, a commitment to fighting inflation suggests that the government avoid using monetary and fiscal policy to push the unemployment rate below 6 percent. Given the uncertainty over the specific level of U*, policymakers must choose between taking the risks of overheating the economy or operating with additional slack. A policy to reduce the inflation rate implies shifting the unemployment rate target toward the high end of the U* range. Such a policy, however, does not require a recession. Slow real GNP growth of approximately 2.5 percent would raise the unemployment rate to the new target. Thereafter, real GNP growth of approximately 3.0 could be resumed. A policy of slowly reducing the full-employment budget surplus should reduce the inflation rate without a recession and avoid the high cyclical unemployment rates that accompany a recession.

The 6 percent unemployment rate target, however, is only the target for monetary and fiscal policies. The goal should be to achieve a lower unemployment rate and a faster GNP growth rate by adopting structural measures aimed at improving the supply side of the labor and capital markets. These policies would shift the federal tax and expenditure policies to favor investment in human and physical capital rather than direct job creation and consumption. One important example of this approach would be a major redirection of funds from public service jobs to manpower training in the private sector.

Structural Unemployment

It is frequently argued that 5.5 percent unemployment is unacceptably high for economic and political reasons. Yet some of the explanations of why it is too high as well as the policy measures that can reduce unemployment are questionable.

A typical way of calculating the economic cost of unemployment is to determine the amount of output that is not produced because the workers and capital that produce the goods and services are unemployed. The usual argument, from Okun's law, of a 1 to 3 relationship between unemployment and GNP, would claim that the United States economy will lose approximately $65 billion if unemployment is 5.5 rather than 4.5 percent. If U* is 5.5 percent, however, there is no permanent output loss when the economy is at that level of unemployment. Higher output and lower unemployment at current levels are not sustainable and only cause higher inflation. An analysis of the data over the decade of rising inflation rates suggests that the government's commitment to full employment has not succeeded in either raising the real GNP growth rate or lowering the unemployment rate from the rates that existed during the 1950s.

If there is no permanent real output loss, then the cost of the unemployment issue can focus on the individuals who tend to be unemployed. The current unemployment rates for the fourteen age-sex groups used by the Bureau of Labor Statistics illustrate that both the actual and equilibrium unemployment rates are highest for young workers. Indeed, approximately 50 percent of the total unemployment is accounted for by workers from the ages of sixteen to twenty-four. Unemployment rates tend to be highest among low-skilled workers, illustrating the mismatch between the employment and unemployment pools when the economy is at full employment. Three of the lowest-skilled occupational categories—service workers, nonfarm laborers, and operatives—account for 50 percent of the unemployment. On the other hand, these three categories include only 30 percent of the employment pool. Layoffs, the cause of unemployment typically associated with recessions and inadequate demand, composed only 11.5 percent of the unemployment pool. Unemployment spells initiated by voluntary actions of the workers accounted for almost 60 percent of the total unemployment. Moreover, few prime-age skilled workers are in the unemployment pool.

Today, the three main structural problems related to the high equilibrium rate of unemployment are the demographic imbalances resulting from the baby boom, which caused a disproportionate influx of young, unskilled workers into the labor market; the lack of capital expenditure and the high level of capacity utilization relative to unemployment; and market imperfections in certain key industries such as energy, health, and construction. Of particular importance is the demographic shift toward younger and female workers. Young male and female workers have been increasing as a percentage of the labor force as a direct consequence of the baby boom of the late 1950s. For young male workers, labor force participation rates have increased somewhat, so that the increase in their relative population size translates directly into an increase in their relative percentage in the labor force. For young females, including those aged sixteen through thirty-four, rapidly increasing participation rates have swelled the population growth into a dramatic increase in labor force growth. Whereas workers in the age group sixteen to twenty-four accounted for 16.7 percent of the labor force in 1960, they now constitute 25 percent. Of the increase in the equilibrium unemployment rate over the past two decades, a full percentage point is due to the changing composition of the labor force.

A large increase in the flow of young workers into a competitive labor market need not create a structural unemployment problem. Because of the compositional shift, U^* might have increased to 5 percent, but it need not have gone above that level. But do labor markets, especially for unskilled workers, have institutional features that encourage unemployment? Of potential importance are the minimum wage, public assistance, and other transfer programs for the poor. These programs have changed dramatically since the 1960s. The United States, for example, virtually did not have an operational minimum wage policy between 1947 and 1967. Minimum wages were set at a constant ratio to wages paid elsewhere in the economy. The major industries that hired numerous workers at low wages could obtain an exemption from the minimum wage laws by arguing before Congress that significant unemployment would result if they were forced to pay the minimum. The result was a policy exempting most of those workers and industries that might have been affected.

By 1967, the influx of young workers threatened the employment and relative wage status of the older workers in the low-paying secondary markets. The minimum wage coverage in 1967 jumped from 39.9 percent to 53.4 percent of civilian employment, largely extending coverage to low-wage workers. There had been some minor increases in coverage before 1967, but increasing the coverage rate has an impact only when it affects the workers who are actually earning the minimum wage. Throughout the postwar period, by far the most significant change in the minimum wage coverage was the increase in 1967.

At the same time, Congress increased welfare payments. In the 1960s, Aid to Families with Dependent Children (AFDC) payments grew relative to the market wage. The biggest rise in welfare payments was "in-kind" transfers, such as the Food Stamp Program.

As a consequence of the baby boom and the changes in government labor market programs, a pattern of high frequency, low duration bouts of structural unemployment has become the norm. The low-skilled worker is frequently unemployed but for short periods. For example, over the past year the average duration of unemployment was slightly over two months, but approximately half the unemployed were out of work for less than five weeks.

For policy purposes it is useful to divide the noncyclical unemployment pool into two groups—those from families with high income and those from families with low income. The former includes teenagers whose parents have relatively high income levels, married individuals who have spouses in the labor market, and some seasonally employed workers such as high-skilled construction workers with high family income. For policy purposes, the concern centers on the second group, the structurally unemployed who have low family income. In these cases, low wages and frequent unemployment or both lead to poverty.

In the current pattern of structural unemployment, there are two main reasons for being unemployed. First, if workers' potential earnings, based on their skill, are below the minimum wage, they may have difficulty finding stable employment. The minimum wage law reduces the demand for low-wage workers in the covered sector.

Second, because of the increase in the level of transfer payments, some low-skilled people may not want to work full time. It is sometimes argued that these unemployed people are malingering and that the work ethic should be strong enough to force them to work. For the most part, low-wage workers do not have opportunities to work at enriching, creative jobs. They might want to work part time in order to remain eligible for public assistance or unemployment compensation, and to retain their skills. But to work full time, as long as society provides the present level of support, is not rational in the economic sense of the term. Furthermore, many of the structurally unemployed will "outgrow" their unemployment problems. The low work attachment of this group is often associated with the fact that they are teenagers who do not have family responsibilities or females who are heads of households and who have too much family responsibility. Both groups will alter their working behavior as they age.

What is the underlying model of unemployment that yields these results? First, it is not a search model in the strict sense. Very little unemployment is caused by people who do not know the current wage and prices or the location of the job opportunities. It is not inadequate searching that causes people to be unemployed. The problem is that people eligible for welfare and unemployment insurance who decide not to work know full well their wage and job opportunities. Since they are willing to work part time, they would rather wait in line for a relatively attractive job. If they are going to work, they will only do so at a wage that makes work more worthwhile than collecting unemployment insurance or public assistance.

As mentioned above, the unemployment problem must be analyzed in light of the worker's life cycle. Young workers grow up, older workers age, and as all get older their situations change. Young workers especially change their outlook on life, their skills, and their family needs from one year to the next. The unemployment model is not a static one where people look at fixed wages and opportunities; rather, it is a dynamic, demographic one where people age and change. In this model people are structurally unemployed because of low skill levels and hence low wages, not because of a lack of jobs or information.

Policy Implications

One needs to reconsider methods to solve structural unemployment. If unemployment were merely due to a lack of jobs, then the current popular panacea of public service employment would help. But if it is a question of skill and low wages, a whole series of different policies are needed.

Some people say that nothing can be done; the private market works for the best, manpower training is ineffective, discrimination is intractable, and the government cannot encourage capital accumulation. After all, the government has tried numerous programs but has accomplished little. A cost-benefit study of government programs might well conclude that the labor market would be better off if the government left it alone. In addition, part of the problem will disappear as the baby boom is followed by a population decline. As the younger population ages, the overall equilibrium unemployment rate should fall. If this rate is 5.5 percent today, the demographics indicate that it should decline below 5 percent in the late 1980s. This assumes that minimum wages, public assistance, and other exogenous variables that affect the sustainable unemployment rate are kept more or less constant.

It does not seem, however, that the government can improve the structure of the labor market to reduce the equilibrium unemployment rate. Although the demographic trends will finally work in a favorable direction, many problems will remain. An important percentage of the undertrained workers will remain in the sixteen to twenty-four age group through the early 1980s. In addition, over the next decade the percentage of disadvantaged, minority workers in the sixteen to twenty-four age groups will grow significantly. It should become increasingly clear that the underlying problem is not a lack of jobs. Relatively high unemployment rates will remain as a symptom of the real problem—low wages.

The labor market policies stressed by Congress and the Carter administration, however, are geared to problems of aggregate demand and not the structural problems. Indeed, of the funds devoted to labor market problems, a greater percentage in 1977–78 were geared to cyclical rather than structural issues than during the 1960s. Aggregate demand policies have successfully dealt with the cyclical unemployment from the 1974–75 recession, but there has been no dent in the noncyclical component of unemployment—that is, the remaining 6 percent.

Although there is considerable discussion about manpower training, little training is actually being funded by the government. Most government monies are used for public service employment and work experience programs. These programs are not training oriented; they are meant to increase the number of jobs available and lower cyclical unemployment, but they do little to increase the skill of job holders. Whereas direct job creation programs—public service employment (PSE) and work experience—are demand oriented, manpower training is supply oriented, since it is structured to increase the skill level of workers.

The Comprehensive Employment and Training Act of 1973 (CETA) program is the government's major current initiative in the labor market. The percentage of dollars on training, relative to direct job creation, has declined from 25.6 percent in 1975 to 17.0 percent in 1978. Over this same period, the number of PSE job slots has grown from 111,262 to 725,200. Thus, not only do training or supply-oriented programs receive a small percentage of the government's labor market funding, but also the trend in percentage terms is strongly in the direction of demand stimulus through increased direct job creation.

This increase in the number of PSE slots has occurred in the context of a strongly growing economy that approached the equilibrium unemployment rate by 1977–78. A 13.5 percent increase in PSE slots between 1976 and 1978 need not necessarily be viewed as strongly contracyclical rather than countercyclical. The overall CETA program has a large number of objectives, some of them conflicting. The goals include improving the market skills of disadvantaged, unemployed workers, countercyclical job creation, and relief for the hard-pressed cities of the northern states. Thus, any discussion of public service employment must take into consideration that many of the public service slots simply go to maintain regular local government employment. For the hard-pressed northern cities, this job-oriented revenue sharing has helped to maintain public services. This aspect of CETA, however, has little relationship to the goal of reducing structural unemployment.

The variety of goals of the CETA program is an important weakness. For example, the CETA effort to help the distressed cities was not targeted with great accuracy and was probably contracyclical in its timing. The new directions in the proposed 1979 package also have severe limitations. In the context of a slowing economy, a drastic reduction of PSE slots may again be countracyclical. Ideally, for maximum cyclical effect, this program should have been increased in 1974–75 and then cut back in 1977–78. Moreover, the attempt to target the jobs more carefully toward disadvantaged workers encounters the problem that most city services are provided by relatively skilled personnel. In general, the public sector is not amenable to hiring low-skilled workers.

Because of these conflicts, CETA should be divided into three distinct programs—one to help the cities in the northern tier that are in financial distress, a second to provide countercyclical demand stimulus, and a third to encourage employment and training for disadvantaged low-skilled workers. Combining these three problems is almost guaranteed to produce inefficiency and a lack of success in meeting any of the objectives.

In general, if the government is to reduce the equilibrium unemployment rate it must disentangle the three components. The purpose of this essay is only to discuss methods of reducing equilibrium unemployment and to emphasize the need for a separate structural labor market program. Such a program should be funded in an acyclical manner and should be independent of public sector employment. It must be geared to increasing the market skills of workers. Since more than enough private-sector jobs are available to employ all those who want to work, it is necessary to focus on the fact that those jobs are not filled because they are unattractive. Unemployment compensation, food stamps, and AFDC payments are reasonably competitive with the wage level for these unfilled, low-skilled jobs; that is, the cost of being unemployed is very low for an unskilled worker. The solution is to raise the cost of being unemployed by increasing the market skills and hence the potential wages of the low-skilled workers.

Given this framework for explaining the existence of equilibrium unemployment, a number of important weaknesses in PSE programs can be isolated. The basic problem is that it does not provide training. It is little more than traditional Keynesian fiscal policy. But the unemployment problem is a structural problem rooted in demographic developments. The current group of young workers went through a public school system that was not ready for the huge influx of students of the baby boom generation. They did not receive adequate training, and many of them dropped out of school early. In fact, high school enrollment rates began to drop in the late 1960s and have continued to drop until recently. There is a large group of young workers today who have less education than the people who entered the labor market ten years ago. Discrimination and the growing fiscal distress of urban areas have worsened the problems. Providing these workers with public service jobs does not solve the fundamental problem—their lack of adequate marketable skills.

A second problem related to the first one is the issue of transferability. Without training, these people do not have skills that can be transferred to the private sector. Are the structurally unemployed supposed to stay under the protection of a public employment program throughout their lives, or is there some notion of moving to unsheltered employment? How can a transfer be successful if the employment program does not provide training? What are these programs supposed to accomplish for the twenty-one-year-old high school dropout who has no marketable skills?

A third problem concerns the wages paid on these public service jobs. If many of the current structurally unemployed are without work because of the low cost of being unemployed, some current schemes that would create numerous low-wage public service jobs would not significantly reduce the unemployment rate. Many of the people in the unemployment pool have already indicated that they do not want permanent jobs with a wage close to the minimum. If the government creates a million job slots, they may be largely filled by new entrants or reentrants into the labor market. In this case, public service employment would increase the number of workers in the labor market but not significantly reduce the unemployment rate.

Of course, the government could pay more than the minimum wage for public service jobs. This type of program would be attractive not only to the unemployed and those out of the labor force but also to people already employed in the private sector at relatively low wages. A program that hired the best qualified applicants would alrgely take workers from the private sector. The drop in the unemployment rate would not be commensurate with the number of new PSE jobs. Moreover, it is easily shown that attempts to restrict eligibility to those currently unemployed are easily circumvented.

A fourth problem is inflation. Since the wages paid on public service jobs would bear little relationship to the productivity of the workers and increase the demand for labor (with the economy already at full employment), the inflation rate would increase. But the problem is deeper than that. Since public service employment programs are similar to traditional fiscal policy, they will have little impact on the equilibrium rate of unemployment. At the same time, these programs often have the stated objectives of lowering the actual unemployment rate below the implicit sustainable level. In this case, public service employment would result in an accelerating inflation rate.

Even with these problems, it is sometimes argued that PSE programs can still lower the equilibrium unemployment rate by targeting their hiring toward the low-skilled workers. If there are too many unskilled workers when the economy is at U^*, would not the equilibrium rate be lowered by hiring those with the highest unemployment rate? In the Humphrey-Hawkins bill, for example, there is an implicit view that the unemployment rates of teenagers, females, and minorities could be lowered at no cost to the more skilled unionized, manufacturing, construction, and mining sectors. This, however, is not correct. In order to reduce the unemployment rates of the low-skilled groups, the unemployment rates for the more skilled groups would have to increase. That is, if PSE can lower the equilibrium unemployment rate while balancing inflation, it does so by hiring a larger number of unskilled workers than the number of skilled workers who have to be displaced. The quantitative nature of the trade-off is unclear. Could PSE hire ten low-skilled workers and fire only one skilled worker, or would it take seven skilled workers to balance the hiring of ten unskilled workers? The equilibrium age-sex unemployment rates suggest that PSE might be able to hire three teenagers for every adult male that was displaced.

To solve the structural unemployment problem, the skills and hence the market wage of less-skilled workers must be increased relative to the level of transfer payments; that is, the cost of being unemployed must be increased. This is not to say that public assistance and minimum wages should be lowered. The economy can afford a relatively high guaranteed income floor for people who have very low skills or who cannot work. Society is wealthy enough to afford a high level of public assistance as well as a high market wage.

Public policy should focus on increasing the market wage of the workers who have suffered on account of the baby boom, not only the young workers but also disadvantaged workers who were caught in the secondary labor market when the baby boom arrived. To increase the market wage of this group, manpower training is needed. Although some manpower training programs in the past have not succeeded, others have been useful. Much can be learned from past errors, and successful training programs can be created. This is not the place to outline an alternative approach to training. But it should be stressed that the focus for training should be shifted from the government to the private sector. Under the Manpower Development and Training Act, the very low-skilled workers attended government-run classes to learn remedial skills. The classes generally lasted for six months. A common complaint was that companies would not hire these workers after the government trained them. But the real question was whether these workers were actually trained. Six months in a government classroom for high school dropouts do not constitute a major training effort. The graduates of these programs still had employment problems because they still lacked the necessary skills. Even remedial classroom training should therefore be shifted to the private sector, and these programs should be constructed to last for two years. A number of major corporations have indicated a willingness to conduct such programs. These firms can provide a more current vocational training environment. If the program is to work, it should be based on the profit motive of the large firms and not on their social conscience. There is some evidence that the goals of manpower training could be achieved through the use of employment tax credits. The New Jobs Tax Credit that was part of the 1977 stimulus package seemed promising. Alternatively, a voucher system targeted to specific groups of workers could be used.

Firms providing remedial training need not orient their training programs toward fulfilling their own manpower needs. The rationale is that the workers are being trained for general semiskilled employment and that an individual who receives both remedial general training and concentrated industrial training in certain skills will be employable in general. In the recent past, there was a shortage of entry-level workers for manufacturing and semiskilled service jobs when the aggregate unemployment rate fell to 5.5 percent. But a worker who has received training in the private sector could be hired as an entry-level worker. He or she would no longer need unusual entry-level training to fill even the bottom job on the promotion ladder.

An employment policy that encourages capital accumulation is also important. Whereas semiskilled and skilled workers appeared to be the sole bottleneck to the expansion of the late 1960s, capacity has become at least as important a barrier to achieving low unemployment in the 1970s. Even when capital growth does not create more jobs directly, it removes a bottleneck to employment growth.

A major problem with the current expansion is that the strongest sectors have been consumption and residential construction. Given the indication of a capacity shortfall, tax incentives to encourage a capital expenditure boom were needed as far back as 1974. The failure of investment to lead the recovery has been an important factor in the inflationary pressures that developed in 1978 while the unemployment rate was still above 6 percent. The tax package of 1978 was far too late and contained too few supply-side incentives to avoid the last upswing in the inflation rate.

Given the outlook for a sluggish economy in the near future, the inflation rate should be relatively stable. The unemployment–capacity figures still indicate a need to orient policy toward encouraging investment. When the economy begins to rebound, the strength and magnitude of the recovery depends on a strong investment path leading to an increase in the rate of capital accumulation. A consumption-led recovery will again leave the economy with an unnecessarily high equilibrium unemployment rate at the next cyclical peak. Traditionally, stabilization policy has been directed toward controlling aggregate demand. In the current environment, however, a program's impact on aggregate supply is more important than its impact on aggregate demand.

Unemployment, Inflation, and Welfare

An important issue is whether a high level of welfare payments are a barrier to a supply-side policy of increased capital accumulation, productivity growth, and lower equilibrium unemployment rates. Does increasing federal government outlays or welfare programs exert an inflationary bias by suppressing incentives to work and by shifting funds from relatively high savers to high consumers? This is a complex question with considerable merit. It can, however, be pushed too far.

As discussed above, the increase in transfer payments—such as Aid to Families with Dependent Children (AFDC), food stamps, and unemployment compensation—as a percentage of market wages should lead to an increase in the equilibrium unemployment rate. This cannot be shown unambiguously because of the poor quality of the data on transfer payments, but the debate in the economics literature is over the magnitude rather than the sign of the effect. In addition, almost all income transfer programs reduce the aggregate savings and investment rate, since they presumably are designed to transfer income from wealthier to poorer families and individuals. Although there are little data on the issue, it may be assumed that AFDC and other transfer programs do not provide sufficient income for families to save significant amounts. These programs are specifically designed to provide a minimum income floor.

The income transfer programs affect two groups of individuals. The first group, those serviced by welfare programs, are among the lowest skilled individuals in society. The cost of leaving these individuals unemployed is measured by the income transfers they receive. The level of transfer payments in the United States is comparable to those paid by Western European countries. Wealthy societies can afford to maintain a relatively high guaranteed income floor. Bringing these individuals back into the labor market will contribute little to the GNP because of their low skill levels.

For example, the work registration programs, aimed at forcing welfare mothers back to work, are misplaced. The government can force someone to register but not to work. The result will be an increase in the labor force and a resulting increase in the equilibrium unemployment rate. Moreover, since welfare mothers tend to have low-skill levels, the lost GNP is extremely small. As a result, this type of program is likely to be counterproductive; its main effect will be to increase the equilibrium unemployment rates even further above the target levels of U* used by monetary and fiscal authorities.

The unemployment insurance system deals with the second group of individuals. Since unemployment compensation is a percentage of the market wage, high- as well as low-wage individuals may be receiving benefits. The economic evidence suggests that unemployment insurance does tend to increase the duration of unemployment. A component of this increase in duration may improve productivity. It may allow young workers to search for jobs in which they are likely to be most productive. In addition, it allows cyclically displaced workers to await recall to their old jobs. Where specific training is important, productivity over the cycle will be improved by encouraging workers to await recall rather than to take a new permanent job.

On the other hand, the unemployment compensation system encourages firms, are at the maximum tax rate, so there is no additional tax charge for These distortions reduce productivity and increase the equilibrium unemployment rate. The appropriate policy is to adjust the unemployment compensation tax schedules so that virtually all firms face additional taxes (related to the cost of the benefits) if they lay off workers. Too many firms, especially seasonal firms, are at the maximum tax rate, so there is no additional tax charge for an additional layoff.

The unemployment insurance system also encourages those who have lost their jobs but do not want another job to stay unemployed in order to remain eligible for unemployment compensation. That is, individuals who want to work part time are encouraged to report themselves as unemployed rather than as out of the labor force. This again serves to increase the equilibrium unemployment rate but has little impact on productivity.

Since the benefits for unemployment insurance usually extend for only twenty-six weeks when the economy is not in a recession, it is unlikely that relatively skilled workers who want full-time jobs would use the system as a way of avoiding work. Indeed, for workers on temporary layoff the option of turning down a recall almost always results in the termination of benefits.

A potential cost of the transfer programs is the work disincentives to the taxpayers. That is, welfare programs reduce the work incentives not only of the payees of the transfer system but also of the taxpayers. For both groups, the marginal tax rates on wage income are increased. The negative impact on work incentives would yield a reduction in potential output. But the work disincentive effect is general to the overall income tax system and the variety of programs it supports. It is unlikely that the taxes collected to pay for the welfare program would have different work disincentive effects for the taxpayers than would other government programs.

The nation's welfare and unemployment compensation systems, though reasonably liberal, need not be viewed as inflationary. If the government recognized that its transfer policies have the effect of increasing U^* and possibly reducing potential output, there would be no additional inflationary pressures. Of course, this means that the government would have to allow the unemployment rate to increase to the level of the new higher equilibrium rate. One problem for the United States over the past decade has been the desire, for example, to fight a war on poverty and a war in Vietnam without anyone paying the costs. The resulting large government deficit, even at full employment, and large money-supply growth rates caused the increased inflation.

To summarize, the existence of relatively generous welfare and unemployment insurance systems increases the equilibrium unemployment rate and shifts resources from more to less productive members of society. The increases in the equilibrium unemployment rate are a problem, however, largely because its changes are not easily monitored and because the government tends to ignore increases in U^*. If the government recognized the effects of its policies on U^* and potential output, the welfare system could be characterized as noninflationary.

The recent reduction in the growth rates of potential output and productivity, and the increase in the equilibrium unemployment rate, could be offset by shifting from a high consumption to a high investment economy. Investment tax credits, accelerated depreciation, manpower training, employment tax credits, and a reduction in marginal income tax rates could all be part of a proinvestment package. Moreover, the transfer system—excluding social security—is small enough to make these policy changes without reducing the relative level of welfare payments. Over the long run a high investment policy would yield higher skill levels and wage rates, lower equilibrium unemployment rates, and consequently a reduction in the welfare population.

The author's general research in the area of unemployment policies has been supported by the General Electric Foundation and the National Institute of Child Health and Human Development.

Increasing Productivity

JOHN W. KENDRICK

This essay analyzes the sources of economic growth in the United States business economy, with particular reference to productivity increases and present estimates of the contributions to growth of the various sources for the periods 1948–66 and 1966–77. This "growth accounting" exercise reveals the causes of the slowdown in productivity growth since 1966 and serves as a background for the further discussion of the kinds of policies available to accelerate the growth of productivity and output and thus contribute to the winding down of price inflation. Policy suggestions will be offered in connection with the discussion of human investments and other sources of growth.[1]

Aggregate economic growth can be enhanced by increasing the growth of natural resources, labor, and man-made capital goods, as well as by increasing their productivity, but it is the latter that is of particular interest from the viewpoint of combatting inflation. That is, as factor inputs are increased, so too is factor income at prevailing prices. But the increase of factor productivity offsets increases in factor prices with respect to unit costs and prices of outputs. Thus the deceleration of productivity advance was directly related to the acceleration of unit costs and prices after 1966. Conversely, an acceleration of productivity gains could aid directly in decelerating the rate of increase in unit costs and prices if appropriate complementary policies were pursued.

Given the rate of growth of the labor force, there is theoretically some optimal rate of capacity-expanding capital formation that would maintain relatively full employment within an efficient range of capacity utilization rates. Further, it is clear that changes in the composition of demand should be matched by changes in the composition of productive capacity so that rates of utilization in the various industries would also be maintained within efficient ranges through time. Otherwise, unit costs would rise, and in the bottleneck in-

---

[1] For a discussion of policy measures to promote saving, investment, and technological advance, see the essay by Roger E. Brinner in this volume, pp. 147–58.

dustries the more rapid increases of demand relative to production would tend to bid prices up. Although the focus of this essay is generally macroeconomic, several policies are suggested to facilitate mobility of resources in anticipation of, or in response to, changes in the composition of demand.

The Growth Accounting Framework

According to production theory, rates of change in productivity may be calculated as the difference between rates of change in the real gross product and in a weighted average of human and nonhuman factor inputs. This relationship is used as the basis for section A of table 1. Real capital inputs are assumed to move proportionately to real stocks of capital (including land and other natural resources) gross of capital consumption allowances. Labor input is measured in hours of all persons engaged in production. The relative weights of the factor inputs are their shares in gross national income, which average about two-thirds for labor and one-third for property.

As shown in section A of table 1, the real gross product rose by almost 4 percent a year, on average, between 1948 and 1966, but then decelerated to a 3 percent annual rate for 1966–77. Total factor input, on the other hand, accelerated from a 1.2 percent average annual growth rate in the first period to 1.7 percent in the second. This was due entirely to an acceleration in the growth of the labor force, employment, and total hours worked, since capital grew at approximately the same rate in both periods. If the growth rates of total factor input are subtracted from those of real product, the result shows that the growth rates of total factor productivity (TFP) fell sharply from 2.7 percent for 1948–66 to 1.3 percent for 1966–77.

In addition to total factor productivity, the table also shows the more conventional output per labor hour measure, which is published regularly by the Bureau of Labor Statistics. This dropped from the 3.5 percent average annual growth rate for 1948–66 to 1.9 percent for 1966–76. But the preferred measure of changes in productive efficiency is total factor productivity, since it reflects the net saving in total real factor inputs achieved as a result of cost-reducing innovations and other forces to be reviewed later. The reconciliation between the labor and total factor productivity change estimates is the rate of substitution of capital for labor (which equals the rate of change in total input per unit of labor, or in capital per unit of labor times the capital weight).

Section A of table 1 shows that the rate of substitution declined from 0.8 percent a year, on average, for 1948–66 to 0.6 percent for 1966–77. Although this rate fell less than that of the output-labor ratio, even in the later period it accounted for less than one-third of the growth in output per unit of labor input.

The growth of factor inputs as a policy objective will be considered briefly before an examination of the sources of growth in total factor productivity. Although this objective is not directly counterinflationary in the same way that productivity gains are, it is conceivable that acceleration of inputs could have an indirect influence. That is, with a given rate of growth in total factor produc-

TABLE 1

Sources of Growth in Real Gross Product and Productivity, United States Business Economy

	1948–66	1966–77p
A. Output, inputs, and productivity ratios (average annual percentage rates of change)		
Real gross product	3.9	3.0
Factor input—total		
Labor	1.2	1.7
Capital	0.4	1.1
	2.7	2.7
Real product per unit of labor input	3.5	1.9
Substitution of capital for labor	0.8	0.6
Total factor productivity	2.7	1.3
B. Sources of growth in total factor productivity (percentage point contributions)		
Advances in knowledge		
R&D stock	.85	.7
Informal innovation	.30	.2
Rate of diffusion	.25	.1
	1.4	1.0
Changes in labor quality		
Education and training	.6	.7
Health and vitality	.1	.1
Age-sex composition	−.1	−.3
	.6	.5
Changes in quality of land	—	−.1
Resource reallocations		
Labor	.4	.2
Capital	.4	.4
	.8	.6
Volume changes		
Economies of scale	.4	.3
Intensity of demand	.1	−.3
	.5	—
Net government impact		
Public services to business	.1	.1
Regulations of business	−.1	−.3
	—	−.2
Actual/potential efficiency and n.e.c.	−.6	−.6

p = preliminary.
n.e.c. = not elswhere classified.
Source: John W. Kendrick, based in part on estimates by Edward F. Denison, *Accounting for United States Economic Growth, 1929-1969* (The Brookings Institution, 1974).

tivity a faster growth of factor inputs would accelerate the growth of real income per capita, which might have some effect in moderating money-wage demands. Regardless of this possible effect, however, a complete treatment of supply management requires attention to the supply of factors as well as to their productivity.

Investment, including outlays to discover and develop natural resources, adds to the stock of nonhuman capital and thus to productive capacity. This is true of outlays designed primarily to cut unit costs as well as those intended primarily to expand capacity, and most new investment does both. To the extent that an increase in the rate of capital formation accelerates the growth of the real capital stock and its potential services, the rate of capital-labor substitution increases and accelerates the rate of growth of real product per labor hour relative to that of total factor productivity. This provides an additional offset to rising average hourly earnings, tending to decelerate increases in unit labor costs, other things being equal. For example, it has been estimated that if the ratio of business-fixed investment to the GNP were increased by 2.0 percentage points, the rate of growth of real capital stocks would accelerate by 1.2 percentage points, which translates into a 0.4 percentage point higher rate of substitution of capital for labor.

The growth of labor input is a function of the growth of the labor force, employment, and average hours worked per year by each person engaged in production. Given relatively full employment, the chief variable is the growth of the labor force, which depends on the growth of the population of working age, its age-sex composition, and labor force participation ratios. Changes in birthrates would not affect labor force growth for sixteen years into the future. That is fortunate for policy discussion, since this is generally held to be a matter of family policy, not public policy, in a democracy. Although various government policies undoubtedly influence the birthrate, they will not be considered here. But there are policies that can influence the growth of the population of working age and, in particular, labor force participation ratios. In view of the projected substantial decline in the growth of the labor force beginning about 1980, and the eventual significant increase in the ratio of dependent elderly persons to the employed population and in the associated financial burdens on public and private pension funds, more thought is being given to ways in which the labor force growth could be bolstered. Some of the major options will be briefly reviewed here.

The growth of the population of working age could be increased by liberalizing immigration laws. The large number of illegal aliens in the United States indicates that many more people would like to immigrate than are now permitted. Net immigration provides the only source of human capital that is virtually costless to the domestic economy. Increased medical research and health care could also increase the growth of the population of working age, although it would not necessarily reduce the dependency ratio. In addition to decreasing mortality, it would increase productivity.

With respect to labor force participation ratios, the most striking downward trend has been among males fifty-five years of age and over. Apart from increased affluence and individual ability to provide for retirement, this trend has been the result of a number of developments: mandatory retirement rules; liberalization of the Social Security Act permitting earlier retirement with actuarially reduced benefits, substantial increases in real benefits, and expanded coverage of the system; major increases in coverage and benefits of private pension plans, and more provisions for early retirement; increased availability of disability benefits under both public and private systems; discrimination against older workers; and loss of social security benefits by workers who earn more than a given amount.

Some economists maintain that payroll and income taxes, which drive a wedge between the wage paid by employers and that received by the employee or which reduce the after-tax remuneration of the self-employed, tend to contract the labor supply. Further, the progressivity of the personal income tax system tends to decrease hours worked by persons in the upper income brackets.

Tax reforms designed to increase incentives to work, with due regard for equity considerations, and measures to decrease incentives to retire are needed to bolster labor force growth. With respect to the latter, the act of Congress raising the mandatory retirement age from sixty-five to seventy in the private economy and eliminating it in federal employment is a step forward. Raising the amounts that persons between sixty-five and seventy-two can earn without losing social security benefits would also help. Greater availability of flexible work arrangements that would permit a gradual reduction of hours worked might also keep more older workers in the labor force. Other measures, such as vocational counseling, job retraining, and job redesign for older workers, could also alter declining participation rates.

To complete the description of the growth accounting framework underlying this essay, the remainder of section B of table 1 shows the sources of growth in total factor productivity. For half a century, from 1916 to 1966, increases in total factor productivity accounted for well over half of the growth in real gross business product. Although its contribution to the growth rate dropped to about 40 percent between 1966 and 1977, it is still of greater potential significance to future growth than is the increase of factor inputs. But in order to devise appropriate policies for speeding up the growth of total factor productivity, it is essential to identify and measure the major causal forces behind increasing productivity. The most successful attempt to do so to date has been that of Edward F. Denison. Section B of table 1 is based largely on Denison's growth accounting approach, with some modifications. In particular, it includes changes in the quality of labor as one of the sources of productivity increase, rather than as part of labor input. It breaks down "advances in knowledge" into its chief components and estimates it directly after 1966, rather than as a residual. It adds the categories of changes in quality of land, reallocations of capital, and the net impact of government on business-sector productivity.

Finally, it estimates the residual separately, interpreting it as chiefly reflecting changes in the ratio of actual to potential labor efficiency at given levels of technological knowledge.

Some of the estimates of the contributions of the sources of productivity growth are relatively good, particularly the contributions of increased education and of interindustry resource shifts. Others, whether prepared by Denison (the source of most of the members for 1948–66 and a few of the subsequent estimates) or by the author, are quite rough. But they are useful for indicating the relative importance of the various factors, and their changing importance over the periods covered. Certainly the table is a convenient framework for organizing the review of causal factors and the discussion of policy measures available to influence them.

Sources of Growth in Total Factor Productivity

The first group of variables relates to advances in knowledge applied to the ways and means of production. Inventions of cost-reducing producers' goods, or management methods, when adopted as innovations in the productive process, are the most important source of productivity gains. As table 1 shows, advances in knowledge contributed an estimated 1.4 percentage points to growth during 1948–66, which represents about half of the estimated rate of increase in total factor productivity. After 1966 the contribution of advances in knowledge dropped to an estimated 1.0 percentage point. This is best explained in terms of the chief components of advances in knowledge.

The bulk of technological advance stems from formal research and development programs (R&D) in industry. After rising for decades to 3.0 percent of the GNP in the mid-1960s, it declined to 2.2 percent in 1977. The stock of knowledge resulting from R&D, obtained by cumulating outlays over the lifetimes of the resulting new products and processes, decelerated considerably after 1966. It seems likely that informal inventive and innovative activity, largely representing the myriad small improvements devised by plant managers and workers to the major technological changes, also decelerated. So did the rate of diffusion of technological advances, evidenced by the fact that the average age of plant and equipment in the business sector declined by about three years between 1948 and 1966 but by less than one year in the subsequent period according to Bureau of Economic Analysis estimates. Since the most recent technologies are embodied in the newest capital goods, the average age of capital is an important indicator of the rate of diffusion of innovations. An economic environment conducive to capital formation also helps to stimulate private R&D outlays, while tax credits or other measures to increase the latter help create investment opportunities as well.

The next group of factors affects the average quality of the labor force. Of these the most important has been the increase in average education and training of each member of the labor force. Based on changes in the real stock of educational capital per person and the rate of return on the capital, education contributed 0.5 percentage point to growth during 1948–66 and somewhat more since 1966. The increase in training per person added another 0.1 percentage point in both periods.

Increases in real outlays for health and safety, and in the resulting real stocks per worker, promote productivity by reducing time lost due to illness and accident and by raising vitality or reducing debilitating health conditions. Real stock estimates indicate that this factor added almost 0.1 percentage point to the productivity growth rate in both periods. Denison contends that the decline in average hours worked per year also contributed to the energy content of hours worked. But at the levels of average hours worked since 1948 it is doubtful that this factor added significantly to hourly labor efficiency.

Changes in the age-sex composition of the work force became a significant negative factor in the mid-1960s. At that time the proportion of youth began increasing sharply, reflecting the baby boom after World War II, and the increase in the female labor force participation ratio accelerated. Because of the below-average experience of these groups and a lower value-added per person, this trend reduced productivity growth by 0.1 percentage point for 1948–66 and 0.3 for 1966–77. The negative effect was largest in the late 1960s and early 1970s. By 1977 the proportion of labor force members sixteen through twenty-four years of age was declining.

With regard to policy options to increase the quality of labor, it should be noted that the upward relative trend of outlays for education and training is continuing. This trend would be augmented by adoption of policies to promote technological progress that upgrades the structure of demand for labor and tends to raise the prospective rates of return on higher education (which declined in the 1970s).

The passage by Congress of a tuition tax credit may help bolster private educational expenditures. So also would the Carter administration's preferred plan to expand loans from public funds, or loan guarantees, for higher education. Expansion of subsidies for training of youth and disadvantaged workers by the Employment and Training Administration could help increase employment as well as training. Expansion of continuing adult education programs is desirable in view of persistent technological change and the increase in the average age of the labor force projected for the years ahead.

In addition to the continued relative growth of private and public outlays for education and training, an increase in the productivity of the resources devoted to these areas is also important. Major technological advances are being made in the areas of computer-assisted instruction, programmed materials, closed-circuit television, instructional films, and other teaching aids. But diffusion of new technology has been slow. More widespread instruction of teachers in the use of advanced educational technology would help. So, too, would centralization of purchasing of new equipment according to acceptable performance standards at various educational levels, possibly through national associations of state and local governments as well as associations of private educational institutions.

Relative outlays for health and safety are also projected to continue to increase in coming years. More generous deductions for medical expenses on the individual income tax would help bolster private outlays. As in education, however, a major emphasis should be placed on increasing productivity in these activities. Continued expansion of research in the fields of medicine, medical and safety equipment, pharmaceuticals, and health delivery systems is basic. Intensification of health education, particularly for youth, and programs for preventive medicine probably offer the cheapest avenues for an improved health status of the nation.

Changes in the age-sex mix of the labor force do not represent a useful policy objective, by and large, since it chiefly reflects demographic trends and individual decisions. But the reduction of disincentives for older workers to remain in the labor force would alter the age distribution of the labor force, as well as its rate of growth to some extent.

Changes in the average quality of land and other natural resources affect productivity trends in the extractive industries and thus in the business economy as a whole, although the share of those industries in the gross business product is small. Up until the mid-1960s, the net effect of the rule of diminishing returns appears to have been minor and far more than outweighed by technological advance, since productivity in extractive industries grew substantially faster than in the economy as a whole. Since 1970 productivity growth has decelerated in agriculture and actually declined in mining. Although the decline was due in part to safety and other regulations, it appears to have been partly due to the declining average quality of natural resources. This subtracted 0.1 percentage point in the 1966–77 period from the trend-rate in the business economy as a whole.

Reliance on the market system, domestic and international, to promote substitution of relatively more abundant and cheaper natural resources for those that are becoming scarcer and more valuable is the primary avenue for mitigating the tendency toward a diminishing return. The same forces tend to direct R&D toward developing new technologies that reduce natural resource costs. But restrictions on oil imports and greater reliance on domestic energy sources will inevitably tend to accelerate deterioration in the average quality of domestic resources. It is always possible, of course, that major new natural resource discoveries will be made or that technological breakthroughs will slow down or temporarily reverse the trend.

Next is a group of forces affecting reallocations of labor and capital resources in response to differential rates of remuneration in various industries resulting from dynamic changes in supply and demand conditions. These are sometimes referred to as changes in economic efficiency, as distinguished from technological efficiency. Inefficient allocation usually results from impediments to mobility, including differences in industrial organization, practices of firms or unions, and the sheer costs of movement.

For the period 1948–66 Denison estimated that shifts from nonfarm self-employment to employee status added 0.1 percentage point to growth and that shifts of labor from farming to the nonfarm sector added 0.3 percentage point. Interindustry employee shifts added about another 0.1 percentage point, but this was offset by a relative increase in the proportion of the gross product accounted for by industries with below-average productivity change. During the following period, the net effect of these labor shifts was reduced to 0.2 percentage point, reflecting chiefly the virtual disappearance of the farm-nonfarm shift effect as the relative importance of farming became quite minor.

There have also been relative shifts of capital, including land, to uses with above-average rates of return. Based on estimates by Dale Jorgenson and Frank Gollop of capital stocks weighted by over fifty industry divisions compared with their unweighted aggregate, the shift effect can be calculated to have been 0.4 percentage point for 1948–66 and a bit higher in the subsequent period. Jorgenson and Gollop include both labor and capital shift effects (which they call "quality change") in their factor input measures. Denison includes only labor shift effects and does not compute the effects of interindustry shifts of capital.

Continuing reallocations of labor, capital, and land will continue to be required in a dynamic economy, and the requirements may even be greater if proposals to accelerate technological progress and other forces promoting productivity and growth are adopted. Reallocations in response to changing supply conditions and demand patterns could be accelerated in several ways. More vigorous enforcement of antitrust laws and other actions to promote competition would facilitate the flow of capital into those industries and product lines in which rates of return are above average because of restrictions on output. In the regulated industries, allowance of rates of return comparable to those in competitive industries (after allowance for differences in risk) would help the utilities obtain their appropriate share of capital. Actually, establishment of a rate-of-return range, with firms showing above-average productivity gains allowed to earn in the upper end of the range, and those showing below-average productivity gains allowed to earn in the lower end of the range, would more closely approximate the competitive situation and serve to promote productivity.

To the extent that higher rates of return are due to pioneering innovations, a faster rate of diffusion of new technology would help raise capital formation in the affected industries and reduce abnormal profit rates sooner. Progressive firms would, of course, continue to enjoy above-average rates of return as long as they continued to stay ahead of the competition, but this is a legitimate incentive and reward for innovation. More and better economic data and estimates from federal statistical agencies, and better analyses and projections from both governmental and private sources, would facilitate adjustments by firms to changes in both supply and demand conditions.

With respect to labor mobility, actions to reduce restrictions on entry by certain labor unions, professional associations, and other organizations would facilitate movement into industries, occupations, and professions with above-average compensation. Expansion and improvement of programs of the

Employment and Training Administration to train or retrain, place, and relocate unemployed workers would further increase mobility. Maintenance of high-level aggregate economic activity itself facilitates adjustments.

Economies of scale occur as growth opens up opportunities for greater specialization of workers, plants, and machines and permits the spreading of overhead expenses over more units of output. Denison estimates that economies of scale account for about 10 percent of the growth rate. On this basis their contribution dropped from 0.4 percentage point for 1948–66 to 0.3 percentage point for 1966–77. Another volume factor is changes in the intensity of demand. As the ratio of actual to potential real product changes, productivity changes, but to a lesser extent. Capital stock and input estimates have not been adjusted for changes in rates of utilization, so capital productivity is obviously affected. Although employment and hours do fluctuate cyclically with output, a certain overhead component in labor input also causes labor productivity to reflect cyclical movements in aggregate demand. Intensity of demand was somewhat higher in 1966 than in 1948, and Denison estimates a 0.1 percentage point contribution on this score. But the Council of Economic Advisers estimates that the ratio of actual to potential real product in 1977 was about 7 percent lower than in 1966. This subtracted 0.3 percentage point from the productivity growth rate during this eleven-year period.

With respect to policy, the way to realize greater economies of scale is to promote stronger growth than has occurred since the latter 1960s. Even without major new policy initiatives, the Bureau of Labor Statistics projects that the trend-rate of growth in the real GNP will average near 3.5 percent a year in the decade of the 1980s. This is better than in the past decade, but the growth rate will decelerate in the second half of the 1980s as the growth of the labor force and hours worked decelerate sharply. If the kinds of policy measures suggested in this essay were adopted, at least 1 percentage point could be added to the growth rate, which would open up possibilities for somewhat greater economies of scale than were enjoyed in the 1970s.

The influence of changes in intensity of demand will, of course, depend on the economic conditions at the beginning and end of the period over which growth rates were measured. In general, however, adoption of policies to reduce cyclical variations—particularly to avoid contractions as severe as the 1973–75 experience—will help to raise the growth trend. The reduction of investments during recessions obviously slows the growth of capacity, and various empirical studies demonstrate that cyclicality and growth are negatively correlated. There is not space here to discuss the intricacies of countercyclical macroeconomic policy formulation. But it must be stressed that the mitigation of price inflation itself would make an important contribution to more stable economic growth.

The contribution of government services to business, such as roads and labor services as in maintaining security, has averaged about 0.1 percentage point a year since 1948. This rough estimate is based on the relative growth of factor services devoted to public purposes. The contribution was about the same after 1966 as before.

But the increases in unit real costs of business necessitated by government rules and regulations appear to have accelerated since 1966. Based in part on estimates by Denison, the negative impact of environmental and health and safety regulation alone has subtracted about 0.2 percentage point from the average annual growth rate between 1966 and 1975, and by 1976 the negative impact had risen to 0.4 percentage point. If improvements in the natural and working environment could be measured and included in the real GNP, it is possible that the negative net government impact since 1966 would be somewhat smaller. But given the present methods of measuring real product and productivity, public programs contributed to the slowdown.

With respect to policies to turn the net government impact around, continuing analysis is needed to ensure that government outlays are worth their cost. In the case of new public investment, it must be demonstrated that the expected rates of return are at least equal to those in the private sector. Outlays on current services to business should yield as much benefit as if businesses spent the funds themselves. These principles are difficult to apply in practice, but the executive and legislative branches must continually apply standards of this type when budgets are made and obligational authority is granted. Also, governments must continually strive to improve productivity in their own operations, so that they can increase the services rendered for the dollars spent or produce a given level of services at lowered cost. The preparation of productivity measures by the Bureau of Labor Statistics now covering about two-thirds of federal government employees should be continued and expanded, as should the work of the Joint Financial Management Improvement Program established by the Office of Management and Budget to promote productivity improvement in federal agencies. Similar programs now in place in several state and major local governments should be rapidly expanded to all. With respect to the negative impacts of government, further progress must be made toward reducing paperwork, simplifying regulations, and applying strict cost-benefit principles in revising old standards or promulgating new ones.

As is true of all growth accounting exercises, there remains a residual, amounting to -0.6 percentage point in both periods. The other variables thus accounted for the 1.4 percent slowdown in total factor productivity, about two-thirds of it attributable to declines in the advance of knowledge and the lower volume factors. But even though the residual reduced growth to the same extent in both periods, its magnitude is large enough to warrant investigation.

To the extent that it does not merely reflect a net overestimate of the other sources of growth, it reflects primarily a decline in the ratio of actual to potential labor efficiency, holding technology and the other variables constant. One element is the decline in hours actually worked in relation to the hours contained in the labor input measure that are largely hours paid for. The ratio of hours "at work" to hours paid for has declined at an average annual rate of around 0.1 percent. Further, University of Michigan surveys indicate that unproductive time at work, such as coffee breaks and attending to personal business, has increased by an average of at least about 0.2 percentage point since the mid-1960s. Beyond this there is considerable speculation that the efficiency of hours actually worked may have declined relative to the kind of norms established in work measurement studies. Certainly there are many cases of restrictive work rules or practices, although it is difficult to ascertain if their impact has increased. Some observers maintain that efficiency may have been adversely affected during the past dozen years by negative social trends, such as increased crime and drug use, erosion of the work-ethic, and increased questioning of materialism and of most institutions, including business. Denison has adduced evidence to show that increasing crimes against business have reduced the growth rate perceptibly, but less than 0.1 percent a year, on average, since 1960.

Increasing the ratio of actual to potential efficiency of workers is a particularly tempting area in which to suggest policy initiatives. Union work rules are subject to revision in contract negotiations, in which "productivity bargaining" is possible. But more fundamentally restrictive rules and practices have grown out of fear of unemployment. Consequently, maintenance of high employment rates associated with reasonably stable national economic growth, combined with a sound unemployment insurance system and opportunities for retraining and relocation under the Comprehensive Employment and Training Act of 1973 (CETA) as amended, should help to reduce such practices. So, too, should provisions for job security by firms and other employers to the extent that it is economically feasible. Unions and management have adopted measures to cushion the effect of technological and other changes such as retraining, using attrition to reduce jobs, and, when layoffs are necessary, giving advance notice, severance pay, or early retirement. Except for seniority, however, protective programs are not widespread.

An even more important reason for subnormal labor efficiency is lack of motivation to perform better owing to lack of interest in the job or concern for the enterprise—particularly in jobs in which remuneration is not tied to performance. It is here that quality-of-working-life programs, job redesign, labor-management productivity teams or broader company productivity programs, incentive pay or profit-sharing schemes, and other methods to elicit worker cooperation in improving efficiency and cutting unit costs can play an important role. During World War II, at the initiative of the chairman of the War Production Board, about 5,000 joint labor-management committees were formed in plants employing over 7 million workers. Only a small proportion of the committees continued after the war. But, with the productivity slowdown, a renewed interest in this approach has been promoted by the National Commission on Productivity, created by executive order in 1970, and reconstituted in 1975 by Congress as the National Center for Productivity and Quality of Working Life.

At the end of 1977 there were over 240 joint labor-management committees of various types in industry and government units. Some were organized as part of communitywide efforts to improve the industrial relations climate and strengthen regional economies. In 1971 the United Steelworkers of America and the steel companies set up joint labor-management teams in all plants of the industry, renewing the plan in 1974 and 1977 as part of joint efforts to increase international competitiveness of the industry. Some nonunion firms have established productivity improvement programs involving labor-management committees in plants and offices. These efforts have been promoted by several quality of working life institutes, state organizations, and the American Productivity Center, a private-sector nonprofit institution founded in 1977. The measures adopted under these programs include work simplification, job redesign, flexible work schedules and expansion of part-time jobs, autonomous work teams, goal-setting, feedback to workers on performance, incentive pay systems, and increased worker participation in design of tools and products, maintenance, reduction of defects and wastage, and the planning of training programs. Under many of the programs there has been a reduction of tardiness, absenteeism, and turnover, as well as measurable increases in efficiency.

When the National Center for Productivity and Quality of Working Life expired on September 30, 1978, its functions in the human relations area were transferred to the U. S. Department of Labor. In view of the potential of organizational productivity programs of the types described, and the relatively limited scope of current efforts, it would seem desirable for the president, through his secretary of labor, to mount a nationwide campain to promote joint labor-management programs, aided by a multipartite advisory committee composed of leaders of industry, labor, government, and the public. It would represent an important aspect of the anti-inflation effort, as well as helping improve international competitiveness of American production and accelerating increases in real average earnings, which are closely related to productivity gains. Since all of these objectives are shared by labor, management, and the public, it should be possible to obtain the active cooperation of all. A 1974 study by Daniel Yankelovich established that almost all managers and union officials agreed with the statement that "it is possible for the union and management to cooperate on specific programs which will improve productivity." Such programs, together with further recovery of the real GNP to its potential, are the chief means of raising productivity in the short term, that is, the next few years. Over the long run, however, increases in tangible and intangible investments to improve the quality of human and capital resources are the key to accelerating productivity advance.

Government Controls Versus Market Discipline

CARL H. MADDEN

Whether or not monetary and fiscal policies can curb inflation, it is painfully evident that they have not done so. Inflation is accelerating while economic expansion seems to be slowing down. The present threat of stagflation poses a policy dilemma: standard anti-inflation measures may weaken growth and bring on recession, while policies to sustain expansion may also nudge upward the rate of inflation.

In such circumstances, the appeal of nonstandard policy tools grows stronger. It is important to look at political and market factors bearing on stabilization policy and to ask why inflation persists during slack periods. Moreover, a strong case has been made for some form of social contract—an incomes policy—that would mediate between various interest groups that contend with one another over the distribution of income. Also, as the nation appears to be moving toward wage and price controls despite official denials, the sorry record of such controls ought to be recalled. As inflation gets more deeply embedded in the economic base, the consequences of the nation's policy choices get harsher.

The first question about the standard anti-inflation measures is not whether they have failed but whether they have yet been tried. Monetary policy has not stopped inflation. Until recent years, stop-go monetary actions, which accommodated fiscal policy by the prevailing opinion of the top policymakers, increased the money supply too fast. From 1968 to 1974, the dominant policy opinion among top government economists, such as George Schultze, Herbert Stein, and Arthur F. Burns, leaned toward the monetarist view. These economists favored a steady, noninflationary growth of the money stock. They proposed that the growth rate of money be gradually brought down, over a long enough period of years to avoid a sharp recession, to an annual rate of 3 to 4 percent, in order to achieve noninflationary sustainable growth at high employment levels. Yet, during the eight years that Arthur Burns was chairman of the Federal Reserve Board, the money supply rose an average of 5.9

percent a year, and prices rose 50 percent, a rate faster than that during William M. Martin's term.

Both Martin and Burns are self-professed inflation fighters widely portrayed in the press as implacable and relentless, and they were praised and respected when they left office. Even though their efforts to fight inflation were recognized, they failed to achieve results that matched their good intentions. In short, neither the accommodative approach of Martin nor the monetarist approach of Burns produced anti-inflation results.

In 1978, under a new chairman at the Federal Reserve with a business and legal background, G. William Miller, the behavior of the various monetary aggregates indicated that the rate of monetary growth was much too high, in the face of an alarmingly high inflation rate. As a result, the money stock is apparently growing too fast and will continue to do so for some time. The monetary base (member bank reserves at the Federal Reserve plus currency in circulation) increased at a 10 percent rate from July 1977 to July 1978 and at a 10.2 percent annual rate from January to July 1978. This strong expansion rate of the monetary base ensures a rapid expansion of the money stock itself.

The anti-inflation record of fiscal policy is no better than that of monetary policy. The most widely accepted commonsense prescription for fiscal policy holds that it should be effectively countercyclical. That is, government should run deficits in recessions that are approximately offset by surpluses during high-level expansions. The federal government has not followed such a prescription. It has run a deficit on national income accounts from FY 1970 through FY 1977, a period including years of high-level expansion. For some time, total federal expenditures have been rising faster than the economy grows. For the fiscal years 1972–77, the rate of growth of federal expenditures was 11.6 percent (on a national income accounts basis), and in FY 1978 the rate is expected to be 10.3 percent.

For FY 1977 and 1978, which mark the second and third years of a cyclical recovery and expansion, the federal deficits, both in actual and in full-employment terms, were unusually large. Of course, the economy was bigger, so these deficits were relatively smaller. Also, federal spending has shifted from direct purchases toward relatively more transfer payments, which are thought to have a smaller impact on the economy for each dollar of expenditures. Also, two sectors of the economy burden fiscal policies today, in contrast to earlier years; one is the international sector, the other is the state and local government sector. The surpluses accruing to foreigners and the large surpluses of state and local governments have tended to offset the stimulative effects of recent federal deficits.

The policy record for monetary and fiscal measures does not show convincingly that these standard anti-inflation techniques have been used primarily as anti-inflation weapons. Multiple policy objectives include, above all, high employment and economic growth. Indeed, it may well be naive or disingenuous to hold that inflation results from macro-policy "mistakes." Rather, it results from expected outcomes of compromises. Meantime, however, the inflation-unemployment trade-off has worsened. The Keynesian model implies a reliable and positive relationship between real and money income. It also implies an inverse relationship between unemployment and aggregate demand. But recent experience has not been consistent with the Keynesian model. In the 1970s high rates of inflation have been associated with rising unemployment. The worsened trade-off can be seen in the growing size of the combination of inflation and unemployment rates. Economic slack has not been including much slowdown in upward price momentum.

The worsening trade-off is the basis for an argument with ominous meaning, if valid, for future stabilization attempts. The trade-off makes the prospective cost of reducing inflation appear higher than earlier. That cost, of course, is lost output and employment. The converse is also argued; that is, stimulative measures intended to reduce joblessness and spur growth may accelerate inflation more than earlier. In 1960, economists Paul A. Samuelson and Robert M. Solow estimated that money wages would not stop increasing unless the unemployment rate rose to 8 percent, and that wages would rise at a rate of 2 to 3 percent a year with 5 to 6 percent of the labor force unemployed. If productivity were increasing at 2 to 3 percent a year, the economy could maintain price stability with a 2 to 3 percent increase in wages each year. But an economy in semirecession from joblessness of 8 percent is unlikely to generate productivity gains of 2 to 3 percent. More recently, studies by Phillip D. Cagan suggest that if the average slack in the economy were about 1 percentage point in terms of unemployment, then it would take eight to nine years to reduce the inflation rate of 1978 to zero. Cagan's measure of full unemployment is a rate of 3.5 percent for prime-age males, and it corresponds to a gross unemployment rate of 6 percent.

Meantime, inflation accelerates. It picked up speed in the first half of 1978, and it is likely to do so again in the first half of 1979. One reason is government-mandated cost increases in minimum wages and social security tax increases. The other is that 1979 is a big collective bargaining year. Negotiating unions in automobile, rubber, electrical machinery, and trucking industries will be trying to restore real income growth. Three-year, life-of-contract wage settlements could easily run to 30 percent or more in 1979. Union catch-up demands anticipate future inflation at recent past rates and thereby build in cost hikes. They also may set patterns for nonunion wage and salary increases.

Continued deficits and excessive monetary growth year after year are not standard anti-inflation measures. After every major war except World War II, prices that had peaked during wartime fell afterwards. But after World War II there was no price decline at all comparable to what followed previous wars. Throughout the twentieth century the price trend has been upward, but since the end of the Depression and the start of World War II, prices have fallen only twice. Each time—in 1949 after the first postwar recession and in 1955 after the post-Korean war slowdown—the decline was less than 1 percent. The dollar worth 100 cents in 1939 is worth only 21.2 cents in 1978 buying power. Yet the expansive policy over the years has validated price pressures and deepened inflationary expectations. The policy record is no basis for a claim that standard remedies have failed. Rather, it is a reason to ask why the standard remedies have been so little tried. What structural features of our economy have made inflation chronic?

Built-in Chronic Inflation

A strong case holds that, in an inflation-prone society, other objectives of monetary and fiscal policy have taken precedence over anti-inflation. To be sure, a society that strives for rapid economic growth and full employment need not therefore give up price stability. But the United States has done so. Postwar economics texts warned, as Paul Samuelson's did in 1961: "Wages and prices seem to have become sticky as far as downward movements are concerned; also government has become quick to act to stem any depression that is beginning to get under way. If prices rise in good times and they do not fall much in bad times, what is the long-term direction for prices? The question answers itself."[1]

Since 1965, the country has seen the inflationary excesses of the Great Society and its greatly expanded welfare state, as government pumped money into the system through greatly expanded budgets and the Federal Reserve System. By 1969, prices were rising more than 6 percent, unprecedented in the postwar period. Two recessions did not stop inflation despite tight money and wage and price controls. In 1973, poor crops and soaring farm prices added to inflation woes. And by the start of 1974, the fourfold rise in the price of imported oil made matters worse. Failure to pass these costs on to consumers has delayed adjustment to the new era of high-price oil and added to government costs. Since the mid-1960s greatly increased federal regulation on behalf of civil rights, consumerism, environmentalism, and worker safety, combined with increases in crime, have raised business costs. And the inflation-weakened dollar itself has contributed to price rises. Basic inflation, officially estimated at 6 to 7 percent, is now built-in in America and persists during slack periods.

The United States may be moving, as Great Britain has already done, toward a proletarian outlook of its middle class. Paul Johnson describes how government-induced "closed shop" attitudes sharpen adversary bargaining behavior when he argued that "the middle class felt they had no alternative but to unionize themselves efficiently, and even to assume the behavioral characteristics of the working classes in a situation of industrial conflict. . . . Professional workers of all kinds, with exceptionally high codes of conduct, who had hitherto placed their obligations to society above financial rewards, were now driven by rapid impoverishment to abandon their traditional ethics. . . ."[2]

[1] Paul A. Samuelson, Economics, 5th ed. (New York: McGraw-Hill, 1961), p. 203.
[2] Paul Johnson, Enemies of Society (New York: Atheneum, 1977).

In the United States, the Congressional Budget Office acknowledges that "the on-going price advance results principally from various interest groups using their economic and political power to maintain their traditional rates of real income growth." And, of course, it has been even more difficult for Americans to keep up the now-expected pace of real income growth since the share of total national income going to oil-producing countries has so dramatically increased. As a result, the nation has seen an increase in adversary bargaining approaches among many interest groups. They include federal, state, and local government employees, police and firefighter personnel, doctors and nurses, airline pilots, and college professors. Policy approaches that would avoid adversary and economic class perceptions and tactics have long-run importance in avoiding wholesale shifts of middle-class Americans to a proletarian outlook. Inflation incites interest-group action and exacerbates interest-group antagonisms and envy.

Interest groups try to preserve real income growth shares by linking income to consumer prices through "indexing." One estimate holds that 55 million Americans now have some shield of an escalator clause against inflation. They include social security, supplemental social security, federal civilian, military, railroad, disabled coal miner, and postal worker pension recipients. Also, they include employees of firms covered by major collective bargaining agreements, state and local county workers, some workers in small, nonunion factories, and food stamp recipients.

Also, household members work more. In 1978, census data show that of 11.1 million families—one out of five families in the nation—having incomes of $25,000 or more, more than three out of four have at least two people working. One out of three such families has three or more family members earning a salary.

People make efforts to get their taxes reduced. Proposition 13 in California and widespread moves for constitutional limits on government spending illustrate the trend. Also, households increase their borrowing or reduce their assets to stay even.

Indexing wages to consumer prices means that wages rise even in slack periods. Besides contractual indexing of wages and pensions, informal indexing arises, often from threats of unionizing or for competitive reasons. In professions such as medicine, groups use political and economic pressure to keep fees in line with prices. Government measures also keep incomes in line through wage minimums, import floors, and the like.

Of workers covered by major collective bargaining agreements, about 60 percent now include contractual indexing of pay to price changes. Despite diversity in these arrangements, total wage and benefit packages including cost-of-living adjustments placed significant upward pressure on prices during the 1976 bargaining round. Thus, it is fair to conclude that powerful forces lead to widespread demands for money wage increases in excess of productivity gains. Also, wages are resistant to reduction during periods of cyclical slack in the economy.

A recent study by Marvin H. Kosters of wage behavior and inflation in the 1970s documents the relatively stable behavior of average wage increases during the past decade. It happened even though differences in rates of wage increase for major sectors of the economy were often quite large. But these large differences offset each other. Kosters believes that considerable potential exists for an acceleration in the rate of increase of average hourly labor costs in response to cyclical expansion. One reason is the spread of indexing through cost-of-living indexes. Another is the pull on lower wage sectors of rising demand and tightening labor markets toward higher wages when relative wages in high-wage sectors are historically high and seldom fall. A third is the increase in labor costs from government-mandated measures.

It is no mystery that prices have become less and less responsive to cyclical shifts in demand downward. The upward tilt of prices is the outcome of structural features that seldom result in wages responding to slack in the economy. The American workforce is a service and an information processing work force, with two-thirds of jobs in service industries and one-third in information-processing industries. Strong unionism is found in manufacturing, construction, transportation and communications, as well as in government, including unions of teachers, fire and police, and health care workers. Still, only between one-fifth and one-fourth of workers throughout the economy are union members. Labor costs in the whole economy, however, make up an estimated 70 percent of total costs. So a little consideration of the structure of the economy, and of its labor markets, makes it easy to understand how a basic 6.0-to-6.5 or more percent inflation rate can become built-in when excessive federal deficits and too rapid money creation keep such an economy awash with liquidity.

In manufacturing, which has a cost structure built on top of rising and often indexed money wage costs, price rises are held in check only through efficiency gains from economies of scale, greater capital intensity, and such other nonlabor efficiencies as improved processes, product or service innovation, and cost savings from finance and marketing advances. In these industries, the cost of regulation mounts because of heavy use of capital equipment, materials, water, and chemicals in manufacturing processes and the expense of security systems in large plants. In these industries, cyclical downturns in demand, with few exceptions, result first in cuts in jobs and output. Variable costs of production are cut first, while prices remain sticky. It now takes prolonged and convincing pressure downward by authorities on overall monetary demand to slow down price rises.

A further word about regulation in manufacturing industries may be in order. Added to recent pressure on prices since the OPEC oil embargo in 1973 quadrupled oil prices are nonoutput-producing cost increasing for manufacturing to meet regulatory standards and to protect facilities and personnel from crime. According to Barry Bosworth, director of the federal Council on Wage and Price Stability, government regulations add about one-half of a percent annually to the rate of inflation. New regulations on industrial noise, worker exposure to cancer-causing substances, transportation facilities requiring expensive alterations to serve the handicapped, and dozens of others forecast for 1979 would cost business and consumers another $35 billion a year and $60 billion in equipment, construction, and engineering.

In service and information-processing industries, wage bargaining, while following patterns set in manufacturing, may be more volatile in the absence of unions, since wages respond upward more quickly to increases in demand or to increases in inflation than when set under three-year union contracts. In government, the wage-setting principle of "comparability" with private industry transmits demand pressures on private sector wages directly to federal pay. Federal money wage increases are now mandated by law each year based on such considerations except when Congress or the president explicitly limits or delays increases. Federal pensions as well as social security payments are indexed, one formally and the other through congressional action, usually every two years. Even the pensions of the Federal Reserve System employees are indexed, a suggestion of the realistic judgment of expert Federal Reserve officials concerning the likelihood of future inflation. While wage determination in these industries of the production of services and information-processing follows a pattern similar to but at times more volatile than manufacturing, productivity gains in these industries are less dependable, systematic, or measurable in some of these industries. In government, of course, productivity gains are not measured, since the output of government is considered equal in value to the price of inputs, a practice that makes neglect of productivity considerations more likely to occur without managerial action.

A lot of people gain from inflation. They include homeowners, mortgage holders, borrowers, businessmen, and politicians. These people benefit, or they think they do, from price rises. A large number of people may be involved, since 60 percent or more of American families own their homes. Most of these owners also hold mortgages. Other individual borrowers number in the millions. And business heads and politicians, though less numerous, are influential. Homeowners have better inflation hedges—real estate—than owners of equities. The deduction of mortgage interest from tax bills gets more valuable as inflation pushes people into higher tax brackets. As inflation pushes tax rates and tax revenues higher, politicians in Congress can spend more and at the same time vote for "tax relief." In effect, Congress abandons its responsibility to legislate tax rate increases to the anonymous and nonaccountable officials of the Federal Reserve. To be sure, whether a particular person benefits from inflation on balance depends on the net outcome of his or her own debtor-creditor-owner position. Still, enough evidence exists to suggest that millions benefit on balance.

People who lose by inflation, except perhaps for the aged, are not politically popular. Bankers and other lenders among institutions are by and large mysterious and distant figures. Brokers and investors on Wall Street are equally remote from the concerns of millions of Americans. Workers whose pay is not formally or informally indexed are likely to be among the minority of 12 percent of families who are officially designated as poor. The aged, who have been increasing in number and living longer, are becoming less popular, while they become politically more active and influential. There is a growing recognition that the ratio of aged to working people is continuing to move adversely to workers. That is, the ratio of aged to working people will rise with the increase and longer survival of the aged, combined with the slowdown in the number of young workers moving into the labor force. Attitudes toward more retirement and sick benefits for older, retired people get less popular and more subject to political controversy as younger people realize the mounting costs per worker of intergenerational wealth and income transfers.

So inflation has its uses. Where growth and high employment are key political goals, a little inflation may help. It creates business optimism, validates investment and inventory decisions, and increases money profits and wages above long-term trends in real income. In an economy where money wages are bargained by interest groups that are more often than before proletarian in outlook, combined demands of these interest groups expressed in wage bargaining and other wage determination processes more often exceed the real resources available to meet them. Easy monetary and fiscal policy validate the money claims while obscuring the outcome for real income shares. Both government subsidy of underpriced imported oil and increased costs to industry of new government regulation add to costs in the economy. In a nutshell, the American economy becomes a secular victim of cost-push inflation, of the wage-price spiral, and the spiral is validated by official action in achieving growth, employment, and welfare goals.

A Guide to Inflation Antidotes

The Carter administration anti-inflation plan of April 1978 relied on symbolism in wage-price setting, jawboning by Presidential Counselor Robert S. Strauss, pressure to cut costs by governmental regulation, and moves to cut the federal deficit. To encourage business and labor to exercise restraint, President Carter proposed to limit salary increases of federal workers in 1978 to 5.5 percent, down from 7.0 percent in 1977, and to freeze top federal employee salaries at $47,500. Strauss, using high-pressure persuasion, sought a limit on pay raises of top business executives to 5 percent, and a number of companies, including General Motors, Ford, American Telegraph, Aetna Life, W.R. Grace, and Time, Inc., as of early June had agreed to limit executive pay from its 12 percent increase of 1977. Straus also persuaded the steel industry to limit price increases in the second half of 1978 to 3 percent. Meanwhile, George Meany of the AFL-CIO flatly refused to promise restraint in wage demands, and in late July Douglas E. Fraser, president of the United Automobile Workers, pulled out of the administration's chosen vehicle for labor-management cooperation in inflation and other economic problems, the unofficial "Labor-Management Group," composed of sixteen top business and labor executives. Fraser labeled the group as a useless "facade" to disguise a "one-sided class war" by business interests.

Besides voluntary wage and price restraints, the administration is seeking ways to cut the cost of government regulation. One way is to deregulate, as with the airlines. Another is a proposal of several top administration economic policymakers for a "regulatory budget," an annual report to document both costs as well as benefits of a year's regulatory actions and the next year's expected ones. The budget would force better decisions and more coordination of action among independent agencies now regulating in their own vacuums without regard for costs or prices.

Budget-cutting, while not an avowed weapon against inflation of the Carter administration, has become more popular with the president. The "taxpayer revolt" spreading across the nation and forcefully affecting primary elections is no doubt one reason. Another is no doubt the Kemp-Roth tax reduction bill, introduced by Republican Senators Kemp and Roth to cut federal tax rates 33 percent, phased on over three years, as well as corporate cuts.

The president by late September 1978 forecast a stronger program to fight inflation that would not injure either management or labor. It included wage-price guidelines, tax-based income policies, and other measures short of compulsory wage and price controls. Still, leading observers foresaw a drift in direction of compulsory price controls, and some saw it as "inevitable."

Business and labor leaders, along with President Carter, profess not to want wage and price controls, although the fact that a majority of the public favors them cannot be ignored. According to three Gallup polls taken consecutively during the first six months of 1978, a majority of the American people favored wage and price controls. In reply to the question, "Would you favor or oppose having the government bring back wage and price controls?" Gallup reported in August that 53 percent favored controls, 34 percent were opposed, and 13 percent were undecided.

In view of accelerated inflation in the coming years, the majority of the public that favors controls is likely to increase. Indeed, for the past forty years, the American people have approved wage and price controls in times of severe inflation. In 1971, when President Nixon disregarded the advice of his economic advisers and followed the urgings of political aides such as Treasury Secretary John B. Connally and imposed controls as part of his economic program, Americans supported him by a 6 to 1 margin. When the controls proved unsatisfactory, the people favored even stricter controls. As Lloyd Shearer wrote in *Parade* magazine on September 24, 1978, "Freezing wages and prices is an anti-inflationary method that most Americans believe infinitely more practical and productive than jawboning."

Labor leaders believe that controls penalize union workers while they let nonunion employees whose wages are more immediately responsive to increases in demand or in the price level off the hook. And as labor leaders see things, business and finance are in the same category. George Meany of the AFL-CIO has consistently stated that he would support direct controls on wages only if they were also imposed on all other forms of income, such as profits, interest, rents, and speculative capital gains. But—as Meany has emphasized—if these other controls were imposed, labor would support controls on wages.

Business leaders oppose controls because, like most economists, they believe controls simply do not work. Business wants freedom to raise prices to respond to market signals; costs rise and fall for reasons other than inflation and deflation, as does demand. Business also fears that controls mean permanent government power over markets. Most economists (J.K. Galbraith is a notable exception) oppose controls for reasons of principle. Controls take away freedom of people and business firms in the market place. They lead to inefficient use of resources by disrupting the information system that markets supply. Controls lead to artificial shortages by underpricing goods and limiting their production. They lead to waste of energy in huge bureaucratic regulatory agencies that are themselves costly and that impose huge cost burdens on industry. Controls tend to multiply and get more specific, arbitrary, and discretionary, leading to government intrusion into the production process in often ludicrous ways.

Above all, business and many economists agree, controls do not in fact stop inflation; they only control its symptoms. No one would propose cooling a hot room by legislating that the thermometer ought not be permitted to rise. Much evidence shows that controls in both war and peace end with prices accelerating upward when they are abandoned. Economic texts for decades have pointed out the simple principle violated by controls: "A legal maximum price, without rationing, leaves a gap between demand and supply. . . . At the artificial ceiling price, supply and demand do not balance and some method of rationing, formal or informal, is needed to allocate the short supply and bring the effective demand down. . . ."[3] The difficulty of rationing is that its success hinges on a real consensus to support the goals and the rules of a controls policy. Only during wars or national emergencies, and then only with a threat of punishment, do people widely agree on sacrifices.

Even though controls may not work, their public popularity ought not to be underestimated. John B. Connally in a lecture in September 1978 expressed regret that he had argued for controls within the Nixon administration in 1971.[4] However, the fact is, this astute political leader did recommend controls and carried the day, probably doing so for appealing political reasons. Other astute political leaders, while in power and while pondering the public support a program of controls might bring a president beset by rising inflation or its perception, might do the same in the future. Even the United States Chamber of Commerce, long opposed in principle to controls, when faced with Nixon's August 1971 *fait accompli* of a wage-price freeze and looking to other legislative battles to be fought, felt it was in no position for its principled opposition to be effective, and so it minimized its stated objections to Nixon's new policies.

If direct and general wage and price controls do not work even though popular, what about measures short of such controls? One such measure has been employed by Great Britain, Sweden, and West Germany. They are all more heavily unionized than is the United States. Britain and Sweden have been

[3] Samuelson, p. 426.
[4] *Washington Post*, September 25, 1978.

marked politically by "democratic socialism" for more than a generation. While all three countries depend on market mechanisms, they all involve more public ownership interest in industry than the United States. And, being more heavily unionized, they go further in sharing industrial power with unions, either through codetermination, as in West Germany, or in labor participation in government, as in Sweden and Britain. And all these countries have well-established welfare state benefits and pursue full employment policies of a highly pragmatic character.

The measure common to these countries is a negotiated wage "cap" determined by bargaining sessions of government with business and labor leaders. In Britain, the Callaghan Labor government for a second year gained a wage agreement of 5 percent. In Sweden, the new "bourgeois" coalition that supplanted the Social Democratic rule of two generations gained union agreement to hold pay increases for eighteen months to levels between 2 and 3 percent. In Germany, at the beginning of each legislative session, business and labor leaders sit down with the government and agree on broad wage and price standards that are compatible with the government plans for growth of the economy.

These countries have moved an important step beyond the United States in self-conscious government policy management of their "mixed" economies. Their approach is elitist and political. All three countries have maintained high employment, but the record of West Germany has exceeded nearly every other Western country in its record of controlling inflation. Yet the process of trying to control inflation has led policical leadership in these countries to negotiate shares of income gains in real terms that at times involve reductions in real income for workers. Bernard D. Nossiter cites Per Olaf Edin, described as a "left-wing, highly regarded economist for the huge metal workers' union," as saying: "Almost every person in our membership understands this means a fall in income but they understand that it is necessary for our long-term good. Yes, it is good for the government, too, but we must always choose what is good for our members."[5] And, in practical terms, as Nossiter writes, the cut in income last year "simply means that a Volvo worker will run his own car longer, postpone building another wing on his second summer house and vacation five weeks on Swedish lakes rather than the Mediterranean."

Whether the United States wishes to move so far as to set wage (and therefore, to some degree, price) policy by elitist agreement is an issue raised by wage-price guidelines and their enforcement. Despite variations, these guidelines or guideposts set acceptable price and wage increases, to be enforced either voluntarily or coercively. The history of Kennedy-Johnson guideposts flows from the inadequacy of Keynesian anti-inflation measures. For Keynes, full employment could be achieved by adequate increases in aggregate demand, and only after full employment was reached would excess demand spill over into inflation. By contrast, the Kennedy-Johnson guideposts were based on the theory of the Phillips curve. In a 1958 article, A.W. Phillips reviewed British ex-

[5] Ibid., June 1, 1978.

perience from 1861 to 1957 with the relationship between changes in unemployment and money wage rates. He found a stable, long-run and inverse relationship between the two. Others found a similar inverse or negative relationship between the two rates of change, money wages, and unemployment in the United States and in other countries for various time periods, both long-run and short-run.

The major policy implication of the Phillips curve is that there is a trade-off between inflation and unemployment. The nation can no longer achieve full employment without inflation. Stabilization policy must be defined by the amount of involuntary joblessness associated with the highest allowable inflation rate. The Keynesian model attributes inflation to excess demand in product markets. Phillips, on the other hand, emphasized the role of rising money wages in tight labor markets as the impetus to price increases. The 1960s, in a sense, was the decade of the Phillips curve. The idea that wage increases should be limited to increases in labor productivity while at the same time aggregate demand ought to be adjusted to keep unemployment at its natural noninflationary rate was the basic idea behind the Kennedy-Johnson guideposts. This fine tuning was supposed to keep the economy at full employment, without inflation, but it also allowed real income to rise at the rate of productivity growth. The policy would be neutral regarding the distribution of income as between wages and profits, since an increase in both output per manhour and wages of, say, 3 percent would allow for about 70 percent of the added income to go to wages and about 30 percent to other costs, including profits.

One assumption of the guidepost policy is that business firms set prices in relation to cost per unit of output. Some theories of oligopoly pricing in industries dominated by few firms hold that such firms use factor price changes (wages and materials costs) as "signals" for price increases, since they are uncertain about the price policies of their rivals. Empirical studies have shown that in the manufacturing sector—where oligopoly is the predominant form of market structure, at least statistically—prices do respond to changes in factor costs without regard to productivity changes. This could mean that wage guideposts without price guideposts would be inflationary by allowing prices to "float." It also could mean that the profit share of the increase in prices, which would rise by the same percent as wages under wage-price guideposts, could rise relative to that of the wage share in real terms.

Another assumption of wage-price guideposts is that wage changes are the principal source of inflationary pressure on costs. Over the long run of post-World War II period, the judgment may be correct empirically. However, in the short run, the inflation of the 1970s has been marked by rising materials costs, food prices, and basic resource prices such as energy. Already, market forces are redistributing income to agriculture and the extractive industries at home and abroad away from manufacturing.

A third assumption of Kennedy-Johnson type guideposts is that controls are the best way to limit wage increases. But are wage increases determined principally by demand conditions in the labor markets? More and more it seems that expectations of future inflation play a leading role. Direct controls on wages will not be politically acceptable to labor without accompanying measures to reduce inflationary expectations.

Finally, any scheme of wage and price controls, including guideposts, presupposes that the source of inflation comes from a wage-price spiral, without regard for shifts in supply underlying the labor and materials markets. However, price changes, including increases as well as decreases, also serve to move toward balance the state of demand and supply in markets. The inflation of the 1970s, as world industrialization spreads, as world population grows, and as gains worldwide are made in human survival, has been marked—in contrast to the inflation of the 1960s—by shortages during periods of peak demand.

It is not merely that guideposts interfere with the market system by involving government in the wage-price decision making process as a partner. It is not merely that guideposts work best when inflation is not already in full swing —that is, they work best when needed less. If prices are already rising at 5 percent a year, and if real productivity gains are 2 percent, then wage increases of only 3 percent, representing a decline in real wages of 2 percent, are hard to justify in the face of productivity gains. If labor does not get these gains at all, then who does get them? Clearly, inflation should drop or else the gains in productivity go to profits. It is that guideposts may not work well in a period when inflationary expectations are widespread and firmly grounded in experience.

Moral suasion may have had some positive role in the 1960s. Economists Gary Fromm and George Perry both testified before Congress that their studies showed such a role. Fromm estimated that the guideposts reduced the average yearly increase of wages by 1.25 percent, unit labor costs by 2 percent, and the wholesale price index by 1.4 percent, during the period from 1962 to 1966. Still, by the early 1970s, Nixon administration economists were skeptical of guideposts because of at least one new factor. It was that chronic inflation had made an inflationary psychology widespread. Indeed, the Nixon controls program was based on an "accelerationist" view of inflation that above all attempted to break the vicious circle of inflationary psychology.

The Nixon controls emphasized controlling prices more than it did wages, although it had wage guidelines. It sought involvement of consumers in policing price movements. It was aimed at consumer psychology. And most economists agree that the Nixon controls did reduce inflation between the last half of 1971 and the end of 1972. But in 1973, exogenous factors such as successive currency devaluations, the corn blight, the Middle East conflict, the Russian wheat deal, and the Peruvian anchovy die-off all occurred when price controls prevented price rises that would have increased supply to match demand pressures. Supply pressures, often from elsewhere in the world, intervened in United States control efforts.

Empirical studies, based on American data for the post-Korean war period, suggest that bringing inflation down by monetary and fiscal policy would produce costs in output and employment that are high and long-lasting. The rising interest in supplementing monetary and fiscal policy with some form of direct government intervention in the wage and price structure comes from those who take for granted the continuation of past relationships among the various elements of the economy concerned. As Arthur M. Okun said recently: "The fundamental issue here is whether people regard the present hand of policy as viable, or whether they're ready to throw it in and deal a new one. The evidence I see indicates that there is no happy ending to the present economic scenario, and that conclusion is becoming increasingly clear to other people with an open mind on these issues."[6]

A tax-based incomes policy (TIP) is a way to preserve the market mechanism but supplement standard policy. It provides a penalty or reward through the tax system that is intended to induce people to behave in more restrained ways on wages, prices, or some combination of the two. One variety of TIP was first proposed in 1971 by Professor Sidney Weintraub of the University of Pennsylvania and Governor Henry Wallich of the Federal Reserve Board. It was a penalty TIP, imposing higher corporate tax rates on firms that granted wage increases in excess of some guidelines. "With wages and other compensation of labor amounting to 75 percent of gross national product," Wallich told Congress, "wages are unavoidably the principal factor in prices. A slowing in wage increases, therefore, will necessarily bring about a slowing in price increases."

Arthur Okun's version of TIP involves rewards, not penalties. Okun would offer workers a reward—say, a tax credit or rebate equivalent to 2 percent of pretax income—if they would accept a limit on wage increases of, say, 6 percent. They would qualify through their employer, so the employer would administer the plan. The plan would include employee benefits as well as cost-of-living adjustments. Numerical standards would be set by Congress annually. The guideline would be set at some rate moderately—not drastically—below the present rate of wage increase. In the view of TIP proponents, unwinding inflation must be gradual to avoid major inequities, disparities and major disruptions in markets. To them, a reasonable and feasible objective is a reduction in inflation of 2 percentage points over the three years of such a program. Okun estimates his program would cost a little over $15 billion with full participation of the labor force.

All the TIP proponents expect the plan to be accompanied by classic measures, and it is not a substitute for monetary and fiscal restraint. But they argue that present-day inflation is not excess-demand induced. That view, says Okun, leads to the prescription that he calls "burning down the house to roast a pig" of just relying on monetary and fiscal tightening. They see their proposal as steering a middle course between relying on market forces and government intervention in the public interest. And, whatever its administrative difficulties, they argue, TIP plans are still a lot less cumbersome than direct wage and price controls. They expect that TIP plans would be combined with some monitoring of prices to keep price increases in manufacturing in line with the slowdown in wage increases.

TIP plans have their critics. The plans are based on the theory that in part prices are a fixed mark-up over costs, a viewpoint not entirely lacking in empirical evidence to support it. However, the evidence is interpreted otherwise by proponents of monetarist theories or critics whose value judgments place preservation of market-type wage-price processes paramount. That to administer TIP plans, particularly the penalty type, would be an administrative nightmare is hard to gainsay, even though wage and price controls are worse ones. TIP plans would of course suffer from the weaknesses common to other forms of wage and price guideposts; however, such guideposts would be enforced.

The most fundamental judgment to be made about TIP plans, as it is also concerning other wage and price controls, not excluding so-called voluntary guideposts, is the degree to which present relations among the relevant variables in the inflation equation are or are not permanent. There remains strong support among economists for reliance on disinflation by monetary-fiscal means alone. These economists do not believe inflation is intractable. Instead, they fall into one of two camps. Monetarists, who favor gradual disinflation through monetary-fiscal restraint, hold that, lacking validation of excessive wage demands and other calls upon resources, including excessive government spending, the economy would move toward a balance that included high employment, stable growth, and stable prices. These economists oppose wage and price controls not only in principle but also because they believe that such controls are not effective in reducing inflation except for quite short periods. These economists emphasize long-run and structural adjustments to a moderate rate of growth in the money stock.

The other group among economists opposed to wage and price controls emphasize the theory of rational expectations. This approach, still subject to vigorous debate, holds that activist monetary and fiscal policies cannot generally increase either employment or real output in the economy. Policy is impotent, the theorists of rational expectations hold, because people in the economy act rationally. That is, people act in anticipation of policy effects in such a way as to offset the desired effects. So, any anticipated fiscal or monetary stimulus to increase output is translated into price increases instead, as labor and management scramble to increase prices and wages to offset the loss of income shares that might otherwise ensue from the inflation they believe will surely result.

The monetarists and the rational expectations group both argue that the only appropriate policy response is a consistent and credible policy move toward reducing the rate of increase of money GNP until a noninflationary price trend is restored. At that point policy should then be directed at achieving the highest output and employment rate compatible with this course. The monetarists are more or less convinced that disinflation will take a long time, barring a sharp and dangerous recession. The devotees of rational expectations, however, believe that people will respond faster to a credible anti-inflationary policy than models of the economy based on faulty analytical relationships derived from the past would suggest. They think inflation premiums will come out of both prices and wages quickly with less damage to output and employment than devotees of wage and price controls are willing to believe.

Professor Madden, who died on October 8, 1978, did not have an opportunity to review this essay before publication.

Report of the Williamsburg Conference

Inflation cannot be controlled without first understanding its root causes and the effectiveness of alternative remedies. The first step in developing this understanding was to enlist the research efforts of the experts whose essays appear in this volume. Each author, however, worked independently, and it was important to bring them together for an exchange of views.

Consequently, the American Council of Life Insurance sponsored a four-day conference in Williamsburg, Virginia, February 21–24, 1979, attended by eighty persons, including not only the authors of the essays but also members of university faculties, professional organizations, business concerns, and labor unions. Divided into small working groups, the participants used the essays as a point of departure for open-ended discussions of the dangers of inflation to national survival.

On the final day of the conference the conclusions that had emerged from the discussions were set forth in a series of recommendations that represented the consensus of the participants. They dealt with actions that should be taken regarding the federal budget, monetary policy, equitable burden sharing, government support programs, regulatory improvement, productivity, health care costs, and the international value of the dollar.

The following recommendations should not be attributed to any one individual, nor to the organizations with which they are associated, nor to the Academy of Political Science. Nevertheless, the conference felt that an expression of the views of a group of Americans drawn from various occupations would be helpful in providing a framework within which national debate could take place.

Copies of a statement reflecting the views of the life insurance industry may be obtained from the American Council of Life Insurance, 1850 K Street, N.W., Washington, D.C., 20006.

Preamble

Inflation is rapidly becoming a socially and economically destructive force which, unless counteracted firmly and promptly, will drive the nation to accept extreme measures threatening to our freedoms. The roots of inflation are entwined not simply in economic factors, but in the social, psychological and political layers of American life. Particularly to be noted is the dramatic rise in expectations which is often described as the "psychology of entitlement" and has been institutionalized in both the public and private sectors.

These expectations are translated into ever-rising government expenditures which have outrun revenues and have led to deficits that contribute to inflation. Pressures on the Federal Reserve Board to support these deficits, while simultaneously holding down interest rates, have led to excessive growth in the money supply. During the past decade other factors have also contributed to inflation, including such outside "shocks" to the economic system as the OPEC oil monopoly, widespread crop failures and raw material shortages.

Among the number of long-term changes being fed into the present malaise the following bear special scrutiny: (1) widespread expectations of continued inflation have been dealt into such economic decisions as wage and price determination, with the result that wages and prices accelerate in boom periods but show little deceleration during recession; (2) a slowdown has occurred in the rate of productivity growth; (3) increases in the extent and cost of government regulation have been large; and (4) the rate of savings and capital investment has declined.

In a fundamental sense, everyone is hurt by inflation—some groups much more than others. There is critical damage to the social fabric; uncertainty clouds economic and financial transactions, thrift is penalized, tax laws become more complicated. The net effect is to poison the political and social atmosphere.

In light of these obvious evils, Americans wonder why prompt and forthright solutions have not been applied. There are multiple reasons. One is fear of recession, and with it greater unemployment—especially among minorities and youth. Another is fear that essential social services will be curtailed. Another is structured rigidity within the system. Amidst the uncertainty one thing *is* certain—since inflation has been long in the making, it cannot be halted quickly. We need the patience to give inflation remedies the time to become effective.

Recommendations

The following recommendations are addressed to both short-term and long-term solutions to the inflation problem:

1. *Federal Budget Policy*
The massive budget deficits of the past decade, which have piled up even in prosperous years, must not be permitted to go on indefinitely. A new budget

ethic is required to limit and reduce these deficits. Federal spending should be reduced as a proportion of GNP. Sufficient flexibility must be provided to handle inevitable fluctuations in the economy and in employment. Acceptance of the new budget ethic may compel us to accept temporarily higher unemployment rates and lower capacity utilization.

2. Monetary Policy

To advance the goal of lower inflation, monetary policy should seek to decelerate the growth rate of the money supply. Money supply growth should be reduced to a rate consistent with price stability and economic growth. This goal of monetary policy should be considered more important than short-term interest rate variations.

To help the Federal Reserve achieve such goals and avoid "credit crunches," federal government deficits must be reduced. Lower interest rates will follow the easing of federal credit demands and private inflation-related credit demands.

3. Equitable Burden Sharing

The burden of fighting inflation should be shared as equitably as possible. While stabilization of the price level and satisfactory employment rates are not incompatible in the long run, we recognize that anti-inflation policies risk stimulating temporary increases in unemployment in the short run. Since some groups may be affected more severely than others, we recommend retention of employment training programs and of transfer payments to the unemployed, but we urge thoroughgoing reforms to assure more efficient and responsible design and operation of such programs. We would emphasize the need for government asistance to the unemployed to alleviate substantial hardship on individuals who are not at all responsible for painful policies which affect them.

4. Government Support Programs

Government actions which raise incomes by artificially elevating prices or wages are both inflationary and inefficient. Americans pay for subsidies through taxation and are entitled to know the costs and benefits of these programs. The best way to achieve action on inflation-producing subsidies is by raising the level of public awareness through broad discussion and debate. Therefore we affirm that in general, subsidy programs should be operated through direct payments to the targeted population. Specifically we urge: (a) elimination of agricultural crop restrictions as one example of a desirable subsidy change; (b) that restrictions on foreign trade be reduced or eliminated through international negotiations because such restrictions raise domestic prices and thereby contribute to inflation. If workers and investors are to be provided with transitional assistance to adjust to foreign competition, it should be in the form of direct payments; and (c) that government wage support programs (including the minimum wage, the Davis-Bacon Act and similar acts) be re-examined.

The minimum wage should not be increased further since its effect is to increase prices and to raise unemployment of the unskilled, including teenagers.

We are persuaded that the principle of a minimum wage should be re-examined because there are better ways to help low-income families.

5. Regulatory Improvements

We believe that excessive regulation has impaired productivity growth and should be reversed. Whenever possible, market incentives should be used rather than regulations. This means that our necessary regulatory systems should be examined critically to determine if they are operating efficiently in the public interest. To further this objective, we support: (a) a requirement that each regulatory agency produce cost/benefit analyses for those of its regulations that have major impact on the economy; (b) establishment of mechanisms for external review of proposed new regulations, with a proviso that such reviews be placed in the public record; and (c) a comprehensive review of major regulations and agencies and prompt elimination where appropriate.

6. Productivity

Productivity improvements are the responsibilities of both the public and the private sectors. To reverse the marked slowdown in productivity growth of the past decade and to help decelerate inflation, we recommend policies to improve the rate of return on investment in new plant and equipment, to stimulate outlays on research and development, and to expand job training programs with emphasis on the private sector.

To increase investment incentives, we urge that consideration be given to (a) broadening investment tax credits to include private research and development (R&D) and new construction outlays; (b) increasing federal support for R&D in real terms; (c) increasing the investment tax credit; (d) accelerating tax depreciation allowances; (e) reducing corporate income tax rates; (f) reducing or eliminating double taxation of dividends; and (g) reducing the capital gains tax. All tax relief should depend upon progress toward appropriate overall budget targets.

Further study should be given to restructuring the tax system to reduce or eliminate its bias against saving and investment.

We also favor innovative measures to improve productivity in those industries characterized by declining or lagging productivity: mining, construction, and the service sector (especially health care and education).

To reduce unit costs and improve efficiency, we recommend that more private firms institute (a) quality-of-working-life programs, and (b) joint labor-management productivity committees linked to shared cost-savings with employees.

7. Incomes Policies

To bring down the rate of inflation, primary reliance should be placed on appropriate fiscal and monetary policies. The use of an incomes policy, such as the present wage-price standards, can be a useful supplement. Voluntary wage-price guidelines can be used to decelerate inflation by allowing more time for fiscal-monetary restraint to take hold, but they can only be viewed as transitional since they will not correct inflation over the long term.

We oppose mandatory wage-price controls because they do more harm than good by introducing rigidities into the system and distortions into the economy. Incomes policies that are based on the tax system warrant further study to determine whether they are administratively feasible and sufficiently flexible to avoid the harmful rigidities of controls.

8. Indexation
Since indexation may be counterproductive in combating inflation, no new forms should be encouraged.

9. The Special Case of Health Care
Effective solutions to inflation will have a beneficial effect on most sectors of the economy. However, since the normal forces of supply and demand do not apply to the subsector of health care (with its acute inflationary tendencies), additional solutions will have to be sought as alternatives to conventional market forces. We need to prevent creation and operation of non-essential health facilities, limit unnecessary surgery or hospitalization, emphasize cost awareness including preventive health measures, and stimulate competition by health care providers at every level.

10. International Value of the Dollar
The most effective way to stabilize the international value of the dollar is to decelerate domestic inflation. Some intervention by the Federal Reserve and the Treasury may be desirable to promote orderly foreign exchange markets. In the longer run, some restructuring of the international monetary system may be needed, but controlling domestic inflation would be the most effective means of checking the depreciation of the U. S. dollar and improving our international economic and financial position.

11. The Challenge to Communicate
Americans are deeply troubled by inflation, but there is some question as to how well they understand its causes and what is required for its solution. Such understanding is vital if progress is to be made in changing the social, psychological and political factors contributing to inflation.

We recommend that a program be undertaken promptly to communicate this understanding, including these reference points: (a) the issues must be expressed in terms such that people can readily understand what is involved; (b) the issues should be presented in such a way that people recognize the need for painful decisions which may be at some cost to themselves; (c) a period of time must be allowed for debate on the issues and their remedies; and (d) communication about the inflation fight should be conducted through various forums, including existing organizations.

As a special measure, the Williamsburg Conference recommends that a national forum be established within which major national groups can discuss the problems of inflation. A forum such as this could be very useful in discussing the evolving common solutions to many of our inflation issues because it can operate outside the glare of publicity and pejorative political debate. Such a forum could be structured along the lines of the Conference of National Organizations which operated so successfully during World War II.

Participants in the Williamsburg Conference:

Kenneth R. Austin
Equitable Life Insurance Company of Iowa

John H. Auten
U. S. Department of the Treasury

Martin J. Bailey
University of Maryland

Anatol B. Balbach
Federal Reserve Bank of St. Louis

Joan Bannon
U. S. Conference of Mayors

Ernest T. Baughman
Federal Reserve Bank of Dallas

Morrison H. Beach
The Travelers Insurance Company

Bharat B. Bhalla
The Continental Group

Coleman Bloomfield
Minnesota Mutual Life Insurance Company

Barry P. Bosworth
Council on Wage and Price Stability

Kenneth E. Boulding
University of Colorado

J. W. Brakebill
Provident Life and Accident Insurance Company

William H. Branson
Princeton University

Roger E. Brinner
Data Resources, Inc.

Phillip D. Cagan
Columbia University

A. Michael Collins
International Union of Operating Engineers

George T. Conklin, Jr.
The Guardian Life Insurance Company

Robert H. Connery
The Academy of Political Science

Robert W. Crandall
The Brookings Institution

John J. Creedon
Metropolitan Life Insurance Company

Fred DeLuca
American Council of Life Insurance

Larry L. Dildine
U. S. Department of the Treasury

Alfred S. Eichner
State University of New York

Marten Estey
The Wharton School

Edgar R. Fiedler
The Conference Board

Richard I. Fricke
National Life Insurance Company

Paul Gallant
American Council of Life Insurance

Walter B. Gerken
Pacific Mutual Life Insurance Company

K. Edwin Graham
American Council of Life Insurance

Edward M. Gramlich
University of Michigan

William C. Greenough
Teachers Insurance and Annuity Association

William B. Gross
Pacific Mutual Life Insurance Company

Serge Grosset
Duquesne University

Melvin A. Hinick
Virginia Polytechnic Institute and State University

Frank J. Hoenemeyer
The Prudential Insurance Company of America

James R. L. Holdsworth
American Council of Life Insurance

A. Linwood Holton, Jr.
American Council of Life Insurance

Edward R. Irvin
Integon Life Insurance Company

Dean W. Jeffers
Nationwide Life Insurance Company

Donald E. Jondahl
Northwestern National Life Insurance Company

John W. Kendrick
The George Washington University

William E. Kingsley
American Council of Life Insurance

Thomas H. Langevin
Capital University

Hartzel Z. Lebed
Connecticut General Life Insurance Company

Arthur Lifson
The Equitable Life Assurance Society of the United States

Sandra Linck
Mansfield, Pennsylvania

William R. Ludwick
Pilot Life Insurance Company

Barbara Lynch
Demarest, New Jersey

James B. McIntosh
Midland Mutual Life Insurance Company

Paul E. Martin
Ohio National Life Insurance Company

J. Edwin Matz
John Hancock Mutual Life Insurance Company

William F. May
American Can Company

Richard V. Minck
American Council of Life Insurance

Melvin Mister
U. S. Conference of Mayors

Blake T. Newton, Jr.
American Council of Life Insurance

William K. Paynter
American Council of Life Insurance

Louis B. Perry
Standard Insurance Company

Joel Popkin
Joel Popkin & Company

Robert A. Quietmeyer
Newark, Delaware

George G. Radcliffe
The Baltimore Life Insurance Company

Robert A. Rennie
Nationwide Life Insurance Company

Cynthia Ricketts
Montpelier, Vermont

Philip Saunders, Jr.
John Hancock Mutual Life Insurance Company

Francis H. Schott
The Equitable Life Assurance Society of the United States

Leslie P. Schultz
United Services Life Insurance Company

Laurence Seidman
University of Pennsylvania

Richard Selden
University of Virginia

Harry P. Seward
Bankers Life Insurance Company of Nebraska

Courtenay M. Slater
U. S. Department of Commerce

Armand C. Stalnaker
General American Life Insurance Company

Robert E. Stevens
Connecticut Mutual Life Insurance Company

Robert H. Stewart
Gulf Oil Corporation

Catherine D. Sveikauskas
Federal Home Loan Bank Board

John R. Taylor
Bankers Life Insurance Company

Paul Wachtel
New York University

Robert A. Wallace
Joint Economic Committee

Harvey D. Wilmeth
Northwestern Mutual Life Insurance Company

Daniel Yankelovich
Yankelovich, Skelly and White

Conrad S. Young
United Benefit Life Insurance Company

James Zabel
First National Tennessee Corporation

Project Director:
  Clarence C. Walton

Administrative Staff:
  Milton Amsel
  George A. Bishop
  Kenneth M. Wright

Index